# Jean Rhys's Modernist Bearings and Experimental Aesthetics

**Historicizing Modernism**

**Series Editors**

Matthew Feldman, Professorial Fellow, Norwegian Study Centre, University of York, UK; and Erik Tonning, Professor of British Literature and Culture, University of Bergen, Norway

Assistant Editor: David Tucker, Associate Lecturer, Goldsmiths College, University of London, UK

**Editorial Board**

Professor Chris Ackerley, Department of English, University of Otago, New Zealand; Professor Ron Bush, St. John's College, University of Oxford, UK; Dr Finn Fordham, Department of English, Royal Holloway, UK; Professor Steven Matthews, Department of English, University of Reading, UK; Dr Mark Nixon, Department of English, University of Reading, UK; Dr Julie Taylor, Northumbria University; Professor Shane Weller, Reader in Comparative Literature, University of Kent, UK; and Professor Janet Wilson, University of Northampton, UK.

*Historicizing Modernism* challenges traditional literary interpretations by taking an empirical approach to modernist writing: a direct response to new documentary sources made available over the last decade.

Informed by archival research, and working beyond the usual European/American avant-garde 1900–45 parameters, this series reassesses established readings of modernist writers by developing fresh views of intellectual contexts and working methods.

**Series Titles**

*Arun Kolatkar and Literary Modernism in India*, Laetitia Zecchini
*British Literature and Classical Music*, David Deutsch
*Broadcasting in the Modernist Era*, Matthew Feldman, Henry Mead and Erik Tonning
*Charles Henri Ford*, Alexander Howard
*Chicago and the Making of American Modernism*, Michelle E. Moore
*Ezra Pound's Adams Cantos*, David Ten Eyck
*Ezra Pound's Eriugena*, Mark Byron
*Ezra Pound's Washington Cantos and the Struggle for Light*, Alec Marsh
*Great War Modernisms and The New Age Magazine*, Paul Jackson

*Historical Modernisms*, Jean-Michel Rabaté
*Historicizing Modernists*, Edited by Matthew Feldman, Anna Svendsen and Erik Tonning
*James Joyce and Absolute Music*, Michelle Witen
*James Joyce and Catholicism*, Chrissie van Mierlo
*John Kasper and Ezra Pound*, Alec Marsh
*Judith Wright and Emily Carr*, Anne Collett and Dorothy Jones
*Katherine Mansfield and Literary Modernism*, Edited by Janet Wilson, Gerri Kimber and Susan Reid
*Late Modernism and the English Intelligencer*, Alex Latter
*The Life and Work of Thomas MacGreevy*, Susan Schreibman
*Literary Impressionism*, Rebecca Bowler
*Modern Manuscripts*, Dirk Van Hulle
*Modernist Lives*, Claire Battershill
*The Politics of 1930s British Literature*, Natasha Periyan
*Reading Mina Loy's Autobiographies*, Sandeep Parmar
*Reframing Yeats*, Charles Ivan Armstrong
*Samuel Beckett and Arnold Geulincx*, David Tucker
*Samuel Beckett and the Bible*, Iain Bailey
*Samuel Beckett and Cinema*, Anthony Paraskeva
*Samuel Beckett and Experimental Psychology*, Joshua Powell
*Samuel Beckett's 'More Pricks than Kicks'*, John Pilling
*Samuel Beckett's German Diaries 1936–1937*, Mark Nixon
*T. E. Hulme and the Ideological Politics of Early Modernism*, Henry Mead
*Virginia Woolf's Late Cultural Criticism*, Alice Wood
*Christian Modernism in an Age of Totalitarianism*, Jonas Kurlberg
*Samuel Beckett and Experimental Psychology*, Joshua Powell
*Samuel Beckett in Confinement*, James Little
*Katherine Mansfield: New Directions*, Edited by Aimée Gasston, Gerri Kimber and Janet Wilson
*Modernist Wastes*, Caroline Knighton
*The Many Drafts of D. H. Lawrence*, Elliott Morsia
*Samuel Beckett and the Second World War*, William Davies

# Jean Rhys's Modernist Bearings and Experimental Aesthetics

Sue Thomas

BLOOMSBURY ACADEMIC
LONDON • NEW YORK • OXFORD • NEW DELHI • SYDNEY

BLOOMSBURY ACADEMIC
Bloomsbury Publishing Plc
50 Bodford Square, London, WC1B 3DP, UK
1385 Broadway, New York, NY 10018, USA
29 Earlsfort Terrace, Dublin 2, Ireland

BLOOMSBURY, BLOOMSBURY ACADEMIC and the Diana logo are
trademarks of Bloomsbury Publishing Plc

First published in Great Britain 2022
This paperback edition published 2023

Copyright © Sue Thomas, 2022

Sue Thomas has asserted her right under the Copyright, Designs and
Patents Act, 1988, to be identified as Author of this work.

For legal purposes the Acknowledgements on pp. xi–xiii constitute an
extension of this copyright page.

Cover design: Eleanor Rose

All rights reserved. No part of this publication may be reproduced or transmitted
in any form or by any means, electronic or mechanical, including photocopying,
recording, or any information storage or retrieval system, without prior
permission in writing from the publishers.

Bloomsbury Publishing Plc does not have any control over, or responsibility for, any
third-party websites referred to or in this book. All internet addresses given in this
book were correct at the time of going to press. The author and publisher regret
any inconvenience caused if addresses have changed or sites have ceased
to exist, but can accept no responsibility for any such changes.

A catalogue record for this book is available from the British Library.

A catalog record for this book is available from the Library of Congress.

ISBN:   HB:     978-1-3502-7575-1
        PB:     978-1-3502-7579-9
        ePDF:   978-1-3502-7576-8
        eBook:  978-1-3502-7577-5

Series: Historicizing Modernism

Typeset by Integra Software Services Pvt. Ltd.

To find out more about our authors and books visit www.bloomsbury.com
and sign up for our newsletters.

*in memory of*
*Hazel June Smith*
*23 June 1934–15 April 2021*

# Contents

| | |
|---|---|
| Preface | x |
| Acknowledgements | xi |
| Introduction: Jean Rhys's modernist bearings and experimental aesthetics | 1 |
| 1 Routes to Rhys's early fiction | 27 |
| 2 The tropical reaches of *After Leaving Mr Mackenzie* | 51 |
| 3 Temporality, history and memory in *Voyage in the Dark* | 73 |
| 4 Depressive time and jazz modernism in *Good Morning, Midnight* | 97 |
| 5 Composing 'Till September Petronella' and 'Tigers Are Better-Looking' | 117 |
| 6 The *doudou* and doudouism in Rhys's fiction | 143 |
| 7 Hurricane poetics in *Wide Sargasso Sea* | 165 |
| Coda | 189 |
| Selected Bibliography | 193 |
| Index | 213 |

# Preface

This book series is devoted to the analysis of late nineteenth- to twentieth-century literary modernism within its historical contexts. *Historicizing Modernism* therefore stresses empirical accuracy and the value of primary sources (such as letters, diaries, notes, drafts, marginalia or other archival materials) in developing monographs and edited collections on modernist literature. This may take a number of forms, such as manuscript study and genetic criticism, documenting interrelated historical contexts and ideas, and exploring biographical information. To date, no book series has fully laid claim to this interdisciplinary, source-based territory for modern literature. While the series addresses itself to a range of key authors, it also highlights the importance of non-canonical writers with a view to establishing broader intellectual genealogies of modernism. Furthermore, while the series is weighted towards the English-speaking world, studies of non-Anglophone modernists whose writings are open to fresh historical exploration are also included.

A key aim of the series is to reach beyond the familiar rhetoric of intellectual and artistic 'autonomy' employed by many modernists and their critical commentators. Such rhetorical moves can and should themselves be historically situated and reintegrated into the complex continuum of individual literary practices. It is our intent that the series' emphasis upon the contested self-definitions of modernist writers, thinkers and critics may, in turn, prompt various reconsiderations of the boundaries delimiting the concept of 'modernism' itself. Indeed, the concept of 'historicizing' is itself debated across its volumes, and the series by no means discourages more theoretically informed approaches. On the contrary, the editors hope that the historical specificity encouraged by *Historicizing Modernism* may inspire a range of fundamental critiques along the way.

Matthew Feldman<br>
Erik Tonning

# Acknowledgements

The larger research project of which this monograph is part, 'Jean Rhys: Her Literary Life', has been funded by the Australian Research Council through its Discovery Projects scheme (DP140103817). My earlier research on Rhys, which has also supported this new project, was funded by Australian Research Council small grants in 1993–4 and 1999. The major outcomes on Rhys from the earlier grants were *The Worlding of Jean Rhys* (1999), essays, articles and the chapter on Rhys in *England through Colonial Eyes in Twentieth-century Fiction* (2001), a book I co-authored with Ann Blake and Leela Gandhi, and discussion of 'Triple Sec' in its first chapter 'Colouring the English'. In 2014 I held a visiting position at the Oxford Centre for Life Writing at Wolfson College and thank Hermione Lee and the college for their hospitality.

The English Program at La Trobe University has an extraordinary standard of collegiality. I am profoundly appreciative of its and my colleagues' encouragement and of Vice-Chancellor John Dewar's support at a crucial time. I am also deeply grateful to the members of the Australian Association for Caribbean Studies and the Australasian Modernist Studies Network and the international community of Rhys scholars. Working with Russell McDougall and Anne Collett on the collection *Tracking the Literature of Tropical Weather: Typhoons, Cyclones and Hurricanes* was particularly inspirational for my research on and writing of Chapter 7, 'Hurricane Poetics in *Wide Sargasso Sea*'. In the Rhys research community, I owe special thanks to scholars who have commissioned me to write on Rhys for collections and special issues – Mary Lou Emery, Erica L. Johnson, Juliana Lopoukhine, Patricia Moran, Frédéric Regard, Elaine Savory and Kerry-Jane Wallart – and to Helen Carr, Peter Hulme, Scott McCracken, Evelyn O'Callaghan, Lizabeth Paravisini-Gebert, Anna Snaith and Andrew Thacker. Jeffrey Geiger very kindly shared with me a copy of his *Facing the Pacific: Polynesia and the U.S. Imperial Imagination* when Covid restrictions in Melbourne barred physical access to libraries.

Caryn Rae Adams, Rebecca Waese and Juliane Römhild in Melbourne, Marl'ene Edwin in London and Emily Magrath in Aberdeen have provided invaluable research assistance towards and on 'Jean Rhys: Her Literary Life'. Caryn Rae Adams worked on the Discovery project over the duration of its funding.

Staff at the Borchardt Library at La Trobe University, the McFarlin Library at the University of Tulsa, the Wilberforce House Museum, the British National Archives, the British Library, the Oxford University Library, the University of Aberdeen Library and Special Collections and Archives at Hamilton College have been particularly helpful.

I have presented writing in progress towards *Jean Rhys's Modernist Bearings and Experimental Aesthetics* at a number of conferences and in research seminar series and thank participants for their questions and encouragement and the conference and seminar series organizers and their teams: Modernism and Multiple Temporalities, Modernist Studies in Asia Network Conference, Aoyama Gakuin University (2019); Caribbean Meridians, Australian Association for Caribbean Studies Conference, Western Sydney University (2019); Modernist Humour, University of Melbourne (2018); International Jean Rhys Conference: Transmission Lines/Lignes de transmission, Paris Sorbonne University (2018); Remaking the New: Modernism and Textual Scholarship, Queen Mary, University of London (2017); Modernist Life, University of Birmingham (2017); Interiors, Australian Association for Caribbean Studies Conference, Australian National University (2017); Modernist Emotions, University of Paris Ouest Nanterre (2016); Modernist Work, University of New South Wales (2016); *Wide Sargasso Sea* at 50, Goldsmiths, University of London (2016); Western Sydney University (2015); Land and Water, Australian Association for Caribbean Studies Conference, University of Wollongong (2015); Transnational Modernisms, Australian Modernist Studies Network conference, University of Sydney (2014); English Literature outside the Circle, Sebelas Maret University (2014); University of Essex (2014); Oxford Centre for Life-Writing, Wolfson College (2014); Reconstructing Caribbean Lives, Australian Association for Caribbean Studies Conference, La Trobe University (2013). I presented keynotes at Transnational Modernisms and English Literature outside the Circle and thank the conferences for financial support.

'Jean Rhys's Piecing of the Local and the Transnational in *Voyage in the Dark*', a very early version of Chapter 3, was published in *Affirmations: Of the Modern*, vol. 4, no. 1 (2016). Permission to draw on the essay has been granted by *Affirmations: Of the Modern*. Permission to draw in Chapter 5 on strands of argument in 'Thinking through "[t]he grey disease of sex hatred": Jean Rhys's "Till September Petronella"', *Journal of Caribbean Literatures* 3, no. 3 (Summer 2003), has been granted by the editor of the journal. Some material on the *doudou* in 'Jean Rhys getting the "feel" of the West Indies in *Wide Sargasso Sea*', published in *Wide Sargasso Sea at 50*, edited by Elaine Savory and Erica L. Johnson, 2019,

Palgrave Macmillan, is reproduced with the permission of Palgrave Macmillan. Some details of Chapter 3 draw on strands of arguments in '"Tearing Me in Two So Slowly So Slowly": Jean Rhys's Representations of Abortion', *Jean Rhys Review* 12, no. 1 (2002), and 'Jean Rhys and Katherine Mansfield Writing the "Sixth Act"', *Jean Rhys: Twenty-First-Century Approaches*, edited by Erica L. Johnson and Patricia Moran (Edinburgh: Edinburgh University Press, 2015). 'Ghostly Presences: James Potter Lockhart and Jane Maxwell Lockhart in Jean Rhys's Writing', a far fuller account of Rhys's negotiation of Lockhart family memory than that in Chapter 7 was published in *Texas Studies in Literature and Language* 57, no. 4 (Winter 2015). The strands of argument have been thoroughly recontextualized and reframed. In Chapter 7 I quote from manuscript materials held in the Beinecke Lesser Antilles Collection at Hamilton College and in the Wilberforce House Museum in Hull. Permission to quote from the materials has been granted by Special Collections and Archives at Hamilton College and Hull Culture and Leisure Limited respectively. Lines from Derek Walcott's poems 'The Royal Palms … an absence of ruins' and 'Air' are quoted with the permission of The Derek Walcott Estate.

At Bloomsbury I want to thank Ben Doyle, Laura Cope, the book production team, and the editors of the Historicizing Modernism series Matthew Feldman and Erik Tonning. Thanks, too, to Chris Tiffin for preparing the index so meticulously.

I have been sustained by the love and joy of Brendan, Anne, Nathanial and Sebastian Thomas. They, my parents and my sisters and their families have been, as ever, very supportive. Sadly, my mother Hazel died an hour or so before I received readers' reports on *Jean Rhys's Modernist Bearings and Experimental Aesthetics*, which is dedicated to her.

# Introduction

## Jean Rhys's modernist bearings and experimental aesthetics

In *Jean Rhys's Modernist Bearings and Experimental Aesthetics*, I address Rhys's composition and positioning of her fiction and how she invites and challenges us (readers, literary historians and critics) to read the tacit, silent and explicit textual bearings she offers. The word 'bearings' in the title signals relation: points of reference that locate and establish 'connection, correspondence, or contrast' in her composition process and within her oeuvre; that disclose genealogies of filiation and disaffiliation as a writer; and that may guide us through senses of the unfamiliarity, difficulty or complexity of her writing.[1] The approach grounds my revelation of as yet untold histories of Rhys's literary career, the formation and scope of her experimental aesthetics, and the meanings of the Americas and the tropics in her writing. Both *Jean Rhys's Modernist Bearings and Experimental Aesthetics* and my earlier *The Worlding of Jean Rhys* (1999) are historical studies, organized, though, around different problem-spaces. David Scott elaborates a problem-space as 'an ensemble of questions and answers around which a horizon of identifiable stakes (conceptual as well as ideological-political stakes) hang'.[2] In *The Worlding of Jean Rhys* my horizon was how to read Rhys's senses of the world and their inscription in her fiction and the autobiographical strand of her Black Exercise Book. The political stakes were a close and nuanced analysis of her representations of the intersections of the colonial and postcolonial, race, ethnicity, gender and class. In *Jean Rhys's Modernist Bearings and Experimental Aesthetics* the horizon is how to read the distinctiveness of her shifting and developing experimental aesthetics over her career.

The distinctiveness, I argue, may be discerned in her practices of composition, residual traces of which are located in her fiction, extant drafts and self-reflexive comment on her writing. The traces comprise patterns of interrelation, intertextuality, intermediality and allusion, both diachronic and synchronic, cultural histories entwined in them and revision. My close analysis of the patterns – grounded in archival research – reveals new experimental, thematic, generic and political reaches of her fiction and sharpens awareness of her complex writerly affiliations and lineages. The approach demands negotiating variously contested, ambiguous and unstable critical and historical categories. Indeed, modernism itself – an umbrella category applied retrospectively – lends coherence to an extraordinarily diverse range of experimental aesthetic practices and movements. The singularity of Rhys's authorial vision has typically been positioned as the perspective of a white writer born in Dominica in 1890 who is always already 'not quite, not English', and whose diasporic Creole modernism is an 'appropriation of modernism', 'an articulation of difference and a rewriting of influence'.[3] The very term 'Creole' in Creole modernism is ambiguous and contested, having multiple meanings across languages and cultures. Creole can refer to distinctive Caribbean identities and customs and languages that emerge from histories of cross-cultural contact. *Jean Rhys's Modernist Bearings and Experimental Aesthetics* is organized as a series of intricately connected essays on her novels and a range of her short fiction, analysed largely in the chronological order of their publication. The exception to chronological order is Chapter 6, a longitudinal study of Rhys's interest in the figure of the *doudou* and doudouism.

Haunting has become a conceptual metaphor for Rhys's place in literary history and the 'risky' historical consciousness to which Rhys's fiction may bring readers, a descriptor of the affect of reading Rhys's fiction and a means to position affect studies and the transnational, transcultural and diasporic as new cutting edges in Rhys studies.[4] Rhys's unsettling (haunting) of readers and scholars is apparent in recent formulations of the intricacies of placing her in familiar literary histories: 'what really matters is her strangeness'; 'Rhys's work defies periodisation and transcends [such] categories' as 'modernist, postcolonial, Caribbean, British and Creole writer'; 'Rhys's peculiar, multivalent, and difficult canonicity'; a 'strange case'.[5] The complexity, of course, is as much around negotiating the shifting parameters of categories, canonization and periodization as situating her voice and aesthetic reach historically. '[H]aunting indicates that, beneath the surface of received history, there lurks another narrative, an untold story', Jeffrey Andrew Weinstock insists.[6] The literary and cultural archives within which Rhys might be read and remembered are disparate and fragmented. Through connective reading, in *Jean Rhys's Modernist Bearings and Experimental Aesthetics* I address critical and cross-cultural idioms of remembering Rhys, developing new narratives of her place(s) in literary history. Like Gillian Whitlock in her advocacy of 'connected reading' of autobiographies shaped by empire and its 'debris', I value 'supplementation rather than completion' and 'complexity rather than closure'.[7]

The twenty-first-century expansion of Modernist Studies – marked by a widening of focus from national to transnational formations, an acknowledgement of the imbrication of modernism and the (post)colonial, a troubling of standard periodizations of modernism and a questioning of a sharp divide between high and popular culture – has occasioned a 'recent and striking rediscovery' of Rhys within the field.[8] Fresh recognition of her as a transnational modernist – in the wake of monographs on Rhys by Helen Carr, Mary Lou Emery, Carol Dell'Amico, Coral Ann Howells, Delia Konzett, Elaine Savory and myself which position her as a diasporic Caribbean modernist[9] – can be measured less in new monographs devoted to study of her fiction since 2005, than in comparative monographs with a chapter or two on Rhys and essays in edited collections and special journal issues on Rhys.[10] The theoretical approaches to Rhys in contemporary scholarship are diverse: philology; psychoanalysis; narratology; postcolonial feminist theory; postcolonial hybridity theory; Caribbean literary and cultural theory.[11] The thematic approaches – I note only a handful here – reflect the expansion of Modernist Studies: celebrity; censorship; cinema experience; consumer capitalism; fashion; multilingualism; the passport; and the transnational.[12] The rediscovery of Rhys is, Anna Snaith observes in 2014, 'just beginning' to unpack 'the vast range of allusions, musical, visual, literary, factual, from all manner of kinds of texts and cultural forms in Rhys's work'.[13] Literary allusions are generally part of a 'common literary culture and tradition' readers and scholars share with an author.[14] Over time many of Rhys's literary allusions have become more recondite. Traces of 'all manner of kinds of texts and cultural forms' are certainly being increasingly acknowledged in critical scholarship on her, although they tend to be treated collectively. Christopher GoGwilt, for instance, describes allusions apart from one to Joseph Conrad's *Almayer's Folly* in *After Leaving Mr Mackenzie* as 'all sorts of cultural fragments – borrowing, perhaps, from avant-garde surrealist uses of photo-montage and collage', a move consistent with his viewing of Rhys through the prism of the 'English modernism of Ford's and Conrad's generation'.[15] Juliana Lopoukhine, Frédéric Regard and Kerry-Jane Wallart write of the 'crowd of cultural references' in Rhys's work and Snaith of 'snippets of West Indian and African American songs' in *Voyage in the Dark*.[16] I approach such traces, sometimes more tacit than allusion, as purposive, their provenances integral to Rhys's locating of her authorial bearings in relation to her materials and her shaping of them. The traces may negotiate or establish her authorial distance from first-person narrative voices and the points of view of characters.

## Rhys's writerly beginnings

To orient readers of *Jean Rhys's Modernist Bearings and Experimental Aesthetics* not particularly familiar with Rhys's career, I need first to draw together an account of her writerly beginnings. Rhys tells several versions of her early interest in writing. As a child of twelve in Dominica, she began writing poems as 'a cure for sadness'.[17] An avid reader of poetry in both English and French, she recognized that her major creative talents lay in writing fiction. In the manuscript 'Leaving School', Rhys writes about her aunt Clarice Rees Williams encouraging her to write a story in 1909 after she left The Academy of Dramatic Art; it was rejected by the magazine to which her aunt sent it.[18] The narrative of Rhys's emergence as an adult writer, told most fully in *Smile Please: An Unfinished Autobiography* (1979), begins with the depression she experienced after her lover Lancelot Hugh Smith abandoned her in 1912, the year she turned twenty-two. It proved to be a rite of passage in which 'sadness' 'became a part of' her and which she 'would have missed ... if it had gone'.[19] On impulse one day while living in a flat in Fulham, reached on a bus route to World's End, she bought a number of brightly coloured 'quill pens' to 'cheer up' her 'table', black exercise books with red spines, 'an ordinary penholder, a bottle of ink and a cheap inkstand', and that evening headed one of the books:

> *This is my Diary.* But it wasn't a diary. I remembered everything that had happened to me in the last year and a half. I remembered what he'd said, what I'd felt. ... I filled three exercise books and half another, then I wrote: 'Oh, God, I'm only twenty and I'll have to go on living and living and living.' I knew then that it was finished and there was no more to say.[20]

Her 'fingers' and 'palms' 'tingled' as she wrote,[21] the word 'tingled' suggesting a 'stinging or smarting sensation', 'thrill', 'excite[ment]' and, by transference from the 'cheeks', 'under the influence of shame, indignation, or the like'.[22] 'I put the exercise books at the bottom of my suitcase and piled my underclothes on them. After that whenever I moved I took the exercise books but I never looked at them again for many years,' Rhys writes.[23] In 1924 she showed the diaries to an acquaintance, experienced journalist H. Pearl Adam. Adam would, with Rhys's permission, rework the diaries while she was typing them up. The narrative Adam produced was 'Suzy Tells', the protagonist of which is Suzy Gray. Rhys, whose finances were severely straitened at the time of the typing, writes in *Smile Please* that she deferred to Adams's experience as a journalist, 'However, when she showed me the typed manuscript … I didn't really like it. She had divided it up into several parts, the name of a man heading each part.'[24] Adams's editing centralizes not the narrating female voice but Suzy's serial sexual partners.

Adam sent 'Suzy Tells' to Ford Madox Ford, the editor of the *transatlantic review*, telling Rhys that Ford was 'famous for spotting and helping young authors'.[25] Published monthly in 1924, the *transatlantic review* featured writing by, among others, Djuna Barnes, Bryher, E. E. Cummings, Nancy Cunard, H. D., John Dos Passos, Havelock Ellis, Ernest Hemingway, James Joyce, Mina Loy, Ezra Pound, Dorothy Richardson, Gertrude Stein, Tristan Tzara, Paul Valéry and William Carlos Williams. The circular announcing the journal spelt out Ford's commitments to 'widening the field in which the younger writers of the day can find publication' and to promoting the internationalization of 'Literature' and its humanistic reach.[26] In the December 1924 number of the *transatlantic review*, which would be its final issue, Ford published 'Vienne', a three-part story by Jean Rhys. Said in the issue to be part of a larger work 'Triple Sec', it was Rhys's first publication and launched her pen-name. Ivan Beede, the associate editor of the *transatlantic review*, also took an interest in Rhys's career; he had been shown the diaries.[27] 'Triple Sec' was Ford's renaming of 'Suzy Tells'.[28] The extant version of 'Triple Sec' ends in 1919, before the action of 'Vienne' begins, so whether the story was indeed part of 'Suzy Tells' is a moot point. Rhys returned to the exercise books of the 1910s (now lost) rather than 'Triple Sec' to develop *Voyage in the Dark* (1934), which covers about half of the narrative span of 'Triple Sec'.[29] Rhys would revise for publication only one other seven-page section of 'Triple Sec' (or the diaries on which it is based), in a process that took decades, with 'Till September Petronella' first appearing in 1960.

Ford's biographer Max Saunders provides some evidence that Rhys's affair with her literary mentor Ford could have begun as early as December 1924 and ended in (the northern hemisphere) autumn of 1926.[30] Over the course of their relationship Ford encouraged Rhys as a writer by placing confidence in her talent; helping her identify for excision the glib and clichés; and setting her a course of reading, particularly of mid- to late-nineteenth- and early-twentieth-century French fiction. As GoGwilt points out, the 'English modernism with which Ford associated himself, Henry James, and Joseph Conrad was a modernism that translated the techniques of the great French "masters" (Flaubert above all … )

into English'.[31] Ford also offered Rhys practical advice, like translating passages from English into French to assist in cutting verbose prose and setting aside until a later time stories that were proving intractably difficult.[32] He arranged for her to translate Francis Carco's *Perversité* from French to English, a translation its publisher attributed to Ford. Savory notes, too, Rhys's earlier translation of some of her husband Jean Lenglet's stories, which she tried to place for publication through H. Pearl Adam. The practice of translation, Savory argues, heightens awareness of 'language nuances' and 'the demands of genre, internal structure and style'.[33]

In Ford's Preface to Rhys's *The Left Bank and Other Stories*, he points to Rhys's departure from the impressionism he championed. In his view its most consummate practitioner was Henry James, whom he reads as having 'bestowed his sympathies upon no human being and upon no cause', having 'remained an observer, passionless and pitiless'.[34] Ford introduces Rhys as Antillean, 'with a terrifying insight and a terrific – an almost lurid! – passion for stating the case of the underdog', a 'bias of admiration for' Paris's 'midinettes and of sympathy for its lawbreakers' and 'a singular instinct for form'. Her writing is 'so very good, so extraordinarily distinguished by the rendering of passion, and so true'.[35] His identification of her as Antillean, a geographical, ethnic and colonial category, places his patronage of her as part of his mission to internationalize literature. Rhys's biographer Carole Angier points out that Ford thought Rhys had 'black blood in her'.[36] His emphasis on 'passion' in his characterization of her writing – 'terrific', 'almost lurid!' – fits a stereotype of black cultural labour being marked by 'extremes of emotion'.[37] There was a large black French Antillean community of around 10,000 in Paris at the time, mostly settled in Montparnasse,[38] so how contemporary readers might have understood the term 'Antillean' in relation to Paris's Left Bank is an open question.

In *Commonwealth of Letters: British Literary Culture and the Emergence of Postcolonial Aesthetics* (2013), Peter Kalliney positions Rhys as a 'bohemian modernist', urging that she 'emerged as a recognized participant-observer of bohemian life' in 1920s Paris and that her 'status as a dissident helped give her access to the scenes of modernist production' there.[39] The characterization does rather conflate her experience of Paris with that of literary expatriates. Elena Lamberti points out that '[i]n the 1920s, the idea of the Grand Tour had finally been replaced by that of *expatriation*, a self-imposed exile which brought many wandering Yankees to Europe and especially to Paris'.[40] Rhys herself endorses the view of the author of an unidentified book on 1920s Montparnasse that literary expatriates had financial means and were '[a]s immoral as they dare … and when they return to their own countries it's always on the back of Paris they put everything they have done'.[41] Her 'status as a dissident' might be measured by Paul Nash's images of her as 'some woman' of Ford's, 'some more or less new one', and 'The Ghost' without '"any real existence", only a "very pathetic and eventful history"'.[42] As Margarete Rubik points out, for Rhys life in Paris was generally not one of 'bohemian ease and intellectual exchange, but of a struggle for survival'.[43]

Rhys's observer role in relation to bohemian life in London began, though, in her diaries of the 1910s, and she was exposed to many scenes of modernist consumption and production and modernist ideas before meeting Ford. In the 1910s Rhys worked as a chorus dancer, artist's model and movie extra, among other occupations, including kept mistress of Lancelot Hugh Smith. *Voyage in the Dark* is set in part during the ultramodern ragtime craze of 1913–14 which scandalized conservative commentators of the day. Around 1914 Rhys was frequenting the bohemian clubs the Café Royal and the Crabtree Club. In 1915 she holidayed with painter Adrian Allinson and his friend, musician and composer Philip Heseltine (Peter Warlock), whom she had met there. In celebrating London's modernist bohemia of the early twentieth century, Peter Brooker writes of its 'experimental social aesthetic which vied with bourgeois norms', 'creating a unity, however temporary, of ideas, practices and settings and a consequent social solidarity across differences of generation, gender and social class'.[44] Later in *Bohemia in London*, he acknowledges the superficiality of the solidarity, referring to 'blatant and subterranean inequalities, especially as experienced by women in relation to men and by women of different social classes'.[45] These inequalities, drawn out by retrospection, would become material for Rhys's writing about the fringes of bohemian life in England and Europe. In the late 1910s Rhys showed her childhood poems to her then 'first friend' Camille Poupeye (1874–1963), a drama and art critic; their bleakness disturbed him. He is remembered simply as Camille in a 1964 letter and in *Smile Please: An Unfinished Autobiography* (1979).[46] A Belgian refugee in England during the First World War, he lived with his family in the same London boarding house that Rhys did at the time and introduced her to Jean Lenglet. Poupeye was fascinated by Asian theatre and working on a book on Noh drama during his friendship with Rhys. His subsequent published books on theatre – beginning with *Le Théâtre japonais* in 1923 – valorize expressionist avant-garde over naturalistic aesthetics.[47] In 'Triple Sec', the character thinly based on him, Raoul Poupeye, would take Suzy to the Café Royal and each night of their friendship the Poupeyes would discuss literature and art with her.

The bonhomie of the cosmopolitan boarding house in which they live includes a capacity to laugh at the English.[48]

Rhys's writing career extended from 1924 until her death in 1979, with a publishing gap between 1939 and 1960. Before the publication of *Wide Sargasso Sea* in 1966, often hailed as her rebirth as a writer, perhaps her highest accolade came from Evelyn Scott, renowned for early recognition and promotion of James Joyce and F. Scott Fitzgerald in the United States. Scott writes of Rhys for the dust-jacket of the US edition of *Voyage in the Dark*: 'She and Mrs Woolf seem to me the women writers of the British Isles who are, in dissimilar veins, the most individualized, the most continually interesting and the most significant as artists.'[49] Rhys had been writing during the Second World War: a novel-length version of the narrative that would become 'Till September Petronella' (1960), lost in a house move; a collection of short stories *The Sound of the River*, rejected by Constable in 1946; and a 'half finished' early take on the project that would become *Wide Sargasso Sea*, which she destroyed.[50] Revisions of the stories from *The Sound of the River* were published between 1960 and 1976. From the late 1930s onwards Rhys insists that the West Indies of her childhood had 'vanished … never was anything more vanished and forgotten'.[51] In 1958, she gave the name 'Creole' to fictional and autobiographical fragments dating from the late 1930s, 'getting down all I remembered about the West Indies as the West Indies used to be. (Also all I was told, which is more important).'[52] The fragments are a salvage and shoring up of memory and a sense of history and place. Rhys unpicked threads from this material and stitched them into her later fiction.

Rhys's naming the material 'Creole' stakes a claim to a place in the ethnically diverse history of the Caribbean at a time when she felt that the meaning of the word Creole in English was shifting. The concept of the 'Creole is and expresses the result of the Atlantic crossing and colonization', Carolyn Allen writes. Etymologically, the term 'Creole' has been traced to Portuguese, Spanish and Kikoongo words.[53] Creole has local variations in meaning throughout the Americas, variations based on specific imperial and linguistic heritages and its meanings have shifted over time. In the British West Indies, Creole was a 'geocultural designation' of birth in the region,[54] and distinctions were made, for instance, between white, coloured and black Creoles, between African and Creole enslaved people, and between white settlers and white Creoles. The term 'Creole' first appears in extant writing by Rhys in 1938 in draft stories 'The Birthday' and 'Mr. Howard's House. CREOLE.'[55] In 'The Birthday' the expatriate English father of the protagonist Phoebe uses the term to explain a local custom to his disapproving English sister, who disparages what she thinks of as the foreign bloodlines of his white Creole wife and child. In 1953, Rhys comments that '[a]ll Creoles are not negroes. *On the contrary.*'[56] She writes in 1959: 'My mother's family was Creole – what *we* call Creole.'[57] Rhys is picking up on a historical process noted by Catherine Hall: the reconstituting of the West Indian as 'Caribbean, or African-Caribbean, or as black – raising new questions about the inclusion of Indians or Chinese or creole whites'.[58] While in 1940 Rhys declares herself to be West Indian,[59] in 1959 she writes, 'As far as I know I am white – but I have no country really now.'[60] With 'Let Them Call It Jazz' (1962) and *Wide Sargasso Sea*, she writes herself back into the Caribbean. Rhys's memories of her Dominican great-aunt Jane Woodcock's oral stories (and songs) are, she suggests in a 1959 letter about writing *Wide Sargasso Sea*, helping her develop and hone a more precise sense of the scope and cultural valency of a Caribbean lineage, located in the subjective points of view of characters.[61]

Rhys's letters, published and unpublished, reveal her awareness of a range of Caribbean writers: Daniel Thaly, an older fellow Dominican who wrote in French, Claude McKay, Eliot Bliss, Alfred Mendes, Phyllis Shand Allfrey, Derek Walcott (by the early 1960s) and V. S. Naipaul (by the late 1960s).[62] Bliss and Allfrey were friends of hers. In 'The Day They Burned the Books' (1960) she alludes to Alfred Mendes's *Pitch Lake* (1934)[63] and in composing *Wide Sargasso Sea* takes some of her bearings from Walcott's poetry of the early 1960s, as I show in Chapter 7. Like Rhys, he started publishing in the *London Magazine* in the early 1960s, and she clearly kept up with his poetry there, keenly anticipating reading his breakthrough collection *In a Green Night*. Walcott's poetry, she avers in an unpublished 1962 letter to Bliss,[64] convinced her that West Indian literature more generally was indeed on the cusp of what Walcott terms in his 1992 Nobel Lecture a 'self-defining dawn'. 'There is', he observes, 'a force of exultation, a celebration of luck, when a writer finds himself a witness to the early morning of a culture that is defining itself, branch by branch, leaf by leaf, in that self-defining dawn, which is why, especially at the edge of the sea, it is good to make a ritual of the sunrise.'[65] Rhys was intrigued that Walcott was from St Lucia, an island which, like Dominica, had an inter-imperial French and English colonial history. By the early 1960s she knew in general terms of the experiment with vernacular speech by contemporary West Indian writers (possibly Sam Selvon and George Lamming) but had not read their work in preparation for her use of stylized English patois for the narrating voice of Selina Davis in 'Let Them Call It Jazz'. Not having read their fiction signals, rather than disinterest, her inability at the time to afford books and reliance on the limited holdings of small local libraries in Cornwall and Devon for reading matter. There are intriguing overlaps between Rhys's anti-colonial poetics of the 1930s and those of diasporic French Antillean writers in Paris in the late 1920s and the early 1930s, particularly Paulette, Jeanne and Andrée Nardal from Martinique.

## Restorying Rhys's experimental aesthetics

Rhys's authorial voice emerges not only through the example and mentoring of Ford and the perspective of a cultural outsider in Europe, but through her pointed engagements with wider aesthetic crosscurrents. In Chapter 1, 'Routes to Rhys's Early Fiction', I examine these engagements in the 1927 version of 'Vienne', 'Tea with an Artist', and *Quartet*, first published as *Postures* in the UK (1928).[66] Rhys positions this fiction variously for her readers in relation to *Die Brücke*, kineticism, futurism, impressionism, marionette theatre, modernist interest in technology and mind, and R. C. Dunning's poem 'The Hermit'. Kineticism was a Viennese art movement active during Rhys's residence in Vienna in 1920–1. A pedagogical initiative of Franz Cizek at Vienna's School of Applied Arts, kineticism 'fused expressionist, cubist, futurist, and constructivist aesthetics to represent the movement of objects and the dynamic properties of forms and spaces'.[67] These bearings, I argue, reveal a self-conscious sifting of international poetics to find and establish a distinctive artistry.

An emerging set of ideas about the tropics as a region, which geographer David Arnold has influentially characterized as 'tropicality',[68] is crucial to the provenance of the Creole. '[T]he "tropical"', Nancy Stepan elaborates, 'came to constitute more than a geographical concept; it signified a place of radical otherness to the temperate world, with which it contrasted and which it helped constitute. Descriptions and pictures of the tropics in this way contributed to the formation of European identity, as distinct from that of the tropical zone.'[69] In *Tracking the Literature of Tropical Weather: Typhoons, Hurricanes and Cyclones*, Anne Collett, Russell McDougall and I observe that tropicality 'is a telling absence from the key concepts of [Anglophone] postcolonial studies',[70] all the more so because tropicality, as Felix Driver and Luciana Martins point out, has been 'compared with … Orientalism, to the extent that both have conventionally been used to define and legitimize essential differences between cultures and natures, both understood in strongly spatial terms'. 'Whether represented positively (as in fantasies of the tropical sublime) or negatively (as a pathological space of degeneration), tropicality has frequently served as a foil to temperate nature, all that is modest, civilized, cultivated.'[71] The term 'tropicality' is not part of Rhys's lexicon, but her understanding and exposure of its operation are integral to her 'specific and pointed critique of the historical and political geographies that undergird her characters' lives'[72] in a range of fiction. Her first extended critique of tropicality is in *After Leaving Mr Mackenzie* (1931).

In Chapter 2 'The Tropical Reaches of *After Leaving Mr Mackenzie*', I argue that Rhys uses textual bearings to draw out the constitutive roles of family silences, adaptation and evolution in the development of protagonist Julia Martin's subjectivity and of tropicality in modern culture. In relation to tropicality, Rhys takes her explicit bearings from a children's story by Rudyard Kipling, W. S. Van Dyke's film *The Pagan*, Joseph Conrad's *Almayer's Folly* and a painting by Amedeo Modigliani. French critical reflections on the revue *Blackbirds of 1929*, including commentary by Michel Leiris, Georges Bataille and André Schaeffner, are part of a contemporary discursive field around the meanings of the tropics with which Rhys engages. These bearings locate hybridity, cultural hybridity and cross-racial mixing as conceptual underpinnings of Rhys's novel. Only an allusion to *Almayer's Folly* and Modigliani's *Reclining Nude* have been discussed to date in Rhys scholarship. Rhys alludes to a song popularized by *Blackbirds of 1929* and its earlier US iteration *Blackbirds of 1928*. The temporal setting of *After Leaving Mr Mackenzie* can be dated precisely as 1929–30 by Rhys's allusions to songs, placing Julia's 'indifference', as the third-person narrator calls her condition, and her experience of being sexual commodified during the Great Depression.[73] An armadillo analogy is crucial to understanding her relationship with her Brazilian-born mother. I compare Rhys's armadillo analogy with Dora Maar's later *Portrait d'Ubu* (first exhibited in 1936). To set up more fully the genealogy of Rhys's critical treatment of tropicality, I also compare Rhys's treatment of the tropical in *After Leaving Mr Mackenzie* with her representation of it in 'Lost Island: A Childhood. Fragments of Autobiography', an essay offered for publication in 1931 or 1932.[74] Threads from the essay are stitched into *Voyage in the Dark*.

In 'Triple Sec', Suzy Gray seldom remembers her childhood in the Caribbean. It is to assuage the homesickness that she experiences when she is pregnant and ill that she wills herself to remember growing up there, causing corporeal memories of her childhood to well up in her mind. The memories encompass half a page of an extant 230-page typescript. Rhys's pre–First World War diaries rather than 'Triple Sec' provided what Rhys calls the 'foundation' of *Voyage in the Dark*.[75] In *Voyage in the Dark*, Rhys makes her use of material from the diaries new not just by transforming 'structure, perspective, and genre',[76] but, as

I show in Chapter 3, through intertextual design and depth to elaborate a view of the relation between the past and present and of the passage of aesthetic time by engaging with decadence and serial moral panics around decadent poetics and dissident styles of living. For Rhys, 'the past exists – side by side with the present, not behind it; ... what was – is'. In *Voyage in the Dark*, Rhys limns the 'positionality of *beside*', undercutting the 'linear logics' of past and present.[77] She critically highlights the sexual commodification of women, white and black. Her most extended intertextual engagement with decadence, which begins in the opening paragraph, is with Oscar Wilde's *The Picture of Dorian Gray* and revelations around cultures of sexual dissidence in the trials involving Wilde. Repertoires of racialization and class and gender stratification – legacies of British imperialism, plantation slavery and the racism that underpinned them – shape the making of colonial civil society and respectability as represented in the novel.

In 'Depressive Time and Jazz Modernism in *Good Morning, Midnight*', Chapter 4, I address Rhys's experiment with time and tempos in the novel. Published in 1939, *Good Morning, Midnight* is set in Paris in 1937 during the Exposition Internationale des Arts et Techniques Dans La Vie Moderne (International Exposition of Arts and Technics in Modern Life), which strove to 'demonstrate the efforts made by every nation in the world towards new standards of living, materially and morally, according to the conditions created by the present economic crisis', the wake of the Great Depression.[78] The terrace, the site of the only scene set at the Exposition in the novel, 'possessed remarkable visual command' over the national pavilions, 'the world itself laid out in microcosm', for the first time in the history of such events under the banner of the international.[79] Yet, as contemporary observer Anne O'Hare McCormick reports, the pavilions were 'so blatantly ... conceived and executed as "national projections"'.[80] The 1937 song 'Swing High, Swing Low', recorded by at least eight different artists and played as the theme music over the opening credits of the film of the same title that year, is also a key temporal marker in the novel. The song is integral to a popular musical culture of the good time, an everyday ethos of jazz modernism. Music and lyrics from the song first surface as one of protagonist Sasha Jansen's 'musical mind pops', 'one-off occurrences of a musical image'.[81] Sasha later improvises around them as a way of ordering and coping with her feelings about social planes and her depressive memories of the impact of her at times harrowing financial insecurity in post–First World War Western Europe. Rhys, I argue, also frames Sasha's experience of depression through explicit and tacit allusion to Mrs Erlynne in Oscar Wilde's *Lady Windermere's Fan*, Pablo Picasso's rescue series of 1932–3 and weeping woman series of the mid-1930s, and Victorian iconography of the female suicide. These texts and art tend to an aesthetic of the surface. Rhys, by contrast, uses Sasha's first-person memories to give plangent depth to the transnational figures of the depressed (drowning) woman, the crying woman and the outcast.

Much of Ford's mentoring of Rhys focused on the revision process. In *The Work of Revision*, Hannah Sullivan highlights 'revision as a major method of composition' for 'modernist writers', a practice that allowed them 'to iterate towards styles of minimalism and maximalism' and 'to discover many of the stylistic features that we associate with modernism'.[82] Revision became a crucial aspect of Rhys's writing process. In 1949 she writes to Selma Vaz Dias, for instance, of her 'longing for clarity', which she has 'learnt one generally gets … by cutting, or by very slight shifts and changes'.[83] '[T]he association of revision and literary value is the legacy of high modernism and the print culture that nourished it', Sullivan demonstrates. 'Modernist writers revised overtly, passionately, and at many points in the lifespan of their texts.'[84] The textual histories of 'Till September Petronella' (1960) and 'Tigers Are Better Looking' (1962), I argue in Chapter 5, demonstrate how Rhys uses revision/recomposition to discover and thread through fresh layers of meaning in her material and in her retrospection on London's pre–First World War and interwar bohemias. There are several extant drafts of each story to ground the analysis. A version of 'Tigers Are Better Looking' was, like an early version of 'Till September Petronella', part of the rejected collection *The Sound of the River*.[85] The events at the core of 'Till September Petronella' – drawn from Rhys's 1915 holiday with Adrian Allinson and Philip Heseltine – are first fictionalized in the Hebertson chapter of 'Triple Sec'. As she did with *Voyage in the Dark*, Rhys may have drawn on her diaries of the 1910s. There is no record of when she lost them. Fragments of versions of the story are in the Green Exercise Book (late 1930s) and the Orange Notebook (1940s). A fragment of material that may have been part of the 1940s novel or a much longer version of the 1960 story survives. Fragments of an early draft of 'Tigers Are Better Looking' open Rhys's Black Exercise Book of the late 1930s, and further fragments are in the Orange Notebook. 'Till September Petronella' and 'Tigers Are Better-Looking' are in some ways companion stories, despite their different historical settings: both focus on the hostilities between her characters and the ways they are shaped by gender, class, sexuality and racialization. The Apple Tree Club in 'Till September Petronella' is based on the Crabtree Club, founded by Augustus John, that Rhys frequented in the 1910s; the Jim-Jam Club in 'Tigers Are Better-Looking' is based on the Shim-Sham Club, founded by

Jack Isow and Ike Hatch in 1935, and dubbed in the British press 'Harlem in London'.[86] Rhys writes about her membership of the Crabtree Club in *Smile Please*; her frequenting of the Shim-Sham Club is not yet known.

Dominica, a Kalinago island at the time of European imperial expansion in the Caribbean, was settled by people of European and African ancestry from French-speaking Martinique and for periods in the late eighteenth and early nineteenth centuries was formally part of the French Antilles. Cultural traffic between Dominica and neighbouring Martinique has been particularly strong. Dominica's Creole language is, like Martinican Creole, French-based. In a note to 'Lost Island', Rhys states that the Dominican and Martinican Creole languages are identical.[87] Pointedly, in recognition of its inter-imperial history, on gaining its independence from Britain in 1979 Dominica joined both the British Commonwealth of Nations and the Organisation internationale de la Francophonie.

The French imperial imaginary of its Caribbean colonies was profoundly shaped by the stereotype of the *doudou* (sweetheart, sweetie or darling), for Rhys a deeply resonant figure of Dominica's inter-imperial history. The Gallic figure of the *doudou* conflates tropical sexual exoticism, a feminized colonial landscape and a projection of the political dimension of the relationship between the French Antilles and France through a romantic sexual relationship.[88] Literature and arts which draw uncritically and sentimentally on this conflation – which includes a 'reservoir of immediately recognizable tropes to inscribe' the French Antilles 'and to propel readerly desire' – have been labelled doudouist.[89] Edwin C. Hill Jr attributes '[t]he surprising absence of the *doudou*'s song in postcolonial criticism' in part to 'the latter's methodological privileging of textual paradigms' over musical contexts.[90] Rhys's authorial interest in the figure of the *doudou* and in doudouism developed in Paris in the mid- to late 1920s, when both (perhaps coincidentally) were becoming objects of anti-colonial critique on the part of French Antillean diasporic writers, notably the Nardal sisters.

I argue in Chapter 6 that Rhys critically invokes the *doudou* and doudouism through allusions to music hall hits and a vernacular Caribbean musical corpus in 'Trio' (from *The Left Bank and Other Stories*), *Voyage in the Dark*, *Good Morning, Midnight*, 'Let Them Call It Jazz' and *Wide Sargasso Sea*. Before *Wide Sargasso Sea*, Rhys situates the *doudou* in the context of Lesser Antillean labour migration. She places imperial and colonial temporalities of doudouism beside a re-visionary interest in the modern resonances of the Antillean *doudou*, addressing her stakes in the formation and perception of Caribbean female sexual identities. Rhys's most substantial treatment of the *doudou* is in *Wide*

*Sargasso Sea*. The history of the *doudou* stereotype has been traced to the French Antilles of the late 1760s and the Creole song '*Adieu foulard, adieu madras*', which Christophine Dubois sings to Antoinette Cosway in Rhys's novel.[91] She sang it as an enslaved nurse to the child Antoinette and sings it, too, after Antoinette's marriage. In writing Part Two of the novel, Rhys struggled to grasp her Rochester figure's point of view. The composition of a poem, 'Obeah Night', has been read as her breakthrough in her characterization of the Rochester figure, a breakthrough occasioned by reflection on editor Diana Athill's criticism of an early draft of Part Two. She remembers it as 'indeed thin: the marriage' between Rochester and Antoinette 'became a disaster almost immediately, before it had been given time to exist'.[92] In Rhys's account, she then 'realised that he must have fallen for her – and violently too'.[93] What seduces him is Antoinette singing to him in the voice of the *doudou*.

As noted, Rhys wrote an early version of *Wide Sargasso Sea* in the 1930s and 1940s; she began writing the novel again in the late 1950s.[94] Despite the time gap between publication of Rhys's pre–Second World War fiction and *Wide Sargasso Sea*, there are continuities in her compositional methods and in her concerns (most notably, tropicality, the *doudou*, sexual ruin, ascriptions of degeneracy to white Creoles, the past existing beside and in the present). Family secrets and investments in planter family memory around the abolition of slavery surface as themes in *After Leaving Mr Mackenzie* and the final draft of *Voyage in the Dark* respectively. In writing *Wide Sargasso Sea*, Rhys painstakingly and imaginatively works her way through psychological geographies of imperialism in ruin, the particularities of which are rooted in the tropology of hurricanes and transgenerationally inflected personal and Dominican cultural memory. They offer, I argue in Chapter 7, 'Hurricane Poetics in *Wide Sargasso* Sea', crucial insight into what Carine M. Mardorossian would term the 'landscape-function' in the text: 'why landscapes are described the way they are, not in and of themselves but in and through narrative and in relation to the human subject … what "classificatory function" the environment and its representation in the text play'.[95] Building on my elaboration of the function of '*Adieu foulard, adieu madras*' in Chapter 6, I demonstrate how Rhys's Rochester's subjective consciousness of climate and landscape (with which he elides the *doudou*) draws out the operation of tropicality as an othering process. Locating an appropriative hurricane poetics in her Rochester's consciousness, Rhys explores their disruptive formal energies to expose the psychological depredations of a new form of frontier capitalism: the barter of 'good race' – marriage into an upper-class English family – for a substantial dowry.[96] Those energies inspire

Rhys to 'lift the whole thing out of real life into – well *on* to a different plane'.[97] In reimagining her Rochester figure's making sense of climate and landscape through Eurocentric ideas of tropicality, Rhys also addresses questions around the historying of the Caribbean, inspired in part by a topos of ruin in Derek Walcott's early poetry. By turning to the hurricane poetics of *Wide Sargasso Sea* and to Rhys's working through of Lockhart family history, I also draw out fresh dimensions of Rhys's re-vision of *Jane Eyre* and representation of Antoinette's psychological geography.

In 'The Locked Heart: The Creole Family Romance of *Wide Sargasso Sea*', Peter Hulme argues that an examination of 'local' West Indian particularities in *Wide Sargasso Sea* demands that the novel be read 'as a reworking of the materials from *Jane Eyre* inflected by the received traditions of a planter "family history". In other words, literary production is viewed here less as a matter of individual creativity than as a trans-generational formation from "event" to "family memory" to "literary text".[98] Family silences and the fallibility of family memory are themes of the vignette 'Geneva' in *Smile Please*. What was sayable about the economic decline of the Lockhart family across generations was that it had not received British government monies to compensate slaveowners for the emancipation of enslaved labour. A cache of archival material I discovered in 2013 – letters of her slaveowning great grandparents James Potter Lockhart and Jane Maxwell Lockhart, William King and William Brade Lockhart, legal documents, slave registration and slave compensation records, and letters by James's friend Alexander Dalrymple – point to what Nicolas Abraham and Maria Torok would term a crypt in the Lockhart family memory around the shame of massive debt and extravagant living ruining family fortunes. The compensation monies were paid to King, James Lockhart's chief creditor. Abraham and Torok theorize that across generations family secrets may be 'preserved in a crypt within language'.[99] Abraham writes of what he terms the phantom: '[W]hat haunts are not the dead, but the gaps left in us by the secrets of others.' The 'words used by the phantom to carry out its return ... are often the very words that rule an entire family's history'.[100] He insists that haunted language 'constitutes an attempt at exorcism, an attempt, that is, to relieve the unconscious by placing the effects of the phantom in the social realm'.[101] Gabriele Schwab carefully elaborates how crypts may be formed:

> [M]emories are passed on from generation to generation, most immediately through stories told or written, but more subliminally through a parent's moods or modes of being that create a particular economy and aesthetics of care. Formed during the earliest phases of life, the latter are often remembered not

as thoughts or words or stories but existentially as moods or even somatically in the form of embodied psychic life. Often it is through the transgenerational transmission of body memories and forms of somatic psychic life that trauma is unconsciously received and remembered.… An individual or a generation can unwittingly speak the unconscious of a previous individual or generation in a cryptic speech marked by an unspeakable secret.… In order to find the crypt in language, we need to read speech and writing as a 'system of expressive traces'.[102]

Abraham duly notes 'that the "phantom effect" progressively fades during its transmission from one generation to the next'.[103] In *Wide Sargasso Sea*, Rhys's negotiation of the Lockhart crypt, I argue, provides an interested view of Caribbean history realized fictionally in the novel's psychological geographies of plantations and European-settled property in ruin. Aspects of the circumscribed oral stories told of the Lockhart fortunes provide for Antoinette Cosway a sense of the material dimensions of her family's circumstances. Rhys is careful to trace Antoinette's understanding of them to conversations and gossip that she overhears as a child.

Rhys conceptualizes her creative process as meticulously finding and developing literary 'shape' in her materials.[104] In *Jean Rhys's Modernist Bearings and Experimental Aesthetics*, my close analysis of the traces of this creative and compositional process through connective reading reshapes the ways in which the fields of Rhys and modernist scholarship might take new bearings in relation to her experimental aesthetics.

# Notes

1 'relation, *n.* 2.a.', *Oxford English Dictionary Online* (Oxford: Oxford University Press, 2019).
2 David Scott, *Conscripts of Modernity: The Tragedy of Colonial Enlightenment* (Durham, NC: Duke University Press, 2004), 4.
3 '[N]ot quite, not English': Erica L. Johnson, '"Upholstered Ghosts": Jean Rhys's Posthuman Imaginary', in *Jean Rhys: Twenty-First-Century Approaches*, ed. Erica L. Johnson and Patricia Moran (Edinburgh: Edinburgh University Press, 2015), 210. '[A]ppropriation of modernism', 'an articulation of difference and a rewriting of influence': Ankhi Mukherjee, 'Creole Modernism', *Affirmations: Of the Modern* 2, no. 1 (2015), https://affirmationsmodern.com/articles/58, accessed 13 May 2019. '[A] set of nuanced contradictions': H. Adlai Murdoch, 'The Discourses of Jean Rhys: Resistance, Ambivalence and Creole Indeterminacy', in *Jean Rhys: Twenty-First-Century Approaches*, ed. Erica L. Johnson and Patricia Moran, 164.

4  A conceptual metaphor for Rhys's place in literary history: Mary Lou Emery, 'Foreword', in *Rhys Matters: New Critical Perspectives*, ed. Mary Wilson and Kerry L. Johnson (New York: Palgrave Macmillan, 1913), xi; Mary Wilson and Kerry L. Johnson, 'Introduction: Rhys Matters?' in *Rhys Matters*, ed. Wilson and Kerry L. Johnson, xi-xii; Erica L. Johnson and Patricia Moran, 'Introduction: The Haunting of Jean Rhys', in *Jean Rhys: Twenty-First-Century Approaches*, ed. Erica L. Johnson and Patricia Moran, 1–17. A descriptor of the affect of reading Rhys's fiction: as examples, 'Rhys's strange and haunting novels', Jean Rhys, *Smile Please: An Unfinished Autobiography* (1979; repr., Harmondsworth: Penguin, 1981), cover blurb, and Leila Aboulela, 'Jean Rhys's *Voyage in the Dark* haunts everything I write', *Guardian*, 22 February 2019. The 'risky space' to which Rhys transports readers and scholars: Elaine Savory, *Jean Rhys* (Cambridge: Cambridge University Press, 1998), 223. A means to position affect studies as a new cutting edge in Rhys studies: Erica L. Johnson and Patricia Moran, 'Introduction', 8–9. The transnational, transcultural and diasporic: Juliana Lopoukhine, Frédéric Regard and Kerry-Jane Wallart, 'Introduction: On Reading Rhys Transnationally', in *Transnational Jean Rhys: Lines of Transmission, Lines of Flight*, ed. Juliana Lopoukhine, Frédéric Regard and Kerry-Jane Wallart (London: Bloomsbury, 2020), 1.

5  '[W]hat really matters is her strangeness': Emery, 'Foreword', [xi]. 'Rhys's work defies periodisation and transcends [such] categories' as 'modernist, postcolonial, Caribbean, British and Creole writer': Erica L. Johnson and Patricia Moran, 'Introduction', 1. 'Rhys's peculiar, multivalent, and difficult canonicity': Wilson and Kerry L. Johnson, 'Introduction', 2. '[S]trange case': Peter Kalliney, 'Jean Rhys: Left Bank Modernist as Postcolonial Intellectual', in *The Oxford Handbook of Global Modernisms*, ed. Mark Wollaeger and Matt Eatough (Oxford: Oxford University Press, 2012), 429.

6  Jeffrey Andrew Weinstock, '*from* Introduction: The Spectral Turn', in *The Spectralities Reader: Ghosts and Haunting in Contemporary Cultural Theory*, ed. María del Pilar Blanco and Esther Peeren (London: Bloomsbury, 2013), 63.

7  Gillian Whitlock, *The Intimate Empire: Reading Women's Autobiography* (London: Cassell, 2000), 204.

8  Douglas Mao and Rebecca L. Walkowitz, 'The New Modernist Studies', *PMLA* 123, no. 3 (2008): 737–8; Lopoukhine, Regard and Wallart, 'Introduction', 6.

9  Helen Carr, *Jean Rhys*, 2nd edn. (Tavistock: Northcote House, 2012); Carol Dell'Amico, *Colonialism and the Modernist Moment in the Early Novels of Jean Rhys* (New York: Routledge, 2005); Mary Lou Emery, *Jean Rhys at 'World's End': Novels of Colonial and Sexual Exile* (Austin: University of Texas Press, 1990); Coral Ann Howells, *Jean Rhys* (Hemel Hempstead: Harvester Wheatsheaf, 1991); Delia Caparosa Konzett, *Ethnic Modernisms: Anzia Yesierka, Zora Neale Hurston, Jean Rhys and the Aesthetics of Dislocation* (New York: Palgrave Macmillan, 2002);

Elaine Savory, *Jean Rhys* (Cambridge: Cambridge University Press, 1998); and Sue Thomas, *The Worlding of Jean Rhys* (Westport, CT: Greenwood, 1999).

10  Edited collections on Rhys: Wilson and Kerry L. Johnson, eds, *Rhys Matters: New Critical Perspectives*; Erica L. Johnson and Patricia Moran, eds, *Jean Rhys*; Elaine Savory and Erica L. Johnson, eds, *Wide Sargasso Sea at 50* (Cham: Palgrave Macmillan, 2020); Loupoukhine, Regard and Wallart, eds, *Transnational Jean Rhys*. Special journal issues: Mary Lou Emery, ed., Jean Rhys, *Journal of Caribbean Literatures* 3, no. 3 (2003); Jeannette Baxter, Anna Snaith and Tory Young, eds, *Reading Jean Rhys*, *Women: A Cultural Review*, 23, no. 4 (2012); and Juliana Lopoukhine, Frédéric Regard and Kerry-Jane Wallart, eds, *Jean Rhys: Writing Precariously*, *Women: A Cultural Review* 31, no. 2 (2020). Recent comparative studies of Rhys are too numerous to enumerate here. I refer to arguments in many over the course of this book.

11  Philology: Christopher GoGwilt, *The Passage of Literature: Genealogies of Modernism in Conrad, Rhys, and Pramoedya* (Oxford: Oxford University Press, 2011). Psychoanalytic studies: Dell'Amico, *Colonialism and the Modernist Moment in the Early Novels of Jean Rhys*; Cathleen Maslen, *Ferocious Things: Jean Rhys and the Politics of Women's Melancholia* (Newcastle-upon-Tyne: Cambridge Scholars Publishing, 2009); Patricia Moran, *Virginia Woolf, Jean Rhys, and the Aesthetics of Trauma* (New York: Palgrave Macmillan, 2007); Anne B. Simpson, *Territories of the Psyche: The Fiction of Jean Rhys* (New York: Palgrave Macmillan, 2005). Narratology: Nagihan Haliloglu, *Narrating from the Margins: Self-Representation of Female and Colonial Subjectivities in Jean Rhys's Novels* (Amsterdam: Rodopi, 2011). Postcolonial feminist theory: Eri Kobayashi, *Women and Mimicry: A Postcolonial Feminist Reading of Jean Rhys's Five Novels* (Okayama, Japan: Fukuro Shuppan Publishing, 2011). Postcolonial hybridity theory: Cristina-Georgiana Voicu, *Exploring Cultural Identities in Jean Rhys's Fiction* (Warsaw: De Gruyter Open, 2014). Caribbean literary and cultural theory: Carine M. Mardorossian, *Reclaiming Difference: Caribbean Women Rewrite Postcolonialism* (Charlottesville: University of Virginia Press, 2005); Leah Reade Rosenberg, *Nationalism and the Formation of Caribbean Literature* (New York: Palgrave Macmillan, 2007); and a series of substantial essays by Emery. Emery, '"Broken Parts": *Wide Sargasso Sea* and the Poetics of Caribbean Modernism', in *Wide Sargasso Sea at 50*, ed. Elaine Savory and Erica L. Johnson (Cham: Palgrave Macmillan, 2020), 125–39; 'Caribbean Modernism: Plantation to Planetary', in *The Oxford Handbook of Global Modernisms*, ed. Mark Wollaeger and Matt Eatough (Oxford: Oxford University Press, 2012), 48–77; 'The Poetics of Labor in Jean Rhys's Caribbean Modernism', *Women: A Cultural Review* 23, no. 4 (2012): 421–44; and 'Taking the Detour, Finding the Rebels: Crossroads of Caribbean and Modernist Studies', in *Disciplining Modernism*, ed. Pamela L. Caughie (New York: Palgrave Macmillan, 2010), 71–91.

12  Jonathan Goldman, *Modernism Is the Literature of Celebrity* (Austin: University of Texas Press, 2011); Celia Marshik, *British Modernism and Censorship* (Cambridge: Cambridge University Press, 2006); Lisa Stead, *Off to the Pictures: Cinema-Going, Women's Writing and Movie Culture in Interwar Britain* (Edinburgh: Edinburgh University Press, 2016); Alissa G. Karl, *Modernism and the Marketplace: Literary Culture and Consumer Capitalism in Rhys, Woolf, Stein, and Nella Larsen* (New York: Routledge, 2009); Vike Martina Plock, *Modernism, Fashion and Interwar Women Writers* (Edinburgh: Edinburgh University Press, 2017); Juliette Taylor-Batty, *Multilingualism in Modernist Fiction* (Basingstoke: Palgrave Macmillan, 1913); Bridget T. Chalk, *Modernism and Mobility: The Passport and Cosmopolitan Experience* (New York: Palgrave, Macmillan, 2014). On Rhys and the transnational, see Jessica Berman, *Modernist Commitments: Ethics, Politics, and Transnational Modernism* (New York: Columbia University Press, 2012); Lopoukhine, Regard and Wallart, eds, *Transnational Jean Rhys*; and Anna Snaith, *Maiden Voyages: Colonial Women Writers in London, 1890–1945* (Cambridge: Cambridge University Press, 2014).
13  Snaith, *Maiden Voyages*, 151.
14  Gregory Machacek, 'Allusion', *PMLA* 122, no. 2 (2007): 531.
15  GoGwilt, *The Passage of Literature*, 65.
16  Lopoukhine, Regard and Wallart, 'Introduction', in *Transnational Jean Rhys*, 5; and Snaith, *Modernist Voyages*, 143.
17  Rhys, letter to Diana Athill, April 1964, *Letters 1931–1966*, ed. Francis Wyndham and Diana Melly (London: Andre Deutsch, 1984), 267.
18  Carole Angier, *Jean Rhys: Life and Work*, rev. edn. (London: Penguin, 1992), 50.
19  Rhys, *Smile Please*, 120, 129–30.
20  Ibid., 104, 129–30.
21  Ibid., 112–14.
22  *Oxford English Dictionary Online*.
23  Ibid., 114.
24  Ibid., 138–9.
25  Ibid., 138.
26  The circular is quoted in Elena Lamberti, '"Wandering Yankees": The *transatlantic review* or How the Americans Came to Europe', in *Ford Madox Ford, Modernist Magazines and Editing*, ed. Jason Harding (Amsterdam: Rodopi, 2010), 216.
27  Ivan Beede, letter to Jean Rhys, 2 February 1931, Jean Rhys Papers, Department of Special Collections and University Archives, University of Tulsa, US.
28  Angier, *Jean Rhys*, 138.
29  Both Jed Esty and Jonathan Goldman confuse these exercise books and *Voyage in the Dark*, placing the novel as written before 1914. Esty, *Unseasonable Youth: Modernism, Colonialism, and the Fiction of Development* (Oxford: Oxford University Press, 2012), 166; Goldman, *Modernism Is the Literature of Celebrity* (Austin: University of Texas Press, 2011), 142.

30  Max Saunders, *Ford Madox Ford: A Dual Life. Volume II: The After-War World* (Oxford: Oxford University Press, 1996), 282, 295–7.
31  GoGwilt, *The Passage of Literature*, 13.
32  Jean Rhys, 'L'Affaire Ford', Jean Rhys Papers; Angier, *Jean Rhys*, 134–5.
33  Savory, *Jean Rhys*, 40–1.
34  Ford Madox Ford, *Henry James: A Critical Study* (New York: Albert and Charles Boni, 1915), 68.
35  Ford, 'Rive Gauche', in *The Left Bank and Other Stories*, by Jean Rhys (1927; repr., Freeport, NY: Books for Libraries Press, 1970), 24.
36  Angier, *Jean Rhys*, 656.
37  Ronald Radano, 'Black Music Labour and the Animated Properties of Slave Sound', *Boundary 2* 43, no. 1 (2016): 177.
38  Brett A. Berliner, *Ambivalent Desire: The Exotic Black Other in Jazz-Age France* (Amherst: University of Massachusetts Press, 2002), 207.
39  Peter J. Kalliney, *Commonwealth of Letters: British Literary Culture and the Emergence of Postcolonial Aesthetics* (Oxford: Oxford University Press, 2013), 224. According to Neville Braybrooke in a review of a new edition of *Voyage in the Dark* in 1967, Jonathan Cape, which published *The Left Bank and Other Stories*, described it on the dust-jacket as 'Studies and Sketches of Present-Day Bohemian Paris'; this leads Kalliney in an earlier essay 'Jean Rhys: Left Bank Modernist as Postcolonial Intellectual' and Angela Frattarola in *Modernist Soundscapes: Auditory Technology and the Novel* (Gainesville: University Press of Florida, 2018) to conflate Ford's Preface and the dust-jacket copy, giving the title of *The Left Bank and Other Stories* as *The Left Bank: Sketches and Studies of Present-Day Bohemian Paris*. Kalliney, 'Jean Rhys', in *The Oxford Handbook of Global Modernisms*, ed. Mark Wollaeger and Matt Eatough (Oxford: Oxford University Press, 2012), 417; Frattarola, *Modernist Soundscapes*, 119. Braybrooke's review is cited in Elgin W. Mellown, *Jean Rhys: A Descriptive and Annotated Bibliography of Works and Criticism* (New York: Garland, 1984), 4.
40  Lamberti, '"Wandering Yankees"', 222.
41  Rhys, letter to Diana Athill, 24 May 1964, *Letters 1931–1966*, 280.
42  Saunders, *Ford Madox Ford. Volume II*, 282–3. He quotes from 'Memoirs of Paul Nash: 1913–1946'.
43  Margarete Rubik, 'Jean Rhys's Vision of the Left Bank', in *Rive Gauche: Paris as a Site of Avant-garde Art and Cultural Exchange in the 1920s*, ed. Elke Mettinger, Margarete Rubik and Jörg Türschmann (Amsterdam: Rodopi, 2010), 63.
44  Peter Brooker, *Bohemia in London: The Social Scene of Early Modernism* (Basingstoke: Palgrave Macmillan, 2007), 8.
45  Brooker, *Bohemia in London*, 125.
46  Rhys, letter to Diana Athill, April 1964, *Letters 1931–1966*, 267; Rhys, *Smile Please*, 120.

47  On Poupeye, see Pierre Piret, 'Camille Poupeye, ein Vermittler des Modernen Theatres', *Lendemains: études comparées sur la France*, no. 98/99 (2000): 75-86, or 'Camille Poupeye, passeur et miroir de la modernité théâtrale', *Textyles: Revue des lettres belges de langue française* 20 (2001): 25-32. The brief obituary for him in London's *Daily Telegraph* notes his friendships with George Bernard Shaw and Sir James Barrie. 'Obituary', *Daily Telegraph* (London), 30 November 1963, 10.
48  Rhys, 'Triple Sec', Jean Rhys Papers.
49  Quoted by Herschel Brickell, rev. of *Voyage in the Dark*, by Jean Rhys, *Philadelphia Record* 13 March 1935.
50  Rhys, letter to Peggy Kirkaldy, October 1945, *Letters 1931-1966*, 39.
51  Rhys, letter to Selma Vaz Dias, 16 October 1956, *Letters 1931-1966*, 133.
52  Rhys, letter to Francis Wyndham, 29 March 1958, *Letters 1931-1966*, 153.
53  Carolyn Allen, 'Creole: The Problem of Definition', in *Questioning Creole: Creole Discourses in Caribbean Culture*, ed. Verene Shepherd and Glen Richards (Oxford: James Currey, 2002), 50-1.
54  Ralph Bauer and José Antonio Mazzotti, 'Introduction: Creole Subjects in the Colonial Americas', in *Creole Subjects in the Colonial Americas: Empires, Texts, Identities*, ed. Bauer and Mazotti (Chapel Hill: University of North Carolina Press for the Omohundro Institute of Early American History and Culture, 2009), 6.
55  Jean Rhys Papers. 'Mr. Howard's House. CREOLE.' is dated 4 December 1938.
56  Rhys, letter to Vaz Dias, 27 April 1953, *Letters 1931-1966*, 108.
57  Rhys, *Letters 1931-1966*, 172.
58  Catherine Hall, 'What Is a West Indian?' in *West Indian Intellectuals in Britain*, ed. Bill Schwarz (Manchester: Manchester University Press, 2003), 48.
59  Angier, *Jean Rhys*, 413.
60  Rhys, letter to Francis Wyndham, 14 September 1959, *Letters 1931-1966*, 172.
61  See Sue Thomas, 'Jean Rhys Getting the "Feel" of the West Indies in *Wide Sargasso Sea*', in *Wide Sargasso Sea at 50*, ed. Savory and Erica L. Johnson, 111-24.
62  Rhys knew Allfrey and Bliss socially in London and corresponded with them. Rhys refers to Thaly in a 1936 letter (*Letters 1931-1966*, 29). Among her unpublished letters, she extols Walcott's early poetry in a letter to Eliot Bliss, 1962, writes of her admiration for Mendes in a letter to Francis Wyndham on 18 November 1968, mentions her knowledge of McKay's writing in a letter to Oliver Stoner (Morchard Bishop) on 7 August 1970, and expresses admiration for Naipaul's *A House for Mr Biswas* in a letter to Diana Athill on 3 May 1966. Jean Rhys Papers, Tulsa, McFarlin Library, University of Tulsa. On Thaly, see Lizabeth Paravisini-Gebert, '"A Forgotten Outpost of Empire": Social Life in Dominica and the Creative Imagination', *Jean Rhys Review* 10, nos. 1-2 (1998): 13-27. On Rhys's relationship with Allfrey, see Lizabeth Paravisini-Gebert, 'Jean Rhys and Phyllis Shand Allfrey: The Story of a Friendship', *Jean Rhys Review* 9, nos. 1-2 (1997): 25-36.

63  See Sue Thomas, 'Genealogies of Story in Jean Rhys's "The Day They Burned the Books"', *Review of English Studies* 72 (2021): 565–76.
64  Jean Rhys, letter to Eliot Bliss, 1962, Jean Rhys Papers.
65  Derek Walcott, 'The Antilles: Fragments of Epic Memory', in his *What the Twilight Says: Essays* (New York: Farrar, Straus and Giroux, 1998), 79.
66  Rhys's preferred title was restored when *Postures* was republished by Andre Deutsch in 1969. Mellown, *Jean Rhys*, 11.
67  Karl Toepfer, *Empire of Ecstasy: Nudity and Movement in German Body Culture, 1910–1955* (Berkeley: University of California Press, 1997), 360.
68  David Arnold, *The Problem of Nature: Environment, Culture and European Expansion* (Oxford: Blackwell, 1996). See also his '"Illusory Riches": Representations of the Tropical World, 1840–1950', *Singapore Journal of Tropical Geography* 21, no. 1 (2000): 6–18.
69  Nancy Stepan, *Picturing the Tropics* (London: Reaktion, 2001), 17–18.
70  Anne Collett, Russell McDougall and Sue Thomas, 'Tracking the Literature of Tropical Weather', in *Tracking the Literature of Tropical Weather: Typhoons, Cyclones and Hurricanes*, ed. Anne Collett, Russell McDougall and Sue Thomas (New York: Palgrave Macmillan, 2017), 13.
71  Felix Driver and Luciana Martins, 'Introduction', in *Tropical Visions in the Age of Empire*, ed. Felix Driver and Luciana Martins (Chicago, IL: University of Chicago Press, 2010), 4, 3.
72  Jessica Berman, *Modernist Commitments: Ethics, Politics, and Transnational Modernism* (New York: Columbia University Press, 2012), 78.
73  Andrew Thacker suggests that *After Leaving Mr Mackenzie* is 'set c. 1925' on the strength of 'the fact that the café le Select is mentioned, an establishment only opened in 1925'. Thacker, 'The Idea of a Critical Literary Geography', *New Formations* no. 57 (Winter 2005/6): 66 and 66n.56.
74  The first title for the essay was 'Down Along: Fragments of Autobiography'. Rhys explains that Dominica is in the Lesser Antilles or Down Along Islands.
75  Rhys, *Smile Please*, 139.
76  Hannah Sullivan, *The Work of Revision* (Cambridge, MA: Harvard University Press, 2013), 2.
77  Eve Kosofsky Sedgwick, *Touching Feeling: Affect, Pedagogy, Performance* (Durham, NC: Duke University Press, 2003), 8, her emphasis.
78  'Paris 1937 International Exhibition of Arts & Technics in Modern Life' [1937], in *World's Fairs: A Global History of Expositions* (Marlborough: Adam Matthew Digital, n.d.), 3, http://www.worldsfairs.amdigital.co.uk.ez.library.latrobe.edu.au/Documents/Details/HMLSC_upam_BX22_AMD599, accessed 29 September 2019.
79  James D. Herbert, *Paris 1937: Worlds on Exhibition* (Ithaca, NY: Cornell University Press, 2018), 13.

80 Quoted in Robert H. Kargon, Karen Fiss, Morris Low and Arthur P. Molella, *World's Fairs on the Eve of War: Science, Technology, and Modernity, 1937–1942* (Pittsburgh: University of Pittsburgh Press, 2015), 18.
81 Tim I. Williams, 'The Classification of Involuntary Musical Imagery: The Case for Earworms', *Psychomusicology: Music, Mind and Brain* 25, no. 1 (2015): 10.
82 Sullivan, *The Work of Revision*, 3, 2.
83 Rhys, letter to Selma Vaz Dias, 9 November 1949, *Letters 1931–1966*, 60.
84 Sullivan, *The Work of Revision*, 2.
85 Rhys, *Letters 1931–1966*, 40n.
86 Rudolph Dunbar, 'Harlem in London: Year of Advancement for Negroes', *Melody Maker*, 7 March 1936.
87 Jean Rhys, 'Lost Island: A Childhood. Fragments of Autobiography', 1, Jean Rhys Papers. The address on the title page indicates that it was being offered for publication through Rhys's husband Leslie Tilden Smith in 1931 or 1932.
88 Régis Antoine, *Les Ecrivains français et les Antilles, des premiers pères blancs aux surréalists noir*, quoted in translation in Brent Hayes Edwards, *The Practice of Diaspora: Literature, Translation, and the Rise of Black Internationalism* (Cambridge, MA: Harvard University Press, 2003), 159.
89 Edwards, *The Practice of Diaspora*, 159.
90 Edwin C. Hill, Jr, '"*Adieu Madras, Adieu Foulard*": Musical Origins and the *Doudou*'s Colonial Plaint', *Ethnomusicology Forum* 16, no. 1 (2007): 39.
91 Richard D. E. Burton, '"Maman-France Doudou": Family Images in French West Indian Colonial Discourse', *Diacritics* 23, no. 3 (1993): 81. There are some variants of the first line from which the song draws its title.
92 Diana Athill, *Stet* (London: Granta, 2000), 162.
93 Rhys, letter to Francis Wyndham, 14 April 1964, *Letters 1931–1966*, 262.
94 Catherine Rovera has meticulously compared the extant drafts of the novel with the published version. *Genèses d'une folie créole: Jean Rhys et 'Jane Eyre'* (Paris: Hermann Éditeurs, 2015).
95 Carine M. Mardorossian, 'Caribbean Formations in the Rhysian Corpus', in *Jean Rhys*, ed. Erica L. Johnson and Moran, 108. She does not, however, identify tropicality as a landscape-function in *Wide Sargasso Sea*. Nor does Jana Giles in 'The Landscape of the Other: Aesthetics, Representation, and the Post-Colonial Sublime in Jean Rhys's *Wide Sargasso Sea*', *MaComère* 5 (2002): 156–83.
96 Charlotte Brontë, *Jane Eyre*, ed. Margaret Smith, introduction and revised notes by Sally Shuttleworth (Oxford: Oxford University Press, 2000), 305.
97 Rhys, letter to Francis Wyndham, 14 May 1964, *Letters 1931–1966*, 277.
98 Peter Hulme, 'The Locked Heart: The Creole Family Romance of *Wide Sargasso Sea*', in *Colonial Discourse/Postcolonial Theory*, ed. Francis Barker, Peter Hulme and Margaret Iverson (Manchester: Manchester University Press, 1996), 75.

99  Gabriele Schwab, *Haunting Legacies: Violent Histories and Transgenerational Trauma* (New York: Columbia University Press, 2010), 55.
100 N. Abraham, 'Notes on the Phantom: A Complement to Freud's Metapsychology', in *The Shell and the Kernel: Renewals of Psychoanalysis*, by Nicolas Abraham and Maria Torok, trans. Nicholas T. Rand (Chicago: University of Chicago Press, 1994), 171, 174, 176.
101 Abraham, 'Notes on the Phantom', 176.
102 Schwab, *Haunting Legacies*, 51–3.
103 Abraham, 'Notes on the Phantom', 176.
104 Diana Athill, 'Foreword', in *Smile Please,* by Rhys, xi.

# 1

# Routes to Rhys's early fiction

Modernist scholarly cultures of celebrity – those around the Left Bank, Ford Madox Ford, his fabled editorship of the *transatlantic review*, and fin-de-siècle Vienna – have occluded the complexity and scope of Rhys's formation as a writer, which ranges beyond Fordian impressionism.[1] In her early fiction, Rhys uses allusion and intertextual and intermedial resonance to locate and position the particularities of her authorial voice and interests for her audiences. In 'Vienne',[2] at sixty-three pages by far the longest story in *The Left Bank and Other Stories*, Rhys alludes to Ernst Kirchner's paintings of dancers, the Viennese art movement kineticism and Filippo Tommaso Marinetti's 'The Founding and Manifesto of Futurism 1909'. The allusions and resonance point to shared formal interests in representing, respectively, routine; movement, groupings and dynamics; and the function of the machine in thinking through the relation between the past and the future. They also signal Rhys's differences of perspective: her interest, for instance, in the mechanics of the off-stage sexual economies in which dancers circulate; the morbid symptoms of the Austro-Hungarian Empire disintegrating under the terms of the post-war Treaty of St Germain and Treaty of Trianon; the 'huge machine of law, order, respectability';[3] and the inescapability of the past. In the far shorter story 'Tea with an Artist', the narrator visits the studio of a painter she identifies as predominantly impressionist in style. Rhys explores the operation of 'law, order, respectability' in framings and readings of the painter and his partner, using irony to expose gaps between the authorial and narrative voices in the story. In *Quartet*, Rhys's representations of the mechanics of Marya Zelli's major depressive episode draw on broad strands of modernist thinking about the relation between the human and (in)animation through marionette theatre and about technology and mind. She also draws on motifs in R. C. Dunning's poem 'The Hermit', lines from which she uses as the novel's epigraph. Rhys explicitly denounces a 'mania for classification' in everyday social life,[4] representing it as an aspect of the depersonalizing 'machine of law, order, respectability'.

The Austro-Hungarian Empire, the major cities of which were Vienna, Budapest and Prague, the settings of 'Vienne', extended from 1867 to 1918. During the First World War Austria-Hungary was one of the Central Powers allied with Germany, Bulgaria and Turkey. Lonnie Johnson points out that in the talks and diplomacy around the post-war peace settlements of the empire with victorious Allied powers – the Treaty of St Germain with Austria (signed on 10 September 1919) and the Treaty of Trianon with Hungary (signed on 4 June 1920) – 'the defeated states were objects of negotiation among the victors. In this respect, the designation "dictated peace" is an accurate description of the so-called negotiation process.' Under the terms of the treaties, both countries lost territory as a 'new European order', with an 'application of the ethnic principle of national self-determination', was established.[5] Inter-Allied Military Control Commissions were appointed to bring about disarmament, both by demobilizing personnel and through 'seizure of war matériel and a prohibition against the ... disposal of equipment through sales'.[6] Rhys's husband Jean Lenglet worked as a secretary-translator for the Japanese delegation to the Commission overseeing disarmament of 'war matériel'. Rhys and Lenglet lived in Vienna from April 1920 to July 1921 and Budapest from July to late October 1921, travelling then to Prague. By May 1922 they were in Belgium.[7] War matériel comprised machinery: 'army equipment, arms, ammunition, and the means to produce them'. Distinctions were made between the appropriate handling of 'war matériel "properly so-called"' and 'matériel adaptable for civilian purposes', sales of 'which would allow Austria to obtain credits necessary for food and economic recovery'.[8] In 'Vienne', the term 'war material' is cynically applied to dancers by Colonel Ishima of the Japanese delegation to the Inter-allied Commission.[9] In this context it suggests assumptions of dancers having sexual histories of servicing military personnel, adaptability for post-war use and 'sale' of sex to subsist and recapitalize. The assumptions are cogs in the 'huge machine of law, order, respectability', which produces, among other things, 'the fiction of the "good" woman and the "bad" one'.[10] The centrality of the mordant term 'war material' in the story is suggested by Rhys's relocating of 'War Material' as the second vignette of the revised 1968 version of 'Vienne' published in *Tigers Are Better-Looking*. In the story, generally nightclub dancers are assumed to be available as part of a 'common pool' of women in straitened circumstances, the sexual use, exchange and conspicuous consumption of whom in front of other men secures Inter-allied homosociality among Commission members and their entourages.[11]

In a reading of 'Vienne' still haunted by the critical stereotype of Rhys as confessional autobiographer 'unfold[ing] an impressionistic personal remembrance of things past', GoGwilt does not separate the narrative and the authorial voices of the story in arguing that the 'narrative perspective' is 'nostalgically attached to personal memories of postwar Vienna in 1921'.[12] The first and last vignettes of 'Vienne', though, feature dancing in a narrative arc that pointedly positions the story in relation to the poetics of three modernist movements – *Die Brücke*, kineticism and futurism – all of which were animated by experiment with the representation of movement and with abstraction. Not recognizing Rhys's engagement with Ernst Kirchner and kineticism, GoGwilt argues that Rhys elides an 'Austrian German cultural-historical perspective[s]'.[13] The opening vignette of 'Vienne' as published in the *transatlantic review* in 1924 is titled 'The Dancer'.[14] With some changes to the punctuation and a renamed husband for the narrator Frances, the vignette, untitled, opens the far longer 1927 version of 'Vienne', which is set in 1920–1. One of the dancer's spectacular drilled moves – jumping '[f]our, five feet' from the ground and landing 'without a sound' – is drawn from the repertoire and technique of Grete Wiesenthal, a Viennese free dance pioneer and post–First World War choreographer.[15] The unnamed dancer has 'Kirchner girl's legs', an allusion to *Die Brücke* leader Ernst Kirchner's stylized and signature representation of regimented dancers' legs in artworks such as *Tänzerinnen* (*Dancers*) (1906) and *Sechs Tänzerinnen* (*Six Dancers*) (1911).[16] The signature legs, one of his 'linear and planar abbreviations for forms in nature ... which he called hieroglyphs' were developed as part of the 'painting vocabulary' of a more abstract 'two-dimensionalized style'.[17] Later in his career Kirchner would characterize his stylistic innovation as 'a technique of grasping everything while it was in motion ... I practised seizing things quickly ... and in this way I learned how to depict movement itself'.[18] 'The image of dancing was for Franz Cizek the key to achieving' a 'synthesis (or "simultanism") of aesthetic styles' – 'expressionist, cubist, futurist, and constructivist' – that he called kineticism, Karl Toepfer writes.[19] For F. T. Marinetti in 'The Founding and Manifesto of Futurism 1909' the speeding car is a sign of 'the beauty of speed' in a machine age that would be a subject of futurist art and writing and the car ride is a metonym of an aesthetic celebrating 'the love of danger, the habit of energy and fearlessness'.[20] In 'Vienne', the car, chauffeur-driven in Vienna and en route from Budapest to Prague, is a symbol of 'The Spending Phase' of Frances and Pierre's time in the former Austro-Hungarian Empire.[21] For Marinetti, the car 'is attached to ... a sense ... of a present moment that is freed from the drag of the past';[22] the tree-tops 'dancing madly' above Frances in the story's final vignette are a sign of a sudden suicidal impulse to be freed from a future determined by 'the old hag Fate' and the 'huge machine of law, order, respectability'.²³ The story's closure suggests that at the human level the drag or pull of the past is inescapable.

Deborah Holmes and Lisa Silverman observe:

> Vienna's glamorous fin de siècle … is almost invariably presented as a golden age of cosmopolitanism, when subcultures became mainstream and the effects of Viennese innovations reverberated around the world. Most often evoked by the names and achievements of a series of great men (Sigmund Freud, Gustav Mahler, Arnold Schoenberg, Gustav Klimt, Hugo von Hofmannsthal, Arthur Schnitzler), this view of Vienna is not only an idealized version of the fin de siècle itself but has become so overdetermined that it is fixed in our imaginations as the example par excellence of modern cultural intersections in Austria's capital, eclipsing all others.²⁴

Kineticism is one of those eclipsed artistic movements. Cizek produced no manifesto of or essays about kineticism; rather, he elaborated kineticism in the classroom. The primacy of dance in kineticism accords with a wider early twentieth-century interest in dance as 'the key medium of all arts trying to reflect the new technological age as an era defined by motion'.²⁵ A yearly exhibition of student work in Cizek's department of ornamental form theory took place at the *Kunstgewerbeschule* from 1920 to 1924.²⁶ Located in Fichtegasse, the School was very close indeed to places which the Lenglets frequented (the Sacher Hotel) and where they lived in 1921 (the Hotel Imperial). The exhibitions were advertised through visually striking posters. The fullest contemporary account of kineticism is *Der Formwille der Zeit in der Angewandten Kunst*, by Leopold Wolfgang Rochowanski (1922), a slim book of 104 pages with 93 black-and-white illustrations of student art. The book was reprinted in 1980, but it is only in the last eighteen years that contextualizing and substantial studies of kineticism have begun to appear.²⁷

The *Formwille* (will for form) of kineticism is the representation of the beautiful; drawing out its blind spots, Rhys places the beautiful alongside transnational consumption, dispossession and exploitation. Remembering Vienna, Frances takes her gaze from the dancer on stage at the Parisien who has 'it' – 'the spark, the flame in her dancing' – to the place of women who work on stages in sexual economies and cultures of serial sexual predation. Rhys's puns, for example, 'tender passages', mordantly evoke the place of money ('tender') in the mechanisms of these economies.²⁸ Having worked as a chorus girl in the late Edwardian period, Rhys is always an acute authorial observer of such erotic commodification of the professional dancer. Rhys places the materiality of the dancer and the performer–spectator relation historically and socially. Rhys had also used 'it', an idiomatic descriptor of magnetic beauty, in the 1924 version of 'Vienne'. The term 'it' entered a popular sexual lexicon in early 1927 with the release of the highly successful film *It*, loosely drawn from a novel by Elinor Glyn, though Glyn had used the term in *Man and Maid* (1922).[29] Rhys's use of 'it', then, shows her keen ear for contemporary vernacular.

In 'Vienne', Rhys's translation of kineticism across genre (arts and crafts to fiction) is accomplished through the mobile gaze of the reminiscing first-person narrator Frances. Frances narrates the story by moving from vignette to vignette, focusing on shifting compositions of groups and couples, on their mobility across space, time and class, and on currency speculation. Her narrative voice shifts back and forth across languages (English, French and German), at times uncertainly, drawing out English borrowings, particularly from French. The slipperiness of moving across languages is highlighted by phonetic misspellings of words, for example, '*Tänzerinen*' for *Tänzerinnen* (dancers) and 'forgessen' for *vergessen* (forget) and missing capitals, 'blumen' for *Blumen* (flowers), mistakes which emphasize the aurality and orality of Frances's experience of German.[30] Mobility of perspective between author and narrator is stitched into the fabric of the story through irony and word play.

Rhys draws out Frances's turn away from the real to abstraction through highlighting her recourse to typing of characters and ethnicities, a mechanical stylization criticized by husband Pierre. In doing so, Rhys foregrounds the representational surface of the perceptions which form her narrative. John Frow points out that '[t]he character typologies on which fictional texts draw and to which they contribute provide a ready-made model of personhood which is usable, on the one hand, for immediate recognition of characters in texts, and, on the other, for application to persons in the world'.[31] Rhys highlights Frances's recourse to ready-made types and in doing so draws attention to signs of speedy classification and judgement in a story which has speed as a theme. The types are, ironically, produced by the operation of the 'huge machine of law, order, respectability' which Frances criticizes. Frances, for instance, explicitly uses such terms as 'satyr', '*jeune fille*', '*mondäne Tänzerinen*', 'adventuress', the 'gr-r-rande cocotte', '*Femme Sacrée*' and 'goose-girl out of a fairy tale' to describe figures in the narrative. Ethnic and national stereotypes, too, are often invoked, pointing to the brittle veneer of cosmopolitan life in Vienna, Budapest and Prague. At one point Pierre tells Frances, after she makes a blanket statement about Hungarians and Austrians, 'Another type'.[32] His criticism is consistent with Rhys's characteristic exposure of 'deeply ingrained habits of national classification underwriting cosmopolitan spaces' noted by Bridget T. Chalk.[33]

The three main car rides address Frances's future, with ironic nods to Marinetti's 'The Founding and Manifesto of Futurism 1909' on Rhys's part. Frances acknowledges a psychological need to focus on present 'moments' that offer 'compensations' for a hinted-at difficult, relatively impoverished and vitiating past in her late teens and early twenties. The illusion that this past is 'responsible' for her 'damned weakness' is comforting. The 'great god money', in her view, confers not only pleasure and status, but '[e]ven the luxury of a soul, a character and thoughts of one's own'.[34] Senses of empowerment to reach beyond 'compensations' for a '[d]ifferent life' emerge from invocation of more archaic spectral presences in human affairs. The driver on the first two car trips is a German chauffeur Franzi, the pronunciation of whose name is close to 'frenzy'. In the vignette 'Intermezzo', Frances remembers the first car ride with Franzi as the 'last frenzied effort' of her 'guardian angel' to protect her. Her first order is '[g]o quick, Franzi. Schnell'. She fantasizes about her rebirth under the aegis of the 'guardian angel':

Clear off – Different life, different people.
Work.
Go to England – Be quite different.

Frances is torn between desire for rebirth and a defiant embrace of 'compensations'. When the car hits a stone, 'a terrific bump', it does not overturn in a ditch as Marinetti's car does in his manifesto, heralding the arrival of futurism.[35] Peter Nicholls nicely characterizes the arrival as a 'ludicrous fantasy of rebirth, of being born by an act of *self*-generation ... without father, mother, past'.[36] Frances '[f]ell back luckily into the car'.[37] As Pierre, Frances and Franzi are about to depart Budapest for Prague, Frances, 'exhilarat[ed]' by the prospect of 'running away 'patted the quivering side of the car', recalling for readers Marinetti and his friends 'lay[ing] amorous hands' on the 'torrid breasts' of 'three snorting' cars.[38] The journey offers Frances, though, 'no comforting sensation of speed'. Indeed, Frances, who is pregnant, at one point tells Pierre, as he is about to take the wheel, 'don't go too fast'. The pregnancy, which inspires in Frances 'a calm sense of power ... as though' she 'were mysteriously ... a *Femme Sacrée*', portends natural, rather than futurist mechanical reproduction. For Frances, the 'country stretched flatly into an infinite and melancholy distance' but seemed 'sunlit and full of promise, like the setting of a fairy tale'.[39] The timeless stasis of the past is etched into the figures of the people they pass on the journey. The subjectivity of Frances's perspective here is underlined by a range of allusions to political upheaval: Austrians and Czechs at war over the future of post-armistice Bohemia, conflict commemorated in a gory painting; Bolshevik and Romanian occupation of Hungary immediately after the First World War; and King Karl's attempt to reclaim the Hungarian throne in 1921.

Allusions to financial crashes in 'Vienne' also play on Marinetti's car crash in 'The Founding and Manifesto of Futurism 1909'. Pierre's speculative currency trading on the '"change in Zurich' and possibly misappropriation of monies end predictably in his going 'fichu' (down the drain).[40] Pierre's course accords with the commonly held modernist perception that '[t]o be modern … is to live fast and embrace risk'.[41] Pierre's acute financial embarrassments are prognostic of the 'hyperinflation and wild oscillations in currency value' which 'culminated in the crash of the Viennese stock market in 1924', with stocks falling to a quarter of their earlier value.[42] On the third car trip, taken just before Frances and Pierre are to leave Prague, Frances contemplates giving Fate 'the slip', 'scream[ing] with laughter', willing the driver Pierre to 'smash' into a tree by the side of the road. Rather, Pierre slows down and, anticlimactically, admonishes Frances for her drunkenness when they reach their Prague hotel. The car is the vehicle of both sensation and the illusion of 'flying between two lines of dark trees, tops dancing madly in the high wind'. '[T]ops dancing madly' catches up Frances's memory of having been 'cracky with joy of life that summer of 1921'.[43] The word 'cracky' suggests the brittleness of her mood and the repressive relation to the past that draws her to seek refuge in the present moment, but it also means '[s]omewhat cracked in intellect; crazy'.[44]

The concept of a 'huge machine of law, order, respectability' that processes and governs social relations is a signature thread throughout Rhys's oeuvre. The positioning of 'Vienne', in which the phrase 'huge machine of law, order, respectability' appears, as the final story in *The Left Bank and Other Stories* lends a summative quality to the phrase in the collection. The narrative layering and design enabled by the concept in the collection may be further illustrated through consideration of 'Tea with an Artist', which features a reading of Left Bank characters by an unnamed first-person narrator. The narrator scrutinizes the impressionist expatriate Flemish artist Mr Verhausen and his partner Marthe Baesen, partly through an ekphrastic description of Verhausen's painting of a much younger Marthe, whom she is told Verhausen 'picked up in some awful brothel in Antwerp'.[45] The names of the characters may carry meaning: Verhausen means to 'squander' or 'dissipate' and Marthe may be a pun on martyr.[46] Qualities of touch impart depth to the characters that somewhat unsettles representational framings of them. Drawing out the narrator's reliance on ideas of 'law, order', and 'respectability' underpinning social relations, Rhys exposes the gap between narrative and authorial voices in the story.

The two readings of Verhausen placed before the narrator's visit to his studio position him in relation to 'law, order' and 'respectability', highlighting the representational machinery in play and setting up interpretative frames, the limits of which are exposed over the course of the story. Observing the bearing of a 'happy man' in a bar or café, the narrator thinks: 'It was obvious that this was not an Anglo-Saxon: he was too gay, too dirty, too unreserved and in his little eyes was such a mellow comprehension of all the sins and the delights of life.' She is classifying him in relation to an ethnic stereotype and a stereotype of propriety. Her 'companion who knew everybody' tells her that Verhausen is 'mad as a hatter', '[a] rum old bird ... a bit of a back number'. Signs of this for the companion are that he works outside the capitalist market economies of painting by refusing to exhibit his paintings publicly or sell them, reportedly cohabits with an ex-prostitute and opines 'that the Fallen are the only women with souls'. In his studio 'in the real Latin Quarter', 'shabbier' than and 'not cosmopolitan' like 'the Montparnasse district', the English narrator notices Verhausen's 'way of touching the canvases – his loving, careful hands', a motion which suggests that he has a subjective stake in the pictures, that they retain for him the aura of their conception and execution and of his ownership of them. The narrator pronounces Verhausen's portrait of Marthe:

> [...] Great art!
> ... A girl seated on a sofa in a room with many mirrors held a glass of green liqueur. Dark-eyed, heavy-faced, with big, sturdy peasant's limbs, she was entirely destitute of lightness or grace.
> But all the poisonous charm of the life beyond the pale was in her pose, and in her smouldering eyes – all its deadly bitterness and fatigue in her fixed smile.[47]

In the context of the narrator's reading of the painting the 'green liqueur' would be absinthe, a conventional symbol of decadence. The phrase 'fixed smile' suggests a studied pose on the part of the model to meet the artist's desire and hints at emotions and a self hidden behind the façade. In a reading of the story through the lens of ekphrasis, Sarah Downes notes of the painting that 'the placement of mirrors within the image makes conscious the multiple moments of framing that can occur' but does not consider how the companion's talk of Verhausen and Marthe and the narrator's recourses to stereotype frame her observations in the café and studio.[48] The reading reduces Verhausen's stake in his pictures to ownership, control of the spectator's gaze and in the case of the painting of Marthe, 'ownership of the woman presented'.[49]

The ekphrastic description by the narrator draws out the character and muse of the attraction between Verhausen and Marthe and the depth and plenitude of the artist's subject, the 'flame his genius had seen in her and had fixed for ever'. The painting preserves an originary moment of Verhausen's attraction to his posing of Marthe. Their Flemish heritage is maintained in their retention of Flemish as their everyday language at home. After Marthe's return from greengrocery shopping, the narrator observes the older Marthe's 'eyes' to be 'clear with the shrewd, limited expression of the careful housewife – the look of small horizons and quick, hard judgments', the narrator again having recourse to stereotype in reading a character.[50] The domestic relationship between Verhausen and Marthe is relatively conventional, even if Verhausen experiences some frisson when he effectively introduces Marthe to the narrator as his common-law wife. As the narrator contemplates the enigma of Marthe's seeming loss of 'smouldering' 'charm' under the pressure of companionate domesticity, she recalls witnessing another layer of the present relationship between Marthe and Verhausen, a small but compelling ritual gesture of affection and warmth: 'the way in which she had touched his cheek with her big hands. There was in that movement, knowledge, and certain sureness'. Framing the gesture through her café companion's scapegoating characterization of Marthe as an ex-prostitute, the narrator reads it as 'as it were the ghost of a time when her business in life had been the consoling of men'. The narrator's observations partly break down the fiction of the good and the bad woman that underpins her café companion's frame. That the narrator's companion 'knew everybody' raises questions about the reliability of the machinery of his framing judgement and the narrator's too ready early psychologization of Verhausen's objections 'to exhibiting and to selling' his art – 'a perverted form of miserliness, I suppose' – an idea that underpins her stereotypical image of him having 'the look of an old Jew when counting his money'.[51]

The catalyst for the narrator's memory of Marthe's touch and revaluation of the anomaly for her between the female figure in the painting and the present-day Marthe is hearing a gramophone recording of a song from Victor Hugo's *Le roi s'amuse*, on which Guiseppe Verdi based his opera *Rigoletto*: 'Souvent femme varie / Bien fol est qui s'y fie!'[52] The words – 'Woman is often changeable: he who trusts her is quite mad' – play to a stereotype of women being fickle.[53] Implicitly rejecting the stereotype, the narrator recalls the touch, reading it as a 'ghost' of Marthe's former life. Picking up the trope of spectrality, one might suggest that in the narrator's eyes Marthe has to repress more intimate aspects of her identity in the role of the shrewd housewife. The song's warning about trust might also be an ironic authorial comment on the narrator and her penchant for stereotypes and received frames of observation.

In *Quartet*, Rhys figures her protagonist Marya Zelli's apprehensions about the 'little arrangements' that people make to maintain respectability, 'arrangements' 'tucked away', like 'prisons and drains', 'where nobody can see' as reducing her to a 'grey ghost'.[54] H. J. and Lois Heidler have invited her to stay with them while her husband Stephan is in prison, a proposal Stephan finds 'chic'.[55] The 'vague, shadowy world' Marya enters is one of 'unreasoning shame' governed by a 'sense of the utter futility of all things'. The spectacle and sounds of a carnivalesque machine and its 'gay, metallic music', 'a merry-go-round at the Porte d'Orléans', playing 'clank[ingly]' "'Je vous aime'" ('I Love You') change her mood, making 'her feel more normal'.[56] The 'little arrangement' with the Heidlers, normalized initially by proximity to the carnivalesque, morphs for Marya into an obsessive love for H. J., who seduces and later abandons her. H. J.'s wife Lois tolerates and facilitates the affair, while despising Marya and treating her cruelly. Marya writes to H. J. that her place in it, processed socially, as it were, by the 'huge machine of law, order, respectability' as hussy, prostitute or filth (*saleté*),[57] leaves her feeling, she thinks, 'as if all the blood in my body is being drained, very slowly, all the time, all the blood in my heart'. She is '*fichue*'.[58] Tropes of mechanism and this trope of the vampiric are used to figure Marya's shift into a 'new, psychological state of personal alienation, moral incoherence, and emptiness',[59] an abject state of liminality between human animation and the mechanical, between self-possession and being possessed, that brings on a major depressive episode.

Octavio R. González argues that Rhys uses focalization to model 'for the reader how to understand the novel itself as a "vague, shadowy world"', a 'world of shadow and illusion that the novel wants readers to value, to view the "shadow" as "more important than the substance"'.[60] He works to counter readings of *Quartet* that invoke psychopathological descriptors of Marya's sexuality as masochistic, by aligning this critical move with the 'mania for classification' that Rhys criticizes in the novel. He does not, however, examine the everyday language of depression in the text, what Matthew Bell might characterize as '"folk" knowledge (*melancholy*)' as distinct from 'medical knowledge'.[61] In the novel Rhys uses the descriptors 'melancholy', 'sad', 'depressed', 'black', 'blackness', 'miserable', 'unhappy', 'cafard' and '*la misère*' to describe depression of spirits. Stephan, who tells Marya of having had cafards in prison, declares to her after his release, 'You don't know what it is, *la misère*.'[62] In its focus largely on Marya's point of view, the novel offers a counterpoint to this dismissal of suffering. Rhys, as she had in 'Vienne' and 'Tea with an Artist', sharply criticizes too ready and reductive 'classifying' of people, the 'fitting' of them into 'proper places' through classification. H. J. and Monsieur Bernadet, an acquaintance of Stephan, label Marya using gendered popularized psychopathological descriptors, H. J. calling her 'with contempt' 'hysterical', 'this sort of woman' and Bernadet thinking to himself that she is 'neurasthenic', attributing the condition to her being 'a pretty girl, but a girl who thinks too much'.[63] González suggests that Rhys 'champions' 'the hermeneutics of understanding versus classification'.[64] Rhys carefully immerses the reader in the viscerality of shifts in Marya's melancholy. The censorship of the novel in the UK by Boot's circulating library indicates how confronting Rhys's critique of the machine of moral classification and empathetic treatment of Marya's melancholy might be seen to be for conservative readers. Boot's reportedly placed *Postures* (the British title of *Quartet*) on its 'restricted list' ('not stocked at all'). Celia Marshik points out that 'while such censorship seems less devastating than outright suppression, it was also more problematic to fight. ... [I]t was difficult to agitate against commercial censorship because the decision to suppress was neither public nor open to legal challenge.'[65]

Rhys's choice of lines from expatriate US poet R. C. Dunning's sonnet 'The Hermit' as the epigraph of the novel positions the 'little arrangement' with the Heidlers as an act of seeming 'good Samaritans'. Rhys's partner Leslie Tilden Smith, commissioned by her to search out potential epigraphs for *Postures*, had suggested lines from T. S. Eliot's 'The Love Song of J. Alfred Prufrock' or 'Portrait of a Lady'.[66] Dunning's sonnet was originally published in the *transatlantic review*, Ford praising Dunning in the issue in which it appeared for his 'consummate' '[r]egular verse', though such verse 'is obviously little in our line' as the journal's editorial 'sympathies are with the newer sincerities'.[67] Dunning writes:

> Bleed, O my heart, bleed slowly but take care
> That no one hears thy bleeding. In the night
> Let not thy bedfellow divine thy plight
> Bleed softly, O my heart, and in the glare
> And heavy silence of high noon, beware
> Of good Samaritans – walk to the right
> Or hide thee by the roadside out of sight
> Or greet them with the smile that villains wear.
>
> Bleed slowly and bleed softly, O my heart
> Go bide in nameless mountains of the north
> Or deep in monstrous cities play thy part

O Bleeding Heart wherby [*sic*] the world's aflood –
But shun all congregations loving blood
Let some fool on a banner bear thee forth.[68]

Rhys's epigraph from the octave of the sonnet commences at 'beware / Of good Samaritans' and serves to juxtapose the 'newer', formally modernist 'sincerities' of her novel with the 'classical' regularity of Dunning's aesthetic.[69] In the novel, Rhys also draws on Dunning's images of the bleeding heart, playing a part and stifled emotion. 'If this was love – this perpetual aching longing, this wound that bled persistently and very slowly', Marya questions, a feeling that escalates into her sense that the 'little arrangement' and her obsession are vampiric.[70] She is distraught at being expected to 'play the game' of adultery as the Heidlers demand she do 'to keep up appearances'.[71] As Coral Ann Howells points out, Marya often 'retreats into silence as a mask for dissent' from the Heidlers' views of her, her background and her expectations.[72] Stephan courted her with the prospect of marriage to him making her '[h]appy, petted, charming' – 'magical words'. Being 'petted' contrasts sharply and pointedly with Rhys's image of what Marya's relationship with H. J. reduces her to: 'She was quivering and abject in his arms, like some unfortunate dog abashing itself before its master.'[73]

Rhys's invocation of 'good Samaritans' is also one of two oblique allusions to 'Triple Sec'. When protagonist Suzy experiences a major depressive episode, Rhys alludes to the biblical parable of the Good Samaritan to represent her sense of the lack of compassion of the English, who have uncharitably stripped her of livelihood and honour.[74] For a very small audience of people familiar with 'Triple Sec' in 1928 and desirous of reading *Quartet* as a roman à clef, the allusion suggests that the apparently kindly intervention of the Heidlers (who would be read as based on Ford Madox Ford and Stella Bowen) exacerbated a similar depressive crisis. This audience would have included Adam, Ford, Bowen, Ivan Beede and probably Lenglet.[75] Before the Heidlers propose to the destitute Marya that she move in with them, the narrative voice observes that at Lois's Thursday 'parties' Marya 'would watch Heidler, who could not dance, walk masterfully up and down the room to the strains of "If you knew Susie as I know Susie" played on the gramophone', making 'sidelong, cautious glances' that 'slid over her as it were'.[76] The song was a hit for Eddie Cantor in 1925.[77] The singer boasts that, unlike others, he knows a wild and amorous side of the seemingly respectable Susie. The allusions suggest that Ford's conflation of Suzy Gray and the author of 'Triple Sec' in his reading of the novel as a roman à clef whet a sexual interest in Rhys and made Marya into a 'grey ghost'. Later in the novel, as Marya walks past the Heidlers' studio at night she imagines that Lois is playing 'If you knew Suzie like I know Suzie' on the gramophone for her party guests. Reflecting on her current state, she realizes that she is '[q]uite dead. Not a kick left in her.'[78]

Rhys juxtaposes the dancing at Lois's parties with music hall dancing, drawing out spectator assumptions and responses. Lois knows that Marya has, before her marriage, been 'on the stage'. As part of an argument that Marya should accept her and H. J.'s offer that she live with them, Lois advises her against becoming a nude dancer: 'getting down to brass tacks, what exactly do you think of doing? ... Well, I hope you're not thinking of trying for a job as a *femme nue* in a music-hall. They don't get paid anything at all, poor dears.'[79] Lois's next thought, coyly expressed, elides the dancer and the kept mistress, revealing her sexualized assumptions about Marya's history and expectations. Marya rejects both suggestions. The 'figure of the dancer' in this scene acts, as it so often does in the period, as a 'cipher for cultural conflict around gender and class'.[80] Later, when the Heidlers and Marya visit a music hall, Lois relishes the performance of a pair of nude dancers moving against a mise-en-scène Marya thinks has been influenced by the distinctive 'blue and mauve' colours of cubist painter Marie Laurencin. Critical of their dancing style ('hop[ping]', 'bounc[ing]'), Marya prefers the 'Spanish singer who was the star of the evening'.[81] The visit, marked by tension between Lois and Marya, has been made at the instigation of Lois, who thinks the risqué might alleviate her boredom.

Rhys's tropes of mechanism are linked progressively through improvisation in language and image. Reflecting on a confrontational row with H. J. and Lois over their 'torturing' 'arrangement' about her, Marya, the third-person narrator writes, had felt that it 'seemed unreal. She had felt like a marionette, as though something outside her were jerking strings that forced her to scream and strike. Heidler, weeping, was a marionette, too. And Lois, anxious-eyed, in her purple dressing-gown.' Marya had told Lois that the reason why she came downstairs was that she was 'thirsty'.[82] Attempting, at their insistence, to preserve the social propriety of the outwardly respectable, middle-class Heidlers, Marya feels 'like a captive attached to someone's chariot wheels'. Her obsessive desire for H. J., grounded in a psychological need for protection that is evident, too, in her memories of her relationship with Stephan, is then represented as the 'mechanism of her brain' which

> got to work with a painful jerk and began to tick in time with the clock.
> She had made a great effort to stop it and was able to keep her mind a blank for, say, ten seconds. Then her obsession gripped her, arid, torturing, gigantic, possessing her as utterly as the longing for water possesses someone who is dying of thirst.[83]

The trope of mechanism accords with Tim Armstrong's observation that in modernist literature '[t]echnology' often 'supplies metaphors for the operation of mind, even for the unconscious and desire'.[84] Rhys also uses it to figure the 'psycho-motor agitation' of Marya's depression[85] as '[l]ittle wheels in her head that turned perpetually' and 'tortured' her through oscillation between 'love and hate'. Reunited with her husband Stephan, though living apart from him, Marya finds that H. J. becomes a spectral, sexualizing presence in her life: 'She lay down. For perhaps thirty seconds she was able to keep her mind a blank, but then her obsession gripped her, arid, torturing, gigantic, possessing her as utterly as the longing for water possesses someone who is dying of thirst.'[86] The 'blank' 'mind' is the sign of a precarious willing of self-control. The repetition of images works to realize the cyclical dimension of her psycho-motor agitation. The 'obsession' and its imbrication with depressive cycles place Marya's desire for H. J. outside her control. This accords with a historical development noted by Pamela S. Haag: the emergence in the 1920s of the idea of 'a bifurcated female self, whose sexuality belonged to the elusive subconscious rather than to the proprietary, rational female self capable of claiming and acting upon those desires'.[87] Measuring Marya only against a 'proprietary, rational female self', Amy Clukey, by contrast, points to the ways in which Rhys's use of 'free indirect discourse conveys Marya's subjectivity, but also establishes a distance from which to register ... her increasingly illogical rationalizations for her relationship with H. J.'[88]

The figurative trajectory I have charted opens with and is framed by the image of the marionette conveying Marya's subjective sense of the 'little arrangement' manipulating the inanimate parties to it, an image that resonates with wider modernist interest in puppet and marionette theatre. *Quartet* was first written as a play, 'meant to be read not acted. Three Acts two scenes each act.'[89] 'The ability of the puppet and the marionette to offer schematised and non-anthropomorphic representations of the human form,' Olga Taxidou observes:

> [F]eeds very neatly into the preoccupation with abstraction, stylisation and estrangement.... [T]he puppet [or marionette] very clearly relies on a mechanics of production. This 'mechanics of production' itself ... comes to be foregrounded as part of the artistic practice.... Both organic and inorganic, human-like and mechanical it [the puppet] becomes one of Modernism's best vehicles for experimentation with the limits of representation itself.[90]

Taxidou suggests that the modernist puppet or marionette is 'drafted into the search for a performance language that does not rely on the power of the literary text', that is, an anterior script and that it 'sets up modes of reception, which rely on distance and estrangement rather than identification and empathy.'[91] Rhys's invocation of the marionette frames her authorial experiment with the representation of the mechanics of obsession (named as such) and melancholy, foregrounding Marya's liminal state between the human and the mechanical and the question of what mechanisms manipulate the strings of her depersonalized conduct. The simile and metaphor of marionette performance locate the mechanism outside the self in the arrangement with the Heidlers; the later tropes place it disorientingly for Marya within the alienated, morally incoherent and emptied self. After Stephan has left France on being released from prison and Heidler forces a 'rupture' in his relationship with Marya, she passively allows an unnamed 'young man' to pick her up in a café. Before going to the bar she has wanted 'the friendly dark where she could lie and let her heart burst'. '"What's it matter"', she says in response to his sexual proposition, framed euphemistically as 'rest' in his 'room'. 'She went with him silently – like a sleepwalker.' The image of the sleepwalker, like that of the marionette, places sexuality outside her rational control. When she tells the man, '[l]ight hurts me', he ties 'two enormous blue silk handkerchiefs ... round the electric light'.[92] The '[l]ight' that 'hurts' her might be construed as self-knowledge of her actions.

Rhys's graphic tropes of mechanism risk the distancing and estrangement of prospective readers, but also set up routes to affective and sensory understanding of Marya's condition through immersion in it. They make visible the humanity that is made ghostly by the 'huge machine of law, order, respectability', which also to some extent impersonalizes the conduct of the more bourgeois Heidlers. Tropes of mechanism as applied to consciousness contrast markedly with the more familiar modernist idea of the 'stream of consciousness' and with Dorothy Richardson's and Virginia Woolf's characterizations of consciousness. Famously, William James writes of consciousness in 1892: 'Consciousness ... does not appear to itself chopped up in bits. It is nothing jointed; it flows. A "river" or a "stream" are the metaphors by which it is most naturally described. ... *[L]et us call it the stream of thought, or consciousness, or of subjective life.*'[93] Consciousness is 'not a stream, it's a pool, a sea, an ocean', insists Dorothy Richardson. 'It has depth and greater depth and when you think you have reached its bottom there is nothing there, and when you give yourself up to one current you are suddenly possessed by another.'[94] Elsewhere she insists that consciousness 'sits stiller than a tree'.[95] In 'Modern Fiction', Virginia Woolf opines: 'The mind receives a myriad impressions – trivial, fantastic, evanescent, or engraved with the sharpness of steel. From all sides they come, an incessant shower of innumerable atoms; and as they fall, as they shape themselves into the life of Monday or Tuesday, the accent falls differently from of old.'[96]

In Rhys's early fiction, her critical interest in the mechanics of 'law, order, respectability' leads her to draw out 'who or what needs to be "ghosted" to found and maintain a particular' post-war 'subjectivity', the 'subjectivities [that] have been marginalized and disavowed in order to establish and uphold a particular norm'.[97] In 'Vienne', Frances in the role of Pierre's wife is haunted by the spectre of her life between seventeen and twenty-two, a period subjected to routine narrative repression. The repression, founded on fear and trauma, functions like the space off in film, invoking the time and 'space not visible in the frame but' partly 'inferable from what the frame makes visible',[98] or the blurred edges of a photographic vignette. In the story, the vignettes take the form of mobile 'snapshots', memory clips, realized, like Kirchner's art, in 'bold strokes'.[99] The spectre of the younger Frances is, as in Jacques Derrida's theorization of haunting, 'always both *revenant* (invoking what was) and *arrivant* (announcing what will come)'.[100] The subjectivities of '*mondäne Tänzerinen*' are ghosted through monetization by speculating serial sexual predators among Inter-Allied Military Control Commission members and their entourage, for whom the women are ultimately as interchangeable as regimented dancers in a chorus line.[101] The circumstances of the dancers are one of the morbid symptoms of the collapse of the Austro-Hungarian Empire and the terms of the dictated peace. Rhys suggests that the dancers have to ghost 'law, order' and 'respectability' to function in the shadow economy. In 'Tea with an Artist' the narrator reads the housewifely Marthe's touch of Verhausen as a 'ghost' of her reputed past as a prostitute. Through an authorial ironizing of the narrator's voice, Rhys points to the ways in which initial framings of the couple by her café companion haunt the narrator's readings of them. In *Quartet*, Rhys's clusters of imagery around protagonist Marya Zelli's sense of her liminality draw out the links between her sense of being a 'grey ghost walking in a vague, shadowy world' and melancholy.[102] Her husband Stephan has been a protector figure, rescuing Marya from a working life in England as a touring dancer that had become '[a] vague procession of towns all exactly alike, a vague procession of men also exactly alike'.[103] After he is sent to prison, Marya feels herself 'hunted' by 'fear': 'It was a vague and shadowy fear of something cruel and stupid that had caught her and would never let her go. She had always known it was there – hidden under the more or less pleasant surface of things.' She finds their room 'full of shadows'.[104] The 'melancholy pleasure' of a pensive mood 'walking along the shadowed side' of 'narrow' Parisian 'streets' gives way to more frightening and confusing forms of melancholy.[105] During her affair with H. J., her bedrooms become more surreally 'melancholy': 'Sleep was like falling into a black hole', the black background of wallpaper comes to dominate one of the bedrooms as 'flowers … crawled like spiders over the black walls of her bedroom', 'the bed plunged downwards with her – sickeningly – into blackness'.[106] The association of blackness and depression is commonplace, as in the descriptors 'black dog' and 'black bile'.

Threads of 'Vienne', 'Tea with an Artist' and *Quartet* – the operation of the 'machine of law, order, respectability', the dancer and dancing, temporalities, and melancholy and depression – are taken up again in Rhys's later writing in fresh ways. Counter-narrative and contiguity (often contrastive) become crucial bearings in her oeuvre. Her aesthetic innovation would continue to take its bearings from an international avant-garde. Notably, in her later fiction, Rhys explores not just the process and implications of machined stereotyping, but also, innovatively, the psychological and emotional reaches and registers of the othering mechanisms of tropicality in *After Leaving Mr Mackenzie*, *Voyage in the Dark*, *Good Morning, Midnight* and *Wide Sargasso Sea*. Rhys tacitly sets *Voyage in the Dark* in the context of the seriality of moral panics around decadence and sexual dissidence (coalescing in relation to conservative norms of law, order and respectability). Her early fiction evinces exploration of the scope of counter-narrative to reductive and demeaning representations of people. She pointedly counters, for instance, Colonel Ishima's classification of dancers as 'war material' and the dismissal of Marya's melancholy by Stephan, H. J. and Bernadet. Rhys remains keenly aware of the sexual economies and class relations in which dancers circulate. These economies and relations, for instance, place a young Antillean woman in 'Trio' and structure Anna Morgan's experience in *Voyage in the Dark*, underpinning the racialized thresholds she crosses. Rhys develops dance as a means of focalizing Julia Martin's sexual indifference in *After Leaving Mr Mackenzie* and as a metaphor – swing – to highlight Sasha Jansen's efforts to cope with her depression and handle the trauma of memory in *Good Morning, Midnight*. Her experiments with narrative and psychological repression, temporalities and the negotiation of depressive time become more complex in *After Leaving Mr Mackenzie*, *Voyage in the Dark* and *Good Morning, Midnight*.

# Notes

1   On Fordian impressionism, see, in particular, Max Saunders, 'Ford and Impressionism', in *Ford Madox Ford: Literary Networks and Cultural Transformations*, ed. Andrzej Gasiorek and Daniel Moore (Amsterdam: Rodopi, 2008), 151–66; and Rebecca Bowler, *Literary Impressionism: Vision and Memory*

in *Dorothy Richardson, Ford Madox Ford, H. D. and May Sinclair* (London: Bloomsbury, 2016), 17–55. Studies of Rhys's literary impressionism include Todd Bender, 'Jean Rhys and the Genius of Impressionism', *Studies in the Literary Imagination* 11, no. 2 (1978): 43–53; Margarete Rubik, 'Jean Rhys's Vision of the Left Bank', 65–70; and Eva Müller-Zettelmann and Rudolf Weiss, '"La vie toute faite des morceaux": Intermediality and Impressionism in Jean Rhys's *Quartet*', in *Rive Gauche: Paris as a Site of Avant-garde Art and Cultural Exchange in the 1920s*, ed. Elke Mettinger, Margarete Rubik and Jörg Türschmann (Amsterdam: Rodopi, 2010), 79–98.

2   There are three published versions of 'Vienne'. All three are structured as a series of vignettes. The version published in the *transatlantic review* in December 1924, its last issue, has three titled and numbered vignettes 'The Dancer', '"Fischyll"' and 'The Spending Phase'. It has been republished in *The Gender of Modernism: A Critical Anthology*, ed. Bonnie Kime Scott (Bloomington: Indiana University Press, 1990), 377–81. I will refer to this version in endnotes as 'Vienne' (1924). The longer version published in *The Left Bank and Other Stories* (1927; repr., Freeport, NY: Books for Libraries Press, 1970), 193–256, has twelve vignettes, eleven of which have titles. 'The Dancer', untitled, opens the story, '"Fischl": Winter 1920–Spring 1921' is the sixth vignette, and 'The Last Act of Vienna – The Spending Phase' is the eighth vignette. Rhys revised the story in 1967 for inclusion in *Tigers Are Better Looking: With a Selection from* The Left Bank (1968; Harmondsworth: Penguin, 1972), 188–220. This version contains sixteen untitled and unnumbered vignettes. Rhys cut three vignettes from the 1927 version entirely – 'André Again', '"Fischl": Winter 1920–Spring 1921' and '"Gelustige"' – and most of 'Dancing at Eisenstein's with Antoine Renault'. Sentences from one paragraph of the 1927 and 1968 version are revised in the second of the three vignettes of the story 'Temps Perdi' (1969) titled '2. *The Sword Dance and the Love Dance*'. The sentences are drawn from the vignette titled 'War Material' in the 1927 text. 'Temps Perdi' was first published in *Penguin Modern Stories*, ed. Judith Burnley (Harmondsworth: Penguin, 1969), 53–67 and first collected in *Tales of the Wide Caribbean*, ed. Kenneth Ramchand (London: Heinemann, 1986), 144–61.

3   Rhys, 'Vienne', in *The Left Bank and Other Stories*, 241.

4   Jean Rhys, *Quartet* (Harmondsworth: Penguin, 1973). The novel was originally published under the title *Postures* (London: Chatto and Windus, 1928) and then as *Quartet* (New York: Simon and Shuster, 1929).

5   Lonnie Johnson, *Central Europe: Enemies, Neighbours, Friends* (Oxford: Oxford University Press, 1996), 191, 194.

6   Joe C. Dixon, *Defeat and Disarmament: Allied Diplomacy and the Politics of Military Affairs in Austria, 1918–1922* (Newark: University of Delaware Press, 1986), 94.

7   Angier, *Jean Rhys*, 114, 118, 121.

8   Dixon, *Defeat and Disarmament*, 74, 110, 114.
9   Rhys, 'Vienne', 209.
10  Ibid., 241, 197.
11  Eve Kosofsky Sedgwick, 'The Beast in the Closet: James and the Writing of Homosexual Panic', in *Speaking of Gender*, ed. Elaine Showalter (New York: Routledge, 1989), 251.
12  GoGwilt, *The Passage of Literature*, 83–4.
13  Ibid., 83.
14  Jean Rhys, 'Vienne' (1924), 377.
15  Rhys, 'Vienne', 193. On Wiesenthal, see Andrea Amort, 'Free Dance in Interwar Vienna', in *Interwar Vienna: Culture between Tradition and Modernity*, ed. Deborah Holmes and Lisa Silverman (Rochester: Camden House, 2009), 121–5.
16  Rhys, 'Vienne', 193. Images of the artworks may be seen on websites, *Tänzerinnen* (1906) on the Solomon R. Guggenheim Museum website, https://www.guggenheim.org/artwork/8434, accessed 27 June 2019 and *Sechs Tänzerinnen* (1911) on the 1000 Museums website, https://www.1000museums.com/art_works/ernst-ludwig-kirchner-six-dancers-sechs-tanzerinnen, accessed 27 June 2019. Dancers were a favourite theme of Kirchner.
17  Donald E. Gordon, *Ernst Ludwig Kirchner: A Retrospective Exhibition* (Boston, MA: Museum of Fine Arts, 1968), 15.
18  Quoted in Nina Miall, *Kirchner: Expressionism and The City: Dresden and Berlin 1905–1918* (London: Royal Academy of Arts, 2003), 5.
19  Toepfer, *Empire of Ecstasy*, 360.
20  F. T. Marinetti, 'The Founding and Manifesto of Futurism 1909', trans. R. W. Flint, in *Futurist Manifestoes*, ed. Umbro Apollonio, trans. Robert Brain, R. W. Flint, J. C. Hihggitt and Caroline Tinsdall (London: Tate Publishing, 2009), 2.
21  Rhys, 'Vienne', 221.
22  Tim Armstrong, 'Technology', in *A Concise Companion to Modernism*, ed. David Bradshaw (Oxford: Blackwell, 2003), 161.
23  Rhys, 'Vienne', 256, 241.
24  Deborah Holmes and Lisa Silverman, 'Introduction: Beyond the Coffeehouse. Vienna as a Cultural Center between the World Wars', in *Interwar Vienna*, ed. Holmes and Silverman (Rochester: Camden House, 2009), 2.
25  Gabriele Brandstetter, *Tanz-Lektüren: Körperbilder und Raumfiguren der Avantgarde*, trans. H. M. Taylor, quoted by Kristina Köhler, 'Dance as Metaphor – Metaphor as Dance: Transfigurations of Dance in Culture and Aesthetics around 1900', *REAL – Yearbook of Research in English and American Literature* 25 (2009): 163.
26  Bernhard Leitner, 'Viennese Kineticism', in *Beyond Art: A Third Culture: A Comparative Study in Cultures, Art and Science in 20th Century Austria and Hungary*, ed. Peter Weibel (New York: Springer, 2005), 42.

27 Leopold Wolfgang Rochowanski, *Der Formwille der Zeit in der Angewandten Kunst* (1922; rpt. München: Klaus Reprint, 1980). Recent studies of kineticism include Peter Weibel, ed. *Beyond Art: A Third Culture: A Comparative Study in Cultures, Art and Science in 20th Century Austria and Hungary* (New York: Springer, 2005); Gerald Bast, Agnes Husslein, Herbert Krejci and Patrick Werkner, eds, *Wiener Kinetismus: Eine bewegte modern/Viennese Kineticism. Modernism in Motion* (Wien and New York: Springer, 2011); and Agnes Husslein-Arco, Thomas Kühler, Ralf Burmeister, Alexander Klee and Annelie Lütgens, eds, *Vienna – Berlin: The Art of Two Cities. From Schiele to Grosz* (Munich: Prestel, 2013).
28 Rhys, 'Vienne', 194, 199.
29 '*It*', dir. Clarence G. Badger (Paramount Pictures, 1927). Glyn describes 'It' in *Man and Maid* (New York: A. L. Burt, 1922) as an alluring 'intangible something' in a person (158). In *Elinor Glyn as Novelist, Moviemaker, Glamour Icon and Businesswoman* (New York: Routledge, 2016), Vincent L. Barnett and Alexis Weedon note that Rudyard Kipling had used the term 'It' in his 1904 story 'Mrs Bathurst' to suggest 'a broad type of winning popularity' (130).
30 Rhys, 'Vienne', 198, 196.
31 John Frow, *Character and Person* (Oxford: Oxford University Press, 2014), 119.
32 Rhys, 'Vienne', 195, 197, 201, 200, 226, 236, 245.
33 Chalk, *Modernism and Mobility*, 124.
34 Rhys, 'Vienne', 230, 194, 233, 221–2.
35 Ibid., 230, 229, 230, 231.
36 Peter Nicholls, *Modernisms: A Literary Guide* (Basingstoke: Macmillan, 1995), 85–6, his emphasis.
37 Rhys, 'Vienne', 231.
38 Marinetti, 'The Founding and Manifesto of Futurism 1909', 20.
39 Rhys, 'Vienne', 250, 246, 236, 250.
40 Ibid., 237, 238.
41 Ulrike Maude, 'Science, Technology and the Body', in *The Cambridge Companion to Modernist Culture*, ed. Celia Marshik (New York: Cambridge University Press, 2015), 36.
42 Alys X. George, 'Hollywood on the Danube? Vienna and Austrian Silent Film of the 1920s', in *Interwar Vienna*, ed. Holmes and Silverman, 147.
43 Rhys, 'Vienne', 256, 202.
44 *Oxford English Dictionary Online*.
45 Jean Rhys, 'Tea with an Artist', in her *The Left Bank and Other Stories*, 75.
46 William Dwight Whitney, *A Compendious German and English Dictionary* (New York: Henry Holt, 1877), 452.
47 Rhys, 'Tea with an Artist', 73, 75, 78.
48 Sarah Downes, 'Jean Rhys, William Orpen and the Frames of Modernist Representation', *Women: A Cultural Review* 27, no. 3 (2016): 290.

49  Ibid., 293.
50  Rhys, 'Tea with an Artist', 80.
51  Ibid., 81, 73, 80, 75, 80.
52  Ibid., 81.
53  Cormac Newark, '"Ch'hai di nuvo, buffon?" or What's New with *Rigoletto*', in *The Cambridge Companion to Verdi*, ed. Xiaoxia Wei (Cambridge: Cambridge University Press, 2004), 207.
54  Rhys, *Quartet*, 44, 46.
55  Ibid., 98, 107.
56  Ibid., 45, 46, 38, 46.
57  hussy (ibid., 69), prostitute (66, 105, 125, 144), or filth (*saleté*, 141).
58  Ibid., 121.
59  Marina Warner, *Fantastic Metamorphoses, Other Worlds: Ways of Telling the Self* (Oxford: Oxford University Press, 2002), 120.
60  Octavio R. González, 'The Narrative Mood of Jean Rhys' *Quartet*', *Ariel: A Review of International English Literature* 49, no. 1 (2018): 110.
61  Matthew Bell, *Melancholia: The Western Malady* (Cambridge: Cambridge University Press, 2014), 36.
62  'melancholy' (Rhys, *Quartet*, 7, 9, 44, 88); 'sad' (37, 38, 72, 74, 88, 104, 110, 118, 136); 'depressed' (7); 'black' (58, 60, 91); 'blackness' (126); 'miserable' (60, 78, 90, 92, 100); 'unhappy' (61); 'cafard' (27, 36); '*la misère*' (133, 136).
63  Ibid., 48, 81, 135, 134.
64  González, 'The Narrative Mood of Jean Rhys' *Quartet*', 121.
65  Marshik, *British Modernism and Censorship*, 177.
66  Leslie Tilden Smith, letter to Jean Rhys, 16 July 1928, Jean Rhys Papers.
67  Ford Madox Ford, 'Paris Letter: Editorial', *transatlantic review* 2, no. 5 (1924): 549.
68  R. C. Dunning, 'The Hermit', *transatlantic review* 2, no. 5 (1924): 480.
69  Ford, 'Paris Letter', 549.
70  Rhys, *Quartet*, 95–6.
71  Ibid., 70, 90.
72  Howells, *Jean Rhys*, 47.
73  Rhys, *Quartet*, 16, 102.
74  Jean Rhys, 'Triple Sec', 124.
75  Stella Bowen refers to 'Triple Sec' as 'an unpublishably sordid novel of great sensitiveness and persuasiveness', in *Drawn from Life* (1941, London: Virago, 1984), 166. Ivan Beede, who had been assistant editor of the *transatlantic review*, reminds Rhys that he has read both her diary and 'Triple Sec' in his letter to her of 2 February 1931, Jean Rhys Papers. The letter praises *After Leaving Mr Mackenzie*.
76  Rhys, *Quartet*, 50.
77  The song was recorded in 1925 by both Al Jolson and by Eddie Cantor. It was a hit for Cantor.

78 Rhys, *Quartet*, 96. In *Quartet*, the spellings Susie and Suzie are used in the song title.
79 Ibid., 42.
80 Townsend, *The Choreography of Modernism in France*, 133.
81 Rhys, *Quartet*, 67.
82 Ibid., 81, 80, 82.
83 Ibid., 90–1.
84 Armstrong, 'Technology', 160.
85 Jennifer Radden, 'Melancholy and Melancholia', in *Pathologies of the Modern Self: Postmodern Studies on Narcissism, Schizophrenia, and Depression*, ed. David Michael Levin (New York: New York University Press, 1987), 241.
86 Rhys, *Quartet*, 97, 113.
87 Pamela S. Haag, 'In Search of "The Real Thing": Ideologies of Love, Modern Romance, and Women's Subjectivity in the United States, 1920–40', *Journal of the History of Sexuality* 2, no. 4 (1992): 550.
88 Amy Clukey, '"No Country Really Now": Modernist Cosmopolitanisms and Jean Rhys's *Quartet*', *Twentieth-Century Literature* 56, no. 4 (2010): 445–6.
89 Rhys, letter to Selma Vaz Dias, 17 February 1953, *Letters 1931–1966*, 100. H. Pearl Adam read a draft in 1926 and commented on it, but Rhys could not find the original manuscript for Vaz Dias in 1953. Adam, letter to Jean Rhys, 13 December 1926, Jean Rhys Papers; Rhys, letter to Selma Vaz Dias, 17 February 1953, *Letters 1931–1966*, 100.
90 Olga Taxidou, *Modernism and Performance: Jarry to Brecht* (Basingstoke: Palgrave Macmillan, 2007), 12–13, 16.
91 Ibid., 12.
92 Rhys, *Quartet*, 116, 117, 118, 118–19.
93 William James, 'The Stream of Consciousness', in *Classics in the History of Psychology*, ed. Christopher D. Green, http://psychclassics.yorku.ca/James/himmy11.htm, accessed 1 October 2017, his emphasis.
94 Vincent Brome, 'A Last Meeting with Dorothy Richardson', *London Magazine* 6 (June 1959): 29.
95 Dorothy Richardson, 'Autobiographical Sketch', in *Authors Today and Yesterday*, ed. Stanley J. Kunitz (New York: H. W. Wilson, 1934), 562–4.
96 Virginia Woolf, 'Modern Fiction', in *The Common Reader: First Series*, by Woolf, ed. Andrew McNeillie (London: Hogarth Press, 1984), 150.
97 María del Pilar Blanco and Esther Peeren, 'Spectral Subjectivities: Gender, Sexuality, Race/Introduction', in *The Spectralities Reader: Ghosts and Haunting in Contemporary Cultural Theory*, ed. del Pilar Blanco and Peeren (London: Bloomsbury, 2013), 313, 310.
98 Teresa de Lauretis, *Technologies of Gender: Essays on Theory, Film, and Fiction* (Bloomington: Indiana University Press, 1987), 26.

99  Rhys, 'Vienne', 193. Nina Miall quotes the descriptor 'bold strokes' in *Kirchner: Expressionism and the City: Dresden and Berlin 1905–1918* (London: Royal Academy of Arts, 2003), 5.
100  María del Pilar Blanco and Esther Peeren, 'Introduction: Conceptualizing Spectralities', in *The Spectralities Reader*, 13.
101  Rhys, 'Vienne', 201.
102  Rhys, *Quartet*, 46. The link between a sense of liminality and a 'grey' ghostliness is also apparent when Marya sends a telegram to H. J., feeling 'relieved, but numb and grey, like a soul in limbo' (114).
103  Ibid., 15.
104  Ibid., 28.
105  Ibid., 9.
106  Ibid., 58, 91, 126.

2

# The tropical reaches of *After Leaving Mr Mackenzie*

Nancy Stepan notes that 'historically, to European eyes', Brazil, where protagonist Julia Martin's mother grew up, 'has been seen as exemplary in its "tropicality".… From the transfer of the Portuguese Crown in 1808, and especially after 1840, when national consolidation began under Dom Pedro II, two frameworks dominated interpretations of the "imagined nation": the tropical environment and race mixture'.[1] Eurocentric discourses of tropicality linked race mixture with 'tropical degeneration and inevitable backwardness'. Stepan outlines the emergence of a countering 'quasi-official ideology of the modern state': an assimilationist 'narrative of national improvement' and modernization 'via hybridization, or *mestiçagem*'.[2] She argues that 'the Brazilian fantasy of racial regeneration in the tropics through whitening' across generations is exemplified in Modesto Broco y Gomes's painting *The Redemption of Ham* (1895), which represents lactification or epidermal whitening across three generations of a family through the maternal line by representing a black woman giving thanks to God while standing alongside her mixed-race daughter, white-skinned son-in-law and white-skinned granddaughter.[3] Nicolas Abraham points out that 'what haunts are not the dead, but the gaps left in us by the secrets of others'.[4] As a child, Julia had, in the absence of her mother's storying of Brazil, in her secrecy about her family and personal history there, 'woven innumerable romances about her mother's childhood in South America'.[5] As a 'study of mourning',[6] *After Leaving Mr Mackenzie* foregrounds the loss of Brazil for Julia, 'the interpersonal and transgenerational consequences' of Mrs Griffiths's characteristic 'silence' about its meanings.[7] That there might be family secrets about mixed-race heritage is hinted at in the description of Mrs Griffiths as being '[d]ark-skinned, with high cheek-bones and an aquiline nose', and as having 'black eyes'.[8] The description and her Catholicism play on a stock Latin (Catholic)/Anglo-Saxon (Protestant) dichotomy that Robert Stam and Ella Shohat demonstrate has shaped understandings of Brazil as a country of the Americas, by contrast with the United States.⁹

Growing up, Julia had identified the tropics with the sun, but while catching butterflies one day she experienced a strong sense of amorphous threat as she moved from the shelter of tree shadows to the 'glare of white sunlight', 'still, desolate, and arid. And you knew that something huge was just behind you'.¹⁰ The 'darkness' that closes in on Julia is racialized as a dominant, assimilative white middle- to upper-class patriarchal English culture; for her mother the darkness is transgenerational silence and obliqueness about the meanings of Brazil in contexts of state-endorsed 'race' mixing there and assimilative imperatives in the Britain of her day. Through developing the reach of the image of the armadillo, Rhys represents Julia's characteristic depressive indifference and her mother's silence as defensive and protective modes of being, albeit in Julia's case at least a caging of a spirit of freedom. The armadillo analogy cuts against critical arguments that Julia negates the memory of her mother by intimating the scene of loving instruction and loss in which the beginnings of the armadillo were storied for Julia and by suggesting that transgenerationally both women have developed retreat into emotional shells as forms of survival and defence. Efthymia Rentzou usefully draws out the animal and the machine as others of the human in modernist literature. In *Quartet*, Rhys experiments with the human-machine dyad to represent Marya's depression; in *After Leaving Mr Mackenzie* she experiments with the human–animal dyad to represent Julia's and Mrs Griffiths's subjectivities.¹¹ 'Animals become pressure points for the concept of subjectivity, channeling experimentations with literary representation,' Rentzou explains. They 'become both a vector for questioning forms and modes of writing and a cornerstone for an ontological, ethical, and ultimately political reconsideration of the humanist animal'.¹²

Immediately after her mother's death Julia remembers her reading Kipling's 'The Beginning of the Armadilloes', one of his *Just So Stories* (1902), to her, though the story is not named in the novel. Kipling invents the word 'mixy' for his story to describe both being confounded by the new and the evolutionary hybrid. In *After Leaving Mr Mackenzie* Rhys engages critically with the ways in which fantasies and ideas of the mixed are played out through the reach of tropicality. I demonstrate that her intertextual juxtaposition of her novel with other explorations of the tropics establish motifs and the thematic domains of the hybrid, the stakes of assimilation, creative evolution and the species boundary human–animal. The juxtapositions distinguish her creativity around these themes and point to the constitutive role of tropicality across modern arts (children's and adult fiction, film, art, revue and music).[13] She alludes not only to Kipling's 'The Beginning of the Armadilloes', but also to Joseph Conrad's *Almayer's Folly* (1895), the theme song from W. S. Van Dyke's film *The Pagan* (1929), a late 1910s painting by Amedeo Modigliani which makes use of a mask motif germane to European primitivism. The motifs of tropicality resonate with French discursive fields around the revue *Blackbirds of 1929*. The tropicalist reach of these works includes Brazil, the South Pacific, Borneo and a generalized Africa. I compare Rhys's treatments of an armadillo analogy with Dora Maar's in *Portrait d'Ubu* and of the tropical in *After Leaving Mr Mackenzie* with her representation of it in her autobiographical essay 'Lost Island', written around the same time as the novel.

'The Beginning of the Armadilloes' is a playful tropicalist narrative about species mixing: the evolutionary adaptation of the armadillo from a hedgehog and a tortoise. Set in Brazil, nicknamed at the time the 'Minotaur of the South',[14] the story, like the minotaur (which is half-human, half-bull), is of hybrid form: tale, annotated explorer's map, captions, illustration and sea shanty. U. C. Knoepflmacher nicely characterizes the *Just So Stories* as 'tongue-in-cheek Lamarckian fables' featuring 'comical mutations … that dramatize animal and human survival'.[15]

That Rhys has Julia remember her mother reading 'The Beginning of the Armadilloes' to her develops a narrative arc around the stakes of Mrs Griffiths's diasporic assimilation in England, for her a 'cold, grey country', not a place in which to be 'happy'.[16] Julia's plangent memory of being read to returns her to a scene of informal instruction, narrative repression and loss, a scene from a time when her mother had been 'the sweet, warm centre of the world' for her. Julia has on a slightly earlier visit to her mother remembered that time of maternal plenitude 'so vividly that mysteriously it was all there again'.[17] Mrs Griffiths finds voice in English as a reader of a tropical bedtime story by Kipling, a diasporic colonial writer whom Rhys's readers in 1931 would have recognized as pro-imperialist. After Julia has left her mother's deathbed, she hears, while walking along the street, 'a barrel-organ playing' and struggles to fit the words of a remembered poem to the tune. The witnessing of her mother's death has made her feel 'very sleepy, horribly sleepy, as a child would be after a very exciting day'. When Julia arrives home she is 'filled with only one wish – a longing for sleep', yet the dissonance between the street tune and the words is 'still ringing in her head'. The words are from the sea shanty that closes 'The Beginning of the Armadilloes':

> Yes, weekly from Southampton,
> Great steamers, white and gold,
> Go rolling down to Rio

(Roll down – roll down to Rio!)
And I'd like to roll to Rio
Some day before I'm old.[18]

*Just So Stories*, as Linda M. Shires points out, includes 'a storytelling adult and a listening child', drawing readers into 'embrace' of the 'relationship'. The narrator addresses the listening child as 'O Best Beloved', 'accomplishing immediacy and intimacy by inviting the first identification of the fiction to be with a loving voice', and 'enlisting the child's collaborative imagination'.[19] Julia's memory of being read 'The Beginning of the Armadilloes' encompasses this immediacy and intimacy. The lyrics she recalls hint at a desire on Mrs Griffiths's part to return home. Brazil is represented in Kipling's poem in 'The Beginning of the Armadilloes' as a place of exotic 'wonders to behold' (like the jaguar and the armadillo) and British commercial traffic, of which the 'white and gold' colours of the steamer are an emblem.[20]

In 'The Beginning of the Armadilloes' survival and regeneration are achieved by mixing; Mrs Griffiths and Julia, too, mix human and what have been deemed armadillo characteristics. The English word armadillo is borrowed from Spanish, literally meaning 'small armed person'.[21] When under threat of attack armadilloes are renowned for burrowing and, as a last resort, for retreating into their brown plated shells by rolling up into a ball. In *Just So Stories*, Kipling 'invite[s] the child' listener, Shires observes, 'to evolve into a being that can adapt to circumstances that might crush and destroy'.[22] A central conceit of 'The Beginning of the Armadilloes' is that adaptive evolution may be willed. The animals in Kipling's story have the attribute of human speech. Stickly-Prickly Hedgehog and Slow-Solid Tortoise 'clever[ly]' and co-operatively transform themselves by taking on characteristics of each other in the process of outwitting a young predator Painted Jaguar. The story sets the 'real old and clever' hedgehog and tortoise living on the banks of the 'turbid Amazon' against the hedgehogs and tortoises in the narrator's modern English garden.[23] The temperate garden contrasts with the tropical forests represented on the map. The map purports to be that of an early-sixteenth-century English exploration of the Amazon, so does not show plantations worked by enslaved labour. The area mapped is represented as a place of sickness and the home of Indians evoked through heathen and ethnographic stereotypes. A 'jungle upbringing', Kipling suggests, necessitates 'cunning' survival skills on the part of potential prey.[24] Stickly-Prickly's and Slow-Solid's verbal twistings of the instructions of Painted Jaguar's mother on how to hunt hedgehogs and tortoises confuse Painted Jaguar into a state he describes as 'mixy'. In the absence of a 'proper name' for the new mixed creature, Painted Jaguar's mother provisionally names it the armadillo.[25] Mrs Griffiths's leathery shell into which she retreats emotionally is inarticulacy after her 'transplantation' to England and austerity after early widowhood when her children are six and one. Her family status becomes: 'Middle class, no money'. In death her face is mask-like, 'bound with white linen'; the story of her beginnings is never revealed.[26] Julia's shell is a depressive 'indifference' that habitually protects her from her own more self-lacerating emotions.[27] The room of the Hotel St Raphael in Paris in which Julia is living at the novel's opening is for her, for instance, 'a good sort of place to hide in ... until the sore and cringing feeling, which was the legacy' of her sexual relationship with Mr Mackenzie abates. The landlady thinks Julia is 'quiet and very inoffensive',[28] qualities influentially attributed to the armadillo by Charles Darwin reporting the comment of a gaucho in *The Voyage of the Beagle* (1839) and Oliver Goldsmith in *A History of the Earth and Animated Nature* (1774), respectively. Goldsmith also notes the vulnerability of the curled-up armadillo to predators.[29] The colouring of the armadillo shell enables camouflage, assimilation with surroundings.

Conrad's epigraph to *Almayer's Folly* – 'Who of us has not had his promised land, his day of ecstasy, and his end in exile'[30] – is especially pertinent to the lives of the women in Julia's family. As Christopher Lane points out, '[w]hile exploring this question' drawn from Henri-Frédéric Amiel, Conrad 'pays particular attention to the way these factors determine group and racial "bonds"'.[31] Mrs Griffiths's sense of exile is compressed in her laconic description of England as 'cold, grey', an implicit point of reference being her silenced memories of tropical Brazil. Julia thinks her 'inarticulate', 'sickening for the sun', '[a]ustere, unconsciously thwarted perhaps, but not unhappy'.[32] For Julia's more conservative sister Norah, who has nursed her mother through two strokes and old age, the promised land has been personal approbation for being 'wonderful', and her exile is the sense that in the process of earning such praise she has lost 'her youth' and 'her beauty' and 'her soft heart' has 'grow[n] hard and bitter', a mark of which is her hankering after the limited independence that will be made possible by small inheritances after the deaths of her Aunt Sophie and her mother. The passage she reads from *Almayer's Folly*, her current bedtime reading, named in the novel, concerns the Siamese enslaved woman Taminah's exile from 'hope' and a prospect of 'change. She knew of no other sky, no other water, no other forest, no other world, no other life.'[33] In Conrad's novel, Taminah's 'every-day look of apathetic indifference' 'veiled over' sleeping 'feelings' and 'passions'.[34] The literary passage affirms Toni Morrison's argument that an image of embodied blackness often functions as a catalyst for white self-realization[35]: Norah realizes her loss through a transitory identification of her carer role as a form of dehumanizing enslavement. Taminah's disappointment at Malayan prince Dain Maroola's sexual interest in Almayer's mixed-race daughter Nina rouses her passion: 'Her jealousy and rage culminated into a paroxysm of physical pain that left her lying panting on the river-bank, in the dumb agony of a wounded animal.'[36]

Julia's 'promised land' has been adventurous escape from what England and her family represent to her. In childhood she has relished the fantasy sensation of flight as she runs, recognizing, 'I'm happy – happy – happy … '[37] After the First World War she uses a marriage to escape to continental Europe. The child of the marriage dies shortly after birth; the marriage fails. At the opening of *After Leaving Mr Mackenzie*, which is set during the Great Depression, Julia is supporting herself by, in Rhys's words, '[g]oing from man to man'.[38] In the language of the day she is an amateur, a woman who, though not a professional prostitute, accepts gifts of money from wealthier men whose mistress she has been or might become. For the partners represented in the novel, Mr Mackenzie and Mr Horsfield, there is around Julia a sexualized frisson of violence and the wild that places her 'outside' their middle-class 'pale'. Mr Mackenzie remembers sending Julia a letter expressing a desire for a sado-masochistic sexual scenario which began: 'I would like to put my throat under your feet.' While not recalling the name of the song, Mr Horsfield thinks lyrics from the US ballad 'Frankie and Johnny' are 'peculiarly applicable to Julia'.[39] Frankie murders her adulterous lover Johnny. Uncle Griffiths, a wealthy, English paternal uncle places Julia 'outside the sacred circle' of family 'warmth', badgering her on her visit to London over her failed marriage to a foreigner and 'desert[ion]' of her family'. Rhys reinforces the implications of his xenophobia when, on leaving his home, Julia experiences a strong sense of the English upper-class demand for stolid sameness, for propriety, for assimilation: 'Each house she passed was exactly like the last. Each house bulged a little forward. And before each a flight of four or five steps led up to a portico supported by two fat pillars.'[40] Maslen notes how phallic the image is.[41] The repressive xenophobia of family patriarch Uncle Griffiths has, it is implied here, also played out in the married life of Julia's parents and in the life of Julia's mother after her father's death. At this point Julia hears a 'drably vague' male busker near the door of a 'public bar' singing in a faltering voice, often 'complaining and mindless, like an animal in pain', what she identifies, in the context of her pervasive sense of England as a place of 'heavy darkness, greasy and compelling', as a rendition of 'The Pagan Love Song'.[42]

The busker's voice and the darkness here figure as a crux in important readings of the novel by Maslen and Johnson. Neither reading, though, unpacks the meanings of darkness in relation to Rhys's patterns of intertextual and intermedial juxtaposition nor addresses more immediately the allusion to 'The Pagan Love Song'. For Maslen, whose reading of the novel addresses the lost baby motif, the voice represents 'Julia's otherwise unrepresented experience of giving birth' in a 'description ... suggestive of the cries of a woman in labour' that 'hint[s] at the animality of the birthing woman'.[43] To take up Maslen's argument, I note that the busker then, in effect, becomes one of a number of reduplicated figures of the depressed Julia in the novel: 'echoes, doubles, kindred beings who display a passion or a destruction such as the aching woman is not up to putting into words and suffers for being deprived of'.[44] Johnson argues that Julia's subjective indifference here is symptomatic of a death drive that morphs 'into a posthuman ontological state of spectrality'. Rhys's pointed invocation of the armadillo through the allusion to Kipling suggests, rather, that Julia's indifference is self-preserving. Johnson argues that 'Julia absorbs the affect of indifference into herself in such a way that she encrypts herself in it'. She supports this proposition by referring to the moment in the text when Julia's experience of London is seeming 'entombment':[45] 'It was the darkness that got you. It was heavy darkness, greasy and compelling. It made walls round you, and shut you in so that you felt you could not breathe. You wanted to beat at the darkness and shriek to be let out. And after a while you got used to it. Of course. And then you stopped believing that there was anything else anywhere.'[46] The association of London with darkness, which resonates with the ending of Joseph Conrad's *Heart of Darkness*,[47] inverts the conventional associations of England, of European empire and of white middle- to upper-class identity with light and enlightenment.

Julia's image of walls of darkness shutting her in resonates with her memories of a childhood game of 'catching butterflies' and putting them in 'an empty tobacco tin', en route to what she thinks will be a 'comfortable cardboard box' where she will feed and domesticate them. The butterflies, though, die of injuries sustained while beating their wings inside the dark tin, the sound of which Julia finds 'very fascinating'. In predatory role as would-be keeper and tamer of insects, Julia labels the butterfly 'an idiot' for 'break[ing] its own wings', exculpating herself from blame.[48] The butterfly is not 'so clever' like the adaptable hedgehog and tortoise become armadillo in Kipling's fantastic tale.[49] Julia has learnt not to 'beat' her wings too much in 'the darkness' by expressing her 'rage' and 'hatred of the world', has 'got used to it', withdrawing into indifference in the rooms she rents.⁵⁰ To show more of what Johnson calls 'interest', following Silvan Tomkins in *Shame and Its Sisters*,⁵¹ would be too self-lacerating. A scene of Julia dancing with an elderly man with a 'cadaverous' appearance at a club she visits with Mr Horsfield followed by a sexual encounter between Horsfield and Julia draws into focus what the third-person narrative voice calls her bodily 'abandonment of fatigue' rather than 'voluptuous[ness]', signs of the lack of interest. Rhys highlights the mechanical aspect of Julia's comportment: dancing to gramophone music, she is like 'a clockwork toy that has nearly run down'; when Mr Horsfield starts to initiate sex, she has a 'heavy, bewildered, sleepy' look.⁵² Rhys's images of Julia's fatigue show her again using dance as a metaphor of sexual modernity. Julia's 'beat[ing]' of her wings is, however, enabling in Rhys's narrative. It pushes to consciousness a critique of what Moran writes of as the 'social and cultural codes that create systems of oppression and exploitation but then disallow the shame and rage that they inevitably create'.⁵³ The story of the boxed butterflies reframes the image of the card of the Hotel St Raphael on the first page of the novel, positioning cheap hotel rooms as boxes in which Julia beats her wings. Rhys's choice of name for the hotel is careful. As Jeremy Hawthorn points out, 'St Raphael is, among other things, the patron saint of blind people, lovers and travelers, and in a metaphorical sense at least Julia is all three of these.'⁵⁴

The lyrics of 'The Pagan Love Song' from the 1929 film *The Pagan* longingly anticipate a tropical primitivist idyll, but have no seductive affect on Julia, who by the time she hears the song sung in a London street does not believe 'that there was anything else' but darkness 'anywhere'.⁵⁵ *The Pagan* is a hybrid of silent movie and sound. 'The Pagan Love Song', sung by Ramon Novarro, the male star, was on the pre-recorded soundtrack to the film, the synch sound being a relatively new technology. The sheet music of the song, sung to the ukulele in the film, rapidly sold 1.5 million copies.⁵⁶ The film, set in the Tuamotu Islands of French Polynesia, deploys a vast array of tropical and religious stereotypes, stereotypes about the racial atavism of mixed-race people, and modernist primitivist tropes and motifs. Even the casting of *The Pagan* draws out the performativity of sexualized 'race'. Ramon Novarro, who played Henry Shoesmith, Jr, was from Mexico and marketed as a Latin lover; Tito, his love interest, was played by Dorothy Janis, who was rumoured by the Metro studio to be 'half-Native American'.⁵⁷ Novarro, whose homosexuality was an 'open secret' in the 1920s, was, too, performing ostensible heteronormativity.⁵⁸ In narrative terms, the commodified tropical sublime in *The Pagan* emerges at the moment of the extinction of the possibility of a place outside a capitalist and imperial world-system, 'when the belief that there could be an actually existing and autonomous primitive way of life *somewhere else* was at its vanishing point'.⁵⁹ In *After Leaving Mr Mackenzie*, the film, the commercialized song and the dreary busker operate within that capitalist and imperialist world-system as part of the cinematic and musical pleasure industries of an Americanized 'mass culture' that 'defined a "sensory-reflexive horizon for the experience of modernization and modernity"'.⁶⁰ Like other cinematic South Sea romances of the period and Conrad's *Almayer's Folly*, the film foregrounds the stakes of miscegenation in its narrative. One of the intertitles in the opening sequence of *The Pagan* describes the setting as a 'straggling half-breed city ... risen to meet the ruthless march of commerce', a march embodied in the film by the international banking system, trade and Christianization. The degeneracy of that march is figured in Mr Slater, an unscrupulous evangelical white copra trader. He cheats the mixed-race Henry of his paternal inheritance, a coconut plantation.⁶¹ Henry's maternal inheritance is a hut in the hills.

'The Pagan Love Song' reconnects Henry and Tito with their maternal heritages as a locus of desire. It is an eroticized daydream of a place of 'golden' sunshine, 'lazy' dreaming and romantically beautiful evenings; 'Native hills are calling', and there will be 'happy years' of love.⁶² The failure of affect as Julia listens to the busker's rendition of the song in a place and time of existential darkness – for her it is 'complaining and mindless, like an animal in pain' – is especially notable by contrast with the 'voyeuristic eroticism' of the camera work in the film as Novarro sings it.⁶³ The camera work here fetishizes Shoesmith's bare flesh – he usually only wears a pareu in the film. Jeffrey Geiger aptly characterizes the shots of Novarro's body: '[T]he camera crawls across it in a point-of-view shot, moving from feet to head while lingering over Novarro's long legs.'⁶⁴ He rightly notes that the point-of-view shots of the prostitute Madge's gaze at Henry's bared body do not necessarily debar homoerotic exoticism.⁶⁵ The singing has seductive appeal for Tito, the mixed-race ward of Slater, who tries to assimilate her to European values through Christian evangelical instruction. His stroking of her hair during a dramatized lesson – another example of the film's voyeuristic eroticism – points to his sexual fetishization of his racial 'improvement' of her. There are similarities between Conrad's Almayer and Van Dyke's Slater: the fetishization of the 'improvement' of the mixed-race daughter/ward through Christian instruction and the violent repudiation of her after she chooses a romantic sexual relationship with a non-white man. Nina's Christianization is crucial to Almayer's aspirational vision of social redemption on his return to Europe with her and enough wealth to blind people there to her mixed-race heritage;

Tito's Christianization is crucial to Slater's attempt to transform the racialized other into a marriageable sexual object for himself. The first tryst of Henry and Tito shows an atavistic return to a hunter/gatherer way of life in 'Native hills' – Henry's maternal heritage. In one cinema poster their love is characterized through tropicalist clichés that play on the melodramatic contrast between light and dark: 'MOON-LIT LAGOONS! WHISPERING PALMS! LOVE UNTAMED, UNASHAMED! THEN THE SHADOW OF THE CONQUERING WHITE MAN!'[66] Slater – the figure of moral darkness – becomes physically violent towards Tito after she consummates her love for Henry, corrupting his fetish object. In *Almayer's Folly*, a more probing psychological study, darkness encompasses the intrigue, delusion and self-blindness in a contact zone between cultures.

Julia names the darkness spreading from imperial centres the hypocrisy of people imagining that they are superior to animals, Rhys's framing of her comment introducing irony at Julia's expense: 'Animals are better than we are, aren't they? They're not all the time pretending and lying and sneering, like loathsome human beings.... People are such beasts, such mean beasts ... They'll let you die for want of a decent word, and then they'll lick the feet of anybody they can get anything out of.'[67] Other characters often exercise a sense of evolutionary superiority over Julia by positioning her as an animal. Julia's first landlady in the novel thinks she leads the 'life of a dog', being kennelled in a room and taking a daily walk. The dog analogy also draws out Julia's habitual predominantly cyclical rather than linear experience of time. Knowing more of her maternal family's history, Uncle Griffiths thinks of exotic tropical animals – 'zebra', 'giraffe' – in relation to Julia, whom he regards as base. When Julia first meets Norah after her return to London she feels that Norah 'kept looking at her as if she were something out of the zoo'.[68]

Motifs of animalization and beastliness feature in Julia's story of telling her life history to Ruth, a sculptress for whom she posed. The memory proffers readers scope for general reflexivity on relationship between character and reader and relationship between artist/writer and character. The story offers three scenes of critical appraisal: Julia's reading of a reproduction of a painting by Modigliani; Ruth's response to Julia's story; and Julia's phantasmatic experience of the model in the painting judging her. The reproduction of the painting by Modigliani, which Julia thinks a 'rum picture', is part of the mise-en-scène in Ruth's studio. Julia describes the model: 'a woman lying on a couch, a woman with a lovely, lovely body.... A sort of proud body, like an utterly lovely proud animal. And a face like a mask, a long, dark face, and very big eyes. The eyes were blank, like a mask.'[69] The description strongly suggests the reproduction is of *Reclining Nude* (1917). *Reclining Nude* mixes the European genre of the reclining nude and the cubist motif of the mask to represent carnal sexuality. The model as erotic white body is racialized by the mask, the provenance of which in modernist art is tropical (Africa or Oceania), and by Modigliani's posing of her to accentuate her buttocks. As Sander Gilman has shown, the exaggeration of the buttocks is a feature of nineteenth-century and early modernist representations of the female prostitute, a racist sign of the black woman hidden within.[70] Modigliani's nudes of the 1910s were controversial, with French police in 1917 shutting down his only solo public show at the Berthe Weill Gallery because of his representation of pubic hair. Mary Thompson notes that pubic and armpit hair were generally 'only seen on women's bodies in erotic or pornographic art, or on the bodies of women of color'.[71] In *Reclining Nude*, armpit hair is shown near the mouth with slightly parted lips, possibly a playful visual euphemism for pubic hair and a receptive vaginal vestibule. Jane Rogoyska and Frances Alexander explain that Modigliani's 'reduction of narrative and subject matter to nothing but the erotic body, presented for its own sake' was 'considered scandalous'.[72] For Julia, the representation of the model mixes human and animal forms; subjectively, though, for her the sense that the eyes of the mask are 'blank' morphs into a feeling that she was 'looking at a real woman, a live woman'.[73] Rogoyska and Alexander note Modigliani's particular interest in eyes as signs of both 'introspection' and 'observation'.[74] 'Always masks had frightened and fascinated her', the narrator later observes more generally of Julia.[75] Julia remembers feeling that both Ruth and the woman in the painting were judging her as she narrativized her adult life for them, a story which begins with the excitement of her re-inventive adventures after leaving England, adventures in which 'men were mixed up, because of course they had to be'. Ruth's curt, demeaning and disbelieving response, which leaves Julia feeling 'beastly', is, 'You seem to have had a hectic time.' Julia tells Mr Horsfield, to whom she is relating the story of the encounter:

> I felt as if the woman in the picture were laughing at me and saying: 'I am more real than you. But at the same time I *am* you. I'm all that matters of you.'
>
> 'And I felt as if all my life and all myself were floating away from me like smoke and there was nothing to lay hold of – nothing.
>
> 'And it was a beastly feeling, a foul feeling, like looking over the edge of the world. It was more frightening than I can ever tell you. It made me feel sick in my stomach.[']

Julia explains that Ruth as reader, despite her artistic leanings, was not open to what was 'outside her scheme of things'.[76] Emery has drawn attention to the ways in which this scene connects Mrs Griffiths, Modigliani's figure and Julia through 'imagery of masks, bestial bodies, and dark skins', drawing out their being 'dispossess[ed]' of 'narratable' stories by the representational codes underpinning modernist primitivism.[77] Rhys's miscegenation and armadillo motifs in the novel strongly suggest that for Julia and her mother mixed-race heritage is part of a suppressed family history. The words of the model, a reduplicated figure, project Julia's subjective fears, a tacit recognition that she is being reduced to an animalized bodily form, that she carries a recognizable racialized blackness within. As author, Rhys, by comparison with Ruth as artist, respects the subjectivity of her character. With Julia's comment on Ruth as reader, Rhys implicitly invites readers of *After Leaving Mr Mackenzie* to reflect on their own openness to difference and the ways in which lack of this might affect their reception of characters and people with whom they come into contact.

Julia's response to the Modigliani reproduction is not Rhys's only study in the novel of her appraisal of avant-garde art through which Rhys gauges her shifting attitudes to the hybrid and her existential condition. Julia is unsettled by a modernist still life in her room at the Hotel St Raphael, 'an unframed oil-painting of a half empty bottle of red wine, a knife, and a piece of Gruyère cheese, signed "J. Grykho, 1923"', in which each 'object in the picture was slightly distorted and full of obscure meaning'. Her difficulty in evaluating the painting makes her loathe it; for her it has 'a certain depressing quality', is 'alarming in its perversion'. 'Lying in bed, ... she was unable to avoid looking at it.'[78] GoGwilt usefully interprets Julia's perplexity at the painting as 'a studied framing of the problem of reading ... interiority (both interiority of social space and of psychological identity)'.[79] He does not, though, take account of Rhys's pointed framing of Julia's response to the painting by juxtaposing it with her affective responses to the wallpaper design in her room and a modernist image of man confined inside a 'huge mauve corkscrew' that she is fascinated by during one of her walks on the Rue de Seine. Both the design and the paintings are departures from, distortions of realism. A legend has been attached to the image to guide interpretation. It explains that life is a spiral that limits humans to climbing up or down. Contemplating the image and legend leaves Julia feeling 'serene and peaceful'.[80] Julia judges the Grykho painting perverse in relation to her unfamiliarity with the codes of identifying and reading its modernist form. The wallpaper design – commercial art – features the basilisk, a mythological creature, which, like Kipling's armadillo, is a 'composite' of disparate species,[81] here 'a strange, wingless creature, half-bird, half-lizard, which also had its beak open and its neck stretched out in a belligerent attitude' facing a 'large bird ...

with open beak' on a tree 'branch' which 'sprouted fungus and queerly shaped leaves and fruit'.[82] Boria Sax notes that from the early modern period depictions of the basilisk 'emphasized its unnatural character by making it a composite of a vast number of creatures: it might have the comb, wattle and claws of a rooster; the mouth and torso of a toad; the wings of a bat; the horns of a stag; and the tail of a snake'. 'According to various accounts', Sax reports, 'it can kill with its scent, its hiss, the touch of its tail and, above all, its glance.'[83] Bartholomaeus Anglicus records that the basilisk 'drieth and burneth leaves and herbs, not only with touch but also by hissing and blast he rotteth and corrupteth all things about him'.[84] Julia finds the fantastic pattern of the wallpaper 'oddly enough, not sinister but cheerful and rather stimulating' after staying so often in rooms with 'striped papers'. In a reading of Rhys's 'exploration of shame and the growth of the rage that Helen Block Lewis terms "humiliated fury"' in *After Leaving Mrs Mackenzie*, Moran argues that the pose of the basilisk in the wallpaper 'is an image for Julia herself', with 'its belligerent and open beak signal[ling] that the shamed subject in Rhys is now prepared to strike back against would-be aggressors'.[85]

The '[r]acialized, animated, fleshly sound'[86] of the stage revues *Blackbirds of 1928* and *Blackbirds of 1929* popularized 'I Can't Give You Anything But Love, Baby' by the white song-writing team of composer Jimmy McHugh and lyricist Dorothy Fields. It was recorded by, among others, Duke Ellington and the Cotton Club Orchestra in 1928 and by Louis Armstrong in 1929. *Blackbirds of 1928*, the longest running all-black show on Broadway at the time, opened as *Blackbirds of 1929* at the Moulin Rouge in Paris on 7 June 1929. In *After Leaving Mr Mackenzie*, the commercialization of 'I Can't Give You Anything But Love, Baby' through gramophone recordings allows the lyrics to be repurposed as part of a different expressive culture, with Rhys using the repurposing of the song to expose imperial civility to be a sham and to highlight sexual commodification of Julia. When an impecunious Julia rents a particularly shabby Bloomsbury room the 'young man' who shows her over it 'whistle[s] shrilly' in the hallway 'I Can't Give You Anything But Love, Baby.'[87] Pointing to a slippage on the word love, Rhys shows the young man sexualizing and possibly also racializing Julia. In context the unarticulated lyrics are assimilated by the young man as a sneer at Julia, rather than a 'decent word':[88] the impoverished first-person voice of the song explains that 'time' and 'love' rather than expensive presents are all he or she can offer to the addressee, who will need to '[d]ream' and 'scheme a while'.[89] The sneer catalyses Julia's representation of herself as an 'importunate ghost' in a letter to her wealthy ex-lover W. Neil James and feeds a later generalization about human civility: 'People are such beasts, such mean beasts.'[90]

The transatlantic provenance of 'I Can't Give You Anything But Love, Baby' encompasses public debate in France over race mixing. The cast of *Blackbirds of 1929* included a greater variety of African-American skin shades than other black revues, provoking French media discussion of miscegenation. In *Paris Blues: African-American Music and French Popular Culture, 1920–1960*, Andy Fry collates and translates two contemporary commentaries on the cast of the revue, the first by Pierre Brisson in *Le Temps* and the second by André Levinson in *Candide*:

> None of these human products is really black, and you have the most complete range of mulattos … quarteroons, Caribbean Negroes or mongrels …, the unexpected crossbreeds of a crossroads-city … The lightened girls are more beautiful and tempting; the men, muscular and vigorous.… And there is all the same the old tam-tam of the grandparents, the old smell of a bloody feast that racks their loins into a frenzy.
>
> It's *métissage*, whimsical crossing of races, capriciously proportioned and grafted mixing, violent distortion, contamination, transfusion of sap, which multiplies, exasperates – and drains … the vitality of America's colored man.… Among these Afro-Americans, we are in the presence not of an indigenous tribe in a state of heavenly savagery, but of … as motley a mix as possible … the supreme and final explosion of an ethnic singularity decomposing.

'More familiar now', Fry notes, 'African Americans had come to represent not only a source of a vitalizing (or terrifying) primitiveness but also an example of race mixing.'[91] Brisson's image of the 'crossbreeds of a crossroads-city' uncannily echoes the 'half-breed city' of *The Pagan*. Rhys was certainly familiar with the newspaper *Candide* – Marya reads it in *Quartet* – and maintained her habit of writing her fiction in Paris from the late 1920s through to the end of the 1930s.

In the surrealist journal *Documents: Archaeology, Beaux Arts, Ethnography, Variety*, Michel Leiris, editor Georges Bataille and music critic André Schaeffner identify crises and fissures in white culture in reflecting on *Blackbirds of 1929*. The reception of the revue in *Documents* addressed questions about 'modern evolution' (Leiris),[92] the meanings of modernity and baseness (Bataille), and the meanings of tropical Africa and 'creative evolution' of the culturally hybrid 'Afro-Americain', a neologism coined by Schaeffner.[93] For Leiris in his article 'Civilisation', jazz, as exemplified in the performance of *Blackbirds of 1929*, offers a white audience a carnivalesque moment of loss:

> [R]egret for our mediocrity, for living such a mediocre life, so dull and ugly in comparison with these creatures, who are as touching as the trees.

> Thus this music and these dances do not linger on the surface, they plunge deep organic roots into us, roots whose thousand ramifications penetrate us; a painful surgery that nevertheless quickens our blood.[94]

'All our moral habits and polite customs, that delightful coloured cloak that veils the coarseness of our dangerous instincts, all those attractive forms of culture of which we are so proud – since it is thanks to them that we regard ourselves as "civilized" – are', Leiris writes, 'ready to disappear at the slightest turbulence, to shatter at the least impact.'[95] Bataille, too, focuses on audience response in his definition of Black Birds: '[W]e are rotting away with neurasthenia under our roofs, a cemetery and common grave of so much pathetic rubbish.' The 'dance and cry' of the Blackbirds 'are marshy emanations of the decomposition who are set aflame above this immense cemetery'.[96] Schaeffner's review urged that the show demonstrated 'that upper-case Music, meaning the French or European classical tradition, should be abandoned for a lower-case use of the word that acknowledges the validity of all forms'.[97] The readings, like Norah's response to the passage in *Almayer's Folly*, instantiate Morrison's proposition that images of embodied blackness often function as catalysts for 'critical moments of discovery' for white people,[98] here the live performance of *Blackbirds of 1929* bearing what are read as the markers of a tropical African lineage of African-American cultural hybridity that exposes the limits of the evolution of white civilization: 'mediocrity' (Leiris), 'neurasthenia', 'pathetic rubbish', death (Bataille). Schaeffner was confronted by the artificiality of the distinction between high and low. Matthew F. Jordan urges that the reception of the revue by these 'surrealist ethnographers … explod[ed] the barrier between high and popular culture' and launched a fresh 'sensitivity to cultural hybridity'.[99]

A comparison of Rhys's armadillo analogy with Dora Maar's *Portrait d'Ubu*, shown at the *Surrealist Exhibition of Objects* at Charles Ratton's gallery in Paris in May 1936 and rapidly adopted as an emblem of the surrealist movement, is instructive. *Portrait d'Ubu* is a photograph of an armadillo foetus in formaldehyde rendered uncannily abstract by not being identified as such. The title *Portrait d'Ubu* alludes to Alfred Jarry's *Ubu Roi*, first performed in 1896, and part of a modernist canon by the 1930s. Maar's photograph has been read 'as a palimpsest portrait of the unconscious, reptilian, primitive',[100] a foray into 'forbidden territory, where the exotic and grotesque mingle to create a disquieting yet exciting tension'.[101] While Kipling had been world-famous for decades, Rhys alludes to a children's story, not by name, rather than a modernist icon and evokes the armadillo – an emblem of a diasporic subject possibly passing as white – through allusion. Maar was part of a modernist coterie, the interpretative paradigms of which could explicate the transgressive hybridity of *Portrait d'Ubu*. Merging the 'scientific' and the 'poetic and artistic', it is the kind of surrealist image that Andre Breton celebrates in 'Crisis of the object' as 'achieving a total disruption of sensibility by routing all rational habits, erasing the distinction between good and evil, expressing strict reservations about the hegemony of the *cogito*, and revealing the *marvellous* in everyday life'.[102]

In *After Leaving Mr Mackenzie*, Rhys evokes through traces of her intertextual and intermedial bearings 'conventional "grammar[s]" of tropicality'[103] and primitivism, pointing to their constitutive presence across modern arts (children's and adult fiction, film, art, revue and music). The novel draws out the reach and impact of these grammars in the lives of Julia and her mother and pushes back against any pre-mapped, conventional 'anticipatory geography of the tropics' readers might bring to text.[104] Rhys uses contrapuntal juxtaposition to distinguish her creativity around themes of darkness, the hybrid, assimilation and evolution and to develop the reach of the figure of the armadillo to explore the transgenerational stakes of diasporic assimilation for Julia and Mrs Griffiths.

Rhys acknowledges that on completing *After Leaving Mr Mackenzie* 'the West Indies started knocking at' her 'heart. So – "Voyage in the Dark."'[105] Between the two novels she wrote 'Lost Island: A Childhood. Fragments of Autobiography', a three-part essay of around 2,600 words originally titled 'Down Along: Fragments of Autobiography', and 'The Christmas Presents of Mynheer van Rooz', her only story set in the Netherlands, published in the British feminist newspaper *Time and Tide* in 1931. Small details of 'Lost Island', particularly about black women selling fishcakes and Masquerade, were revised for *Voyage in the Dark*. Tropical Dominica is remembered in 'Lost Island' as a place in which racialized thresholds form the aesthetic senses and the ethical and political identifications with which they are implicated. Rhys highlights the emergence of a gendered non-metropolitan sublime in which the transcendent poetics of the sublime is grounded in the fragility of natural beauty in the face of the elements, rather than views to 'mountainous terrain or a sexualized prospect of recapitalization of a plantation economy'.[106] The essay culminates in a moment of mixed feeling: envious celebration of the expressive culture of Masquerade and recognition of the violence of casual racism towards black people and of the coercive socio-economic conditions in which the black majority lives. The racism and impoverishment of a black majority are legacies of 'slavery's denial of Black humanity' manifesting in 'spatial, legal, psychic, [and] material' structures of Dominican life.[107] For Julia, whose family history in Brazil has been silenced, the world has become a place of indifferent darkness (unalleviated by tropicalist romance); the narrator of 'Lost Island' vividly evokes the sensuous plenitude of the tropics (colour, aroma and sound). In *Voyage in the Dark*, corporeal memories of tropical plenitude will provide solace for Anna in England. Bringing together the plenitude of Anna's memory and the greyness of her present, Rhys extends her structural technique of contrapuntal juxtaposition to address the experience of time for the diasporic subject.

Rhys extends her critique of tropicality as she addresses the Caribbean in *Voyage in the Dark* and later fiction. She brings into her compositional practice an exploration of the imperial and inter-imperial bearings of the *doudou* and doudouism in texts which encompass cultural passage between Dominica and Martinique in various ways. In counterpointing *Jane Eyre* and *Wide Sargasso Sea*, Rhys takes up and experiments around Brontë's Rochester's reference to the hurricane. As Sonya Posmentier points out, hurricanes are a 'signature environmental event' of the tropical Caribbean and have become in the decolonizing poetics of the region 'a figure for the problem of literary mimesis' and for a literary 'break from the past'.[108]

# Notes

1 Stepan, *Picturing Tropical Nature*, 124.
2 Ibid., 133, 135–6, 139.
3 Ibid., 42.
4 Abraham, 'Notes on the Phantom', 171.
5 Jean Rhys, *After Leaving Mr Mackenzie* (1930; repr., Harmondsworth: Penguin, 1971), 76.
6 GoGwilt, *The Passage of Literature*, 91.
7 Nicholas T. Rand, in *The Shell and the Kernel: Renewals of Psychoanalysis*, by Abraham and Torok, trans. Rand, 168.
8 Rhys, *After Leaving Mr Mackenzie*, 70, 72.
9 The Catholicism of Mrs Griffiths is revealed when Julia recites the Catholic prayer for the dead at her deathbed (ibid., 88). Robert Stam and Ella Shohat, 'Transnationalizing Comparison: The Uses and Abuses of Cross-Cultural Analogy', in *Comparison: Theories, Approaches, Uses*, ed. Rita Felski and Susan Stanford Friedman (Baltimore, MD: Johns Hopkins University Press, 2013), 126–8.
10 Rhys, *After Leaving Mr Mackenzie*, 115–16.
11 Maslen observes that 'animalisation' and 'ghostliness' are recurring tropes of Julia's dehumanization (*Ferocious Things*, 93, 94).

12 Efthymia Rentzou, 'Animal', in *A New Vocabulary for Global Modernism*, ed. Eric Hayot and Rebecca L. Walkowitz (New York: Columbia University Press, 2016), 32.
13 Graham Huggan and Helen Tiffin, *Postcolonial Ecocriticism: Literature, Animals, Environment* (London: Routledge, 2010), 135.
14 Stam and Shohat, 'Transnationalizing Comparison', 130.
15 U. C. Knoepflmacher, 'Kipling's "Mixy" Creatures', *SEL: Studies in English Literature 1500–1900* 48, no. 4 (2008): 929.
16 Rhys, *After Leaving Mr Mackenzie*, 76.
17 Ibid., 78.
18 Ibid., 90–1.
19 Linda M. Shires, 'Mutual Adaptation in Rudyard Kipling's Letters to His Children and *Just So Stories*', *Children's Literature* 43 (2015): 184, 193.
20 Rudyard Kipling, 'The Beginning of the Armadilloes', in *Just So Stories for Little Children*, ed. Lisa Lewis (Oxford: Oxford University Press, 1998), 90. Not aware of Rhys's allusion to Kipling's story, Emery states that Julia 'seems to insist, yet with heavy irony, on her mother's South American identity and to comment, almost grotesquely, on its "rolling" away'. *Jean Rhys at 'World's End'*, 126.
21 *Oxford English Dictionary Online*.
22 Shires, 'Mutual Adaptation in Rudyard Kipling's Letters to His Children and *Just So Stories*', 196.
23 Kipling, 'The Beginning of the Armadilloes', 87.
24 Jessica Straley, *Evolution and Imagination in Victorian Children's Literature* (Cambridge: Cambridge University Press, 2016), 119.
25 Kipling, 'The Beginning of the Armadilloes', 81, 87.
26 Rhys, *After Leaving Mr Mackenzie*, 76–7, 53, 89.
27 Ibid., 37.
28 Ibid., 9.
29 Darwin reports, 'It seems almost a pity to kill such nice little animals, for as a Gaucho said, while sharpening his knife on the back of one, "son tan mansos" (they are so quiet).' Charles Darwin, *The Voyage of the Beagle* (New York: P. Collier, 1937), 103. In one of Kipling's sources, *A History of the Earth and Animated Nature* (London, 1774), Oliver Goldsmith describes the armadillo as 'a peaceful harmless creature, incapable of offending any other quadruped, and furnished with a peculiar covering for its own defence.... The instant the armadillo perceives itself in the power of its enemies, it has but one last resource, to roll itself up, and thus patiently wait whatever tortures they think proper to inflict' (219, 222–3). Its habitat, he writes, is 'in remote and thinly inhabited countries, where the men are savage, and the quadrupeds various' (218). Alexis Harley kindly pointed me to Darwin's references to armadilloes.
30 Joseph Conrad, *Almayer's Folly: A Story of an Eastern River*, ed. Floyd Eugene Eddelman and David Leon Higdon (Cambridge: Cambridge University Press,

1994), 1. 250 n.1.4–5 discusses Conrad's source, Henri Frédéric Amiel, which he remembers inexactly in translation.
31  Christopher Lane, 'Almayer's Defeat: The Trauma of Colonialism in Conrad's Early Work', *Novel: A Forum on Fiction* 32, no. 3 (1999), 413.
32  Rhys, *After Leaving Mr Mackenzie*, 76.
33  Ibid., 76, 75.
34  Conrad, *Almayer's Folly*, 85.
35  Toni Morrison, *Playing in the Dark: Whiteness and the Literary Imagination* (Cambridge, MA: Harvard University Press, 1992), viii.
36  Conrad, *Almayer's Folly*, 87.
37  Rhys, *After Leaving Mr Mackenzie*, 115.
38  Ibid., 20.
39  Ibid., 69, 21, 43.
40  Ibid., 57, 61.
41  Maslen, *Ferocious Things*, 93.
42  Rhys, *After Leaving Mr Mackenzie*, 62, 61, 62.
43  Maslen, *Ferocious Things*, 93.
44  Julia Kristeva, *Black Sun: Depression and Melancholia*, trans. Leon S. Roudiez (New York: Columbia University Press, 1989), 246.
45  Erica L. Johnson, '"Upholstered Ghosts"', 222.
46  Rhys, *After Leaving Mr Mackenzie*, 62.
47  Joseph Conrad, *Heart of Darkness*, ed. Paul B. Armstrong, Norton Critical Edition (New York: W.W. Norton, 2006), 76.
48  Rhys, *After Leaving Mr Mackenzie*, 115–16.
49  Kipling, 'The Beginning of the Armadilloes', 87.
50  Rhys, *After Leaving Mr Mackenzie*, 62, 97, 9, 62.
51  Johnson, '"Upholstered Ghosts"', 221.
52  Rhys, *After Leaving Mr Mackenzie*, 107, 111.
53  Moran, '"The Feelings Are Always Mine": Chronic Shame and Humiliated Rage in Jean Rhys's Fiction', in *Jean Rhys*, ed. Erica L. Johnson and Moran (Edinburgh: Edinburgh University Press, 2015), 200.
54  Jeremy Hawthorn, 'Travel as Incarceration: Jean Rhys's *After Leaving Mr Mackenzie*', in *Literary Landscapes: From Modernism to Postmodernism*, ed. Attie de Lange, Gail Fincham, Jeremy Hawthorn and Jakob Lothe (Basingstoke: Palgrave Macmillan, 2008), 68.
55  Rhys, *After Leaving Mr Mackenzie*, 62.
56  Richard Barrios, *A Song in the Dark: The Birth of the Musical Film* (Oxford: Oxford University Press, 1995), 107. The ukulele is an instrument usually associated with Hawai'i.
57  Andre Soares, 'Actress Dorothy Janis Dies: One of the Last Silent Screen Performers', http://www.altfg.com/film/dorothy-janis-dies-silent-movies-591, accessed 17 May 2016.

58  Jeffrey Geiger, *Facing the Pacific: Polynesia and the U.S. Imperial Imagination* (Honolulu: University of Hawai'i Press, 2007), 189.
59  Ben Etherington, *Literary Primitivism* (Stanford, CA: Stanford University Press, 2017), 9.
60  James Donald, *Some of These Days: Black Stars, Jazz Aesthetics, and Modernist Culture* (Oxford: Oxford University Press, 2015), 13.
61  *The Pagan*, dir. W. S. Van Dyke, Metro-Goldwyn-Mayer, 1929, Warner Brothers, 2010.
62  'Pagan Love Song', *International Lyrics Playground*, http://lyricsplayground.com/alpha/songs/p/paganlovesong.shtml, accessed 17 May 2016.
63  Geiger, *Facing the Pacific*, 193.
64  Ibid., 187.
65  Ibid., 194.
66  '*The Pagan* (1929)', *IMDb* (Internet Movies Database), http://www.imdb.com/title/tt0020253/mediaviewer/rm645470464, accessed 17 May 2016.
67  Rhys, *After Leaving Mr Mackenzie*, 97–8.
68  Ibid., 9, 57, 52
69  Ibid., 40.
70  Sander Gilman, 'Black Bodies, White Bodies: Toward an Iconography of Female Sexuality in Late Nineteenth-Century Art, Medicine, and Literature', *Critical Inquiry* 12, no. 1 (1985): 219.
71  Mary Thompson, 'Pubic Hair Untamed: Viewership, Body Hair, and Primitivism in Modigliani's Female Nudes', *Summer Research* (2018): 332.
72  Jane Rogoyska and Frances Alexander, *Amedeo Modigliani* (Parkstone International, 2019), 22.
73  Rhys, *After Leaving Mr Mackenzie*, 40.
74  Rogoyska and Alexander, *Amedeo Modigliani*, 18.
75  Rhys, *After Leaving Mr Mackenzie*, 90.
76  Ibid., 40–1, 39.
77  Mary Lou Emery, *Modernism, the Visual, and Caribbean Literature* (Cambridge: Cambridge University Press, 2007), 212.
78  Rhys, *After Leaving Mr Mackenzie*, 8.
79  GoGwilt, *The Passage of Literature*, 90.
80  Rhys, *After Leaving Mr Mackenzie*, 13.
81  Boria Sax, *Imaginary Animals: The Monstrous, the Wondrous and the Human* (London: Reaktion, 2013), 121.
82  Rhys, *After Leaving Mr Mackenzie*, 7–8.
83  Sax, *Imaginary Animals*, 121, his emphasis.
84  Quoted in 'Basilisk', in *The Medieval Bestiary*, http://bestiary.ca/beasts/beast265.htm, accessed 11 September 2016.
85  Moran, '"The Feelings Are Always Mine"', 195.

86   Radano, 'Black Music Labor and the Animated Properties of Slave Sound', 206.
87   Rhys, *After Leaving Mr Mackenzie*, 48.
88   Ibid., 98.
89   'I Can't Give You Anything But Love (Baby)', *International Lyrics Playground*, http://lyricsplayground.com/alpha/songs/i/icantgiveyouanythingbutlovebaby.shtml, accessed 17 May 2016.
90   Rhys, *After Leaving Mr Mackenzie*, 48, 98.
91   Andy Fry, *Paris Blues: African American Music and French Popular Culture, 1920–1960* (Chicago, IL: University of Chicago Press, 2014), 67–8.
92   Matthew F. Jordan, *Le Jazz: Jazz and French Cultural Identity* (Champaign: University of Illinois Press, 2010), 137. The French reception of *Blackbirds of 1929* is also discussed by Fry in *Paris Blues*, 50–69.
93   Matthew F. Jordan, '*Amphibiologie*: Ethnographic Surrealism in French Discourse on Jazz', *European Studies* 31 (2001): 167.
94   Michel Leiris, 'Civilisation', translated by Iain White, in *Encyclopædia Acephalica*, ed. Alistair Brotchie (London: Atlas Press, 1995), 95.
95   Leiris, 'Civilisation', 93.
96   Georges Bataille, 'Black Birds', trans. Iain White, in *Encyclopædia Acephalica*, ed. Alistair Brotchie (London: Atlas Press, 1995), 36.
97   David Evans, '*Documents* against Civilization', in *Empire and Culture: The French Experience, 1830–1940*, ed. Martin Evans (Basingstoke: Palgrave Macmillan, 2004), 74.
98   Morrison, *Playing in the Dark*, viii.
99   Jordan, '*Amphibiologie*', 179.
100  Anne Baldassari, *Picasso: Love and War 1935–1945. Life with Dora Maar* (Melbourne: National Gallery of Victoria, 2006), 76. Image, 97.
101  'A Journey through the Exhibition: Picasso and Dora Maar – A Mercurial Meeting of Minds', *Picasso: Love and War 1935–1945: Education Resource*, National Gallery of Victoria, https://www.ngv.vic.gov.au/picasso/education/ed_JTE_MMM.html, accessed 30 June 2018.
102  André Breton, 'Crisis of the Object', in *Surrealism and Painting*, trans. Simon Watson Taylor (London: Macdonald, 1972), 275.
103  David N. Livingstone, 'Tropical Hermeneutics: Fragments for a Historical Narrative. An Afterword', *Singapore Journal of Tropical Geography* 21, no. 1 (2000): 94.
104  Ibid.
105  Rhys, letter to Francis Wyndham, 14 September 1959, *Letters 1931–1966*, 171.
106  Sue Thomas, 'Jean Rhys Writing White Creole Childhoods', *a/b: Auto/Biography Studies* 19, nos. 1–2 (2004): 209.
107  Christina Sharpe, *In the Wake: On Blackness and Being* (Durham, NC: Duke University Press, 2016), 14.
108  Sonya Posmentier, *Cultivation and Catastrophe: The Lyric Ecology of Modern Black Literature* (Baltimore, MD: Johns Hopkins University Press, 2017), 11, 193.

3

# Temporality, history and memory in *Voyage in the Dark*

In *Voyage in the Dark*, Rhys pointedly engages with texts, movements and sites identified as decadent or degenerate in nineteenth- and early twentieth-century moral panics: French naturalism epitomized by Émile Zola's *Nana*; the work of Oscar Wilde and Aubrey Beardsley (who is explicitly named in the novel); the 'amateur' prostitute in Britain during the First World War and the 1920s; the tropics (othered through the discourse of tropicality as a site of miscegenation and degeneration); plantation slavery cultures; and the ragtime craze in England in the early 1910s (often stigmatized as American decadence). Falling is a crucial motif of the novel, which Rhys described as 'downward career of a girl',[1] from the opening, '[i]t was as if a curtain had fallen', through dreams of people going overboard from a ship to the last sections of Part IV, where fall resonates as sexual fall (represented in delirium as falling from a horse), regaining of consciousness ('down to earth again') and a lie about miscarriage in an effort to cover up an illegal abortion in seeking medical treatment ('you had a fall').[2] Rhys's placing of *Voyage in the Dark* in relation to a transnational genealogy of representation of decadence is a crucial feature of her self-conscious innovation around the relation of past and present (their being side by side) to give plangent depth to protagonist Anna Morgan's experience of dispossession, migration to England and sexual commodification. These bearings sustain a critique of the sexist, classist and ethnocentric ways in which women are positioned in subcultures represented as dissident, decadently other to bourgeois heterosexual norms of relationship and reproduction. Law, order and respectability place and other these women as bad. Stanley Cohen identifies as a moral panic the sensationalization of a 'condition, episode, person or groups of persons' as

> a threat to societal values and interests; its nature is presented in a stylised and stereotypical fashion in the mass media; the moral barricades are manned by editors, bishops, politicians and other right-thinking people ... Sometimes the

panic passes over and is forgotten, except in folk-lore and collective memory; at other times it has more serious and long-lasting repercussions and might produce such changes as those in legal and social policy or even in the way society perceives itself.³

Engaging with theories of moral panic, Simon Watney argues that the British and US media 'address ... an imaginary national family unit which is both white and heterosexual. All apparent threats to this key object of individual identification will be subject to the kinds of treatment which Cohen and his followers describe as moral panics.' He identifies such panics as 'primarily defensive', repetitive, 'fundamentally *serial*', and exhibiting an 'infinite variety of tone and posture'.⁴ Rhys also alludes to moral panics which address imaginary imperial family units in which hegemony is invested in respectable middle-class white English norms and in which perceived crossings of racialized thresholds are denounced. The seriality of the panics resonates with the idea of 'starting all over again, all over again ... ' that closes the novel, linking Anna's experience with a broader sense of the temporality of cultural history.⁵

The opening sentence of *Voyage in the Dark*, which describes the affect of white Creole Anna Morgan's move from Dominica to England, '[i]t was as if a curtain had fallen, hiding everything I had ever known', alludes to Oscar Wilde's *The Picture of Dorian Gray*. The allusion signals Rhys's contestation of Dorian Gray's and Lord Henry Wotton's abjection of the past to sustain a decadent present. Later in the first chapter Anna drops the 'as if': 'A curtain fell and then I was here.'⁶ *The Picture of Dorian Gray* is a quintessential text of 1890s decadence about which Wilde was grilled during the libel trial which publicized allegations of homosexuality. Dorian Gray's barely seventeen-year-old fiancée, actress Sibyl Vane, dies, apparently by suicide by ingesting prussic acid or white lead, after he breaks off their engagement. His disenchantment with her was prompted by a disappointing performance she gave in the role of Juliet in *Romeo and Juliet* in 'an absurd little theatre' in a 'labyrinth of grimy streets and black, grassless squares' in east London. Having come to know real 'love' and 'passion' in her relationship with Dorian, her 'Prince Charming', Sibyl could no longer 'mimic' it on stage. Dorian insists to her that she has 'killed' his 'love'. 'A fit of passionate sobbing choked her', as he looks 'down' on her prostrate form with 'chiselled lips curled in exquisite disdain'. Dorian's initial anxiety about his lack of affect at the news of his fiancée's death, prompts his mentor Lord Henry to try to persuade him that the suicide has been fortuitous as abandoned female partners have an excruciating habit of 'insist[ing] on living on' and 'go[ing] in at once for reminiscences',

> digging up the past, and raking up the future.... The one charm of the past is that it is past. But women never know when the curtain has fallen. They always want a sixth act, and as soon as the interest of the play is entirely over they propose to continue it. If they were allowed to have their way, every comedy would have a tragic ending, and every tragedy would culminate in a farce. They are charmingly artificial, but they have no sense of art.

He opines that 'there is really no end to the consolations that women find in modern life' after love affairs break up.[7] In context reminiscence is implicitly positioned as one of the potential consolations. Katherine Mansfield draws on the passage for the epigraph to 'A Little Episode' (dated as 1909), so it may have had a wider currency in the early twentieth century than it does today.[8] The romance between Sibyl and Dorian had been about to conform to a Cinderella pattern Rhys refers to in her fiction and autobiography: stage girl marries wealthy man; in *Voyage in the Dark*, 'Chorus Girl Marries Peer's Son' and thus 'get[s] on' in life.[9] For Lord Henry, the proper place of the past is beneath the present. He redeems the suicide as a fortunate act of self-sacrifice in Dorian's interest. In conversation with Basil Hallward, Dorian idealizes it as a theatrical triumph: '[S]he passed again into the sphere of art. There is something of the martyr about her. Her death has all the pathetic uselessness of martyrdom, all its wasted beauty.' 'What is past is past' becomes the seductive rationale of Dorian's amoral hedonism,[10] though after Sibyl's death the weight of the past, his corruption, does register in the portrait of him painted by Basil Hallward.

The first few pages of *Voyage in the Dark* offer a counterpoint to the opening of *The Picture of Dorian Gray* in which Lord Henry luxuriates in the present moment. The counterpoint takes up the challenge of the character Gilbert's comment in Wilde's essay 'The Critic as Artist' that the writer 'who would stir us now by fiction must either give us an entirely new background, or reveal to us the soul of man in its innermost workings. ... [T]here is still much to be done in the sphere of introspection.'[11] Jed Esty has nicely pointed to the ways in which Lord Henry's hedonism is grounded in 'cultural privilege that Raymond Williams has called metropolitan perception, that is, the "magnetic concentration of wealth and power in imperial capitals and the simultaneous cosmopolitan access to a wide variety of subordinate cultures"'.[12] Wilde's novel opens in a 'studio ... filled with the rich odour of roses', flowers Rhys always associates with Englishness.

Lord Henry is smoking a 'heavy opium-tainted' cigarette, taking in 'the heavy scent of the lilac', 'the more delicate perfume of the pink-flowering thorn' and the spectacle and sounds of the 'garden' outside. 'The dim roar of London was like the bourdon note of a distant organ.'[13] He is immersed in the corporeal sensations of a present moment in which the 'heightened sensitivity to motion, colour, sound and scent' produced by the drug 'segues into exotic images of the Orient'. Lord Henry's perspective here makes manifest his credo of 'living for and in the moment'.[14] Esty argues that the 'cluster[ing]' and 'thicken[ing]' of 'Orientalist tropes' in this opening sequence and elsewhere in Wilde's text mark 'points where' he 'needs to break with the realist mode of presentation or the linear demands of traditional plotting'.[15]

*Voyage in the Dark* immerses the reader in the first-person narrative perspective of Anna. Rhys's contrapuntal scene of Anna's consumption explicitly evokes white Creole difference from the English. The difference registers in her sustaining modernist primitivist corporeal memories of Dominica and impressionistic evocation of England in her mind as a grim and enclosing place. Anna is unable to 'fit' 'back there' or 'out there' and England 'together'. The lack of fit makes her feel 'as if a curtain had fallen' and challenges her epistemological certainties.[16] Dominica is never explicitly named in *Voyage in the Dark*. Rather, Anna remembers the geographical coordinates of a small island on which she was born and grew up: '$15°\ 10'$ and $15°\ 40'$ N. and $61°\ 14'$ and $61°\ 30$ W.'[17] Interested readers would be sent scurrying for an atlas. Rhys's citing of the cartographic bearings shows up their epistemological distance from Anna and challenges them to reorient their perspectives. Anna's comparative cultural privilege as a white Creole is registered in the memories as difference from labouring black people and capacity to reduce their humanity by casually remembering them as 'niggers', a word Rhys characteristically uses in the novel as a sign of the racism of Anna's English stepmother Hester. Anna's memories warm and nurture her in the relative existential and physical 'cold' of expatriation.[18] Rhys alludes to the scene in Joseph Conrad's *Heart of Darkness* in which the company doctor tells Marlow as he is about to depart for the Congo that 'out there' 'the changes take place inside, you know', '[i]n the tropics one must before everything keep calm'.[19] For Anna's sister chorus girls the tropics are a site of 'shame'.[20] The garden of the boarding house in which she and Maudie are staying is 'walled-in'. What Anna can see from the sofa on which she is reading Zola's *Nana* is less picturesque than Lord Henry's view of the garden from Basil Hallward's studio. Her vista is redolent of her lower-class position: a 'tree by the back wall ... lopped so that it looked like a man with stumps instead of arms and legs. The washing hung limp, without moving, in the grey-yellow light.'[21] The tree is an image of amputation rather than growth.

The image of the walled-in garden resonates with leitmotifs of England as a place of enclosure and as distinguished by a culture of repetition and homogenizing sameness. Anna's subjective sense of her diasporic place and time shapes her retrospective impressions of arrival:

> [A] small tidy look it had everywhere fenced off from everywhere else ... I had read about England ever since I could read – smaller meaner everything is never mind – this is London – hundreds thousands of white people white people rushing along and the dark houses all alike frowning down one after the other all alike all stuck together – the streets like smooth shut-in ravines and the dark houses frowning down.[22]

Alikeness becomes a metonym of English xenophobia and grey blandness, and suggests that, contra Wilde, England is not a site for women of Anna's class of 'sensations that would be at once new and delightful, and possess that element of strangeness that is so essential to romance', sensations that sustain Dorian's embrace of hedonism.[23] Anna's persistent sense of the greyness of England is shown in starkest form in her memory that on tour as a chorus girl,

> You were perpetually moving to another place which was perpetually the same. There was always a little grey street leading to the stage-door of the theatre and another little grey street where your lodgings were, and rows of little houses with chimneys like the funnels of dummy steamers and smoke the same colour as the sky; and a grey stone promenade running hard, naked and straight by the side of the grey-brown or grey-green sea.[24]

The passage illustrates a fine point Erica L. Johnson makes about Rhys's oeuvre: '[T]hat affect structures modernist temporality such that memory ... shifts into an affective mode whereby the present is "saturated by the past."'[25] Walls feature in Rhys's representation of Anna's depression. Anna remembers feeling in Newcastle that the walls of her boarding-house room were closing in on her and that while living in Ethel's flat after her break-up with Walter, 'when you try to think it's as if you're face to face with a high, dark wall'. Walls figure in Anna's sense of the English sneering at women of her class and in her desperate situation: '[T]heir damned voices, like high, smooth, unclimbable walls all round you, closing in on you.'[26] While Walter's cousin Vincent talks to her about an abortion, she observes that 'the look in his eyes was like a high, smooth, unclimbable wall. No communication possible.' When she tries to broach with Vincent the question of her ambivalence about the pregnancy and fear that the child could 'have something the matter with it', he patronizingly dismisses her fears, illustrating that indeed no dialogue is possible: '"My dear girl, nonsense, nonsense."'[27]

In the first chapter of Part One of *Voyage in the Dark*, Laurie Gaynor, a sister chorus girl, chaffs Anna, calling her 'Virgin' and jokes that Walter Jeffries, who had picked Anna up in Southsea, would have to 'borrow the club tin-opener' in dating her.[28] By novel's end Anna has been supporting herself by amateur prostitution, taken to drinking, become pregnant by one of her casual partners and had an abortion. The amateur was the subject of moral panics in the 1910s and the 1920s, in both of which she was represented as 'threatening a racial degeneration'.[29] In tracing Anna's path, Rhys redeploys and engages with aspects of the discourses circulating around the amateur and familiar narrative arcs of seduction plots. Walter Jeffries, whose kept mistress she will later become, first meets her while sexually cruising Southsea pier and buys her two pairs of stockings, 'lisle thread with clocks up the side'.[30] Amateurs were, as here, more part of a gift culture than a professional prostitute, exchanging the prospect of sex for luxuries like the stockings, clothes, jewelry, nights out, car rides – what Walter's cousin Vincent calls 'good times'.[31] Good times, with shifting resonances, become a leitmotif in Rhys's later fiction *Good Morning, Midnight* and 'Till September Petronella'.

The opening of *Voyage in the Dark* places Anna and her labour in relation to transatlantic circulation of capital and to the transatlantic as a site of 'material and economic exchange', 'transmission of aesthetic and ideological forms', and migration and dispossession.[32] Her named lovers Walter Jeffries and Carl Redman make their wealth through transatlantic business. Londoner Walter works in the City and travels to New York; Carl is a married American businessman who travels to mainland Europe, England and Buenos Aires. The extramarital affairs consolidate homosociality among their friends, an interpretation hinted at when Laurie tells Anna that Carl is 'a funny cuss. He only cares about gambling really.' Carl tells Anna that he is married and has a daughter but will not elaborate further.[33] Sean X. Goudie notes a conventional representational use of a 'figure of the West Indian creole woman … as [the US's iconic female] Columbia's constitutive double, Columbia's figuration signifying a Republic that violently exploits for purposes of power and prestige "monstrous", creolizing hemispheric realities that the figure of the West Indian creole woman is made to embody according to her "blood" entanglements'.[34] He traces this to the ways in which 'in the late eighteenth century' 'U.S. Anglo-Americans suppressed their associations with the term "creole" in favor of a specific creole identity designating their liberation from Europe: "American".[35] In this context, Carl's apparently respectable and reproductive American wife functions as an iconic Columbia figure to Anna, who is positioned as a degenerate white Creole.

Rhys also counterpoints other motifs from *The Picture of Dorian Gray* in *Voyage in the Dark*. Like Wilde, Rhys plays on the idea of the corrupting book. Dorian Gray famously becomes 'absorbed' in, 'fascinated' by a 'poisonous' 'yellow book' given to him by Lord Henry, a book often identified as modelled largely on Joris-Karl Huysmans's *A rebours* (1884).[36] Touring chorus girl Maudie, with whom Anna is sharing a room in a boarding house, calls Zola's *Nana*, which Anna is reading, 'a dirty book … it's about a tart', and comments, 'I bet you a man writing a book about a tart tells a lot of lies one way and another. Besides, all books are like that – just somebody stuffing you up.'[37] This is a variant of a scene in which Zola's character Nana reads a novel that had made a 'great sensation', 'the history of a courtesan; and she was disgusted. She said that it was all false, showing, besides, an indignant repugnance for such filthy literature, which had the pretension of being true to nature, as though one could describe everything.'[38] Maudie's reported comment draws attention to narrative repression around propriety and literary representability more generally. Anna, pointedly on Rhys's part, is not a close or attentive reader of *Nana*, as Dorian is of the 'yellow book'. She finds '[t]he print … very small, and the endless procession of words' gives her 'a curious feeling – sad, excited and frightened. It wasn't what I was reading, it was the look of the dark, blurred words going on endlessly that gave me that feeling.'[39] Until the mid-1890s 'the English response to Zola and his fiction had been overwhelmingly and virulently negative'.[40] In 1888 Henry Vizetelly, the publisher of English translations of Zola's fiction, was successfully prosecuted under Britain's obscenity laws and fined; in 1889 he was fined and jailed for three months.

Wilde racializes Dorian's opium addiction; by the end of *Voyage in the Dark* Anna is an alcoholic and Rhys shows how her drinking is racialized. Dorian uses opium to achieve 'a new Hedonism', 'experience itself, and not the fruits of experience', 'sensations that would be at once new and delightful', 'oblivion … where the memory of old sins could be destroyed by the madness of sins that were new'.[41] The addiction, observes Curtis Marez, takes Dorian into

> opium dens on the quays of East London. The craving for opium impels a movement from the fastness of Dorian's home to the edge of the city – and by extension, the island nation – where England opens out onto scenes of threatening racial otherness. … Opium critics represented addiction to the drug

as a form of racial contagion akin to miscegenation; English reformers deemed the drug especially pernicious because it suggested the possibility of a quasi-racial transformation or degeneration.[42]

In the opium dens Dorian mixes with Chinese and Malay people. Critics have noted the stereotyped and hackneyed quality of Wilde's descriptions of Dorian's ventures into London's underworlds. Edouard Roditi, for instance, writes, 'From the brilliantly lit society with which the author seems so well acquainted, we step straight into a dim slum-land of which he seems ignorant, scared or ashamed, whose denizens are all stock characters from almost "gothic" melodrama.'[43] In Chapter 5 of Part 1 of *Voyage in the Dark*, Anna and Walter have a conversation about 'drink[ing]' being in Anna's 'blood', and he calls her a 'rum little devil'.[44] The liqueur triple sec and rum are ingredients of the cocktail called Little Devil. The name of the liqueur provided a title for H. Pearl Adam's first reworking of Rhys's diaries about her life in the 1910s, an ingredient of *Voyage in the Dark*. The history of rum, a spirit distilled from sugar-cane, is deeply imbricated with the sugar plantation cultures of the Caribbean.[45] Rhys puns on 'rum'. As an adjective, rum means 'Odd, strange. Also: bad, spurious, suspect'.[46]

Walter represents what is in Anna's blood as 'too lush', yet in inviting her to his bedroom says, 'You sound a bit tight ... you rum child.'[47] Offering women alcohol, usually spirits, is a routine part of the scenarios of seduction and sexual pick up dramatized in the novel, used to loosen moral inhibitions around extramarital sex. The dust jacket of the copy of *Nana* that Anna reads has 'a coloured picture of a stout, dark woman brandishing a wine-glass. She was sitting on the knee of a bald-headed man in evening dress.'[48] The wine glass here is a sign of her consumption of sex; 'dark' is a reference to brunette features. Walter has plied Anna with wine on their first date at the Hoffner Hotel and Restaurant, Hanover Square; the private dining room has an adjoining bedroom concealed by a curtain. Carl asks her whether she 'take[s] ether', as she 'look[s] a bit as if' she 'took something'. 'Cold – cold as truth, cold as life. No, nothing can be as cold as life', Anna thinks about her condition as Carl tries to warm her hands.[49] 'Effects of drinking' ether 'are similar to those produced by **alcohol** but appear faster and last briefly', notes Richard Lawrence Miller.[50]

Anna's movement further into London's demi-monde after Walter drops her is signalled in the resonant histories of two establishments to which Carl takes her – Kettner's and Oddendino's – and of Berners Street, where Laurie is living. 'Rhys is always so particular about the names of streets, cafés, and restaurants,' observes Andrew Thacker in his study of the 'spatial style of her fiction'.[51] The future Edward VII conducted his affair with actress Lillie Langtree at Kettner's. The reference to Kettner's also places Anna's experiences with Carl beside the conduct of sexually dissident subcultures revealed in the courtroom appearances of Wilde, suggesting the sedimentation of practices within such homosexual or heterosexual subcultures over time. Wilde's practice of entertaining 'young male prostitutes in private upper rooms' at Kettner's was a sensational courtroom revelation at the libel trial.[52] Oddendino's in Soho, where Carl, Joe Adler, Laurie and Anna dine in 1912–13, listening to the named Melville Gideon singing and playing the piano, is a historical marker of the transatlantic commercialization of ragtime and its reach into white performance and dance cultures. 'Beginning in the years before the Great War, Soho', Marc Matera writes, 'became one of the principal sites associated with the pleasures and anxieties sparked by the consumption of imported cultural forms and the presence of foreign bodies'.[53] Gideon, a ragtime performer who relocated from New York to London, struck a deal with the owner of Oddendino's that he would be paid 25 cents for the per capita increase in trade his performances brought to the restaurant.[54] He reportedly earned £7,000 in his first year of performing in England[55] and Oddendino's became one of Soho's 'magnets for demi-mondes and young bloods on the town'.[56] A resonant ragtime song 'Waiting for the Robert E. Lee', which was in the historical Gideon's repertoire,[57] haunts Anna as an earworm, 'musical memory'.[58] A sign of the disturbance created by the ragtime version is that C. R. W. Nevinson's painting *Waiting for the Robert E. Lee* shown at the 1913 Post-Impressionist and Futurist Exhibition in London – a representation of dancing to the song – was printed in black-and-white 'upside down' in the *Daily Sketch*, labelled 'ragtime art that perfectly expresses the feelings aroused by five barrel organs playing that inescapable tune under one's windows'.[59] That Laurie lives in Berners Street when she first introduces Anna to Carl and Joe points to a scandal about the street's history current in 1934. Charles Dickens helped set up his mistress, actress Ellen (Nelly) Lawless Ternan and her sister Maria, at No. 31. The relationship between Dickens and Ternan had featured in the salacious novel *This Side Idolatry: A Novel Based on the Life of Charles Dickens* (1928), by C. E. Bechhofer Roberts. Michael Slater outlines the slew of publicity about the relationship that ensued after the death of the last surviving child of Dickens in 1933, noting, for instance, Ralph Straus's article of 23 January 1934, in which he wrote that '"in his later years"' Dickens 'enjoyed frequenting "a careless Bohemian world" where he met "attractive young actresses whom he would playfully call 'little periwinkles'"'.[60]

Rhys's allusion to the history of Wilde's patronage of Kettner's draws out a fetishization of youth and economies of procurement in the sexually dissident subcultures she places alongside each other. Wilde's testimony under cross-examination revealed a penchant for the youth of his casual partners and suggested that the sexual coterie for which Alfred Taylor procured young men from lower social classes was organized around gifts – money, silver cigarette cases, books and dinners, for example.[61] Edward Carson, the defence lawyer for the Marquis of Queensberry, made such a point of asking about the amount of alcohol available for the young men that Wilde eventually responded, 'any one who dines at my table is not stinted in wine. If you mean, did I ply him with wine, I say "No!" It's monstrous, and I won't have it.'[62] By the time Laurie meets Americans Carl Redman and Joe Adler, she is 'getting about a bit' by 'showing' men 'round' 'a bit', and introducing them to potential fresh partners. Structurally Rhys positions Laurie in Parts Two, Three and Four as a monitory image for Anna and her life as a metonym of the material underpinnings of the circulation of amateur prostitutes around London. Laurie 'went on about how lucky she had been and what a lot of men with money she knew and what a good time she was having'. Laurie prudently 'bank[s] half of everything' her male friends give her. 'I never pay for a meal for myself.... I get along with men. I can do what I like with them. Sometimes I'm surprised myself. I expect it's because they feel I really like it and no kidding,' she boasts.[63] The euphemism 'it' suggests the difficulty of fully acknowledging her amateur prostitution and procurement. In context here, too, Rhys puns on kidding, meaning becoming pregnant and having babies. Laurie inveigles Anna into going out with Carl, Joe and her, telling Anna, '"I'm sure you'll go well with Carl because you look awfully young and he likes girls that look young."'[64] So, too, does Walter Jeffries. Vincent, his cousin, even greets Anna: '"Well, how's the child? How's my infantile Anna?"'[65] Laurie has also earlier brought another 'kid', Renée, along on a date with Carl and Joe, playing to Carl's sexual taste.[66] When Carl takes Anna to Kettner's, she does 'everything to the tune of *Camptown Racecourse*'.[67] The ragtime version which she performs is haunted by the song's history in blackface minstrelsy. The first record of the slang word 'camp' meaning '[o]stentatious, exaggerated, affected, theatrical; effeminate or homosexual; pertaining to or characteristic of homosexuals' has been traced to James Redding Ware's *Passing English of the Victorian Era* (1909); this meaning had greater currency by the early 1930s when *Voyage in the Dark* was published.[68] In association with Kettner's the puns in the title *Camptown Racecourse* are, then, clearly intended.

Gideon and Oddendino's capitalized on the phenomenal popularity of ragtime in the commercial arrangement into which they entered. The ragtime craze in pre–First World War Britain is epitomized by the success of the revue *Hullo, Ragtime!*, with score and lyrics by Louis Hirsch (1881–1924), which ran at the Hippodrome from 23 December 1912 to *c.* 13 April 1914. '[I]n the decades before the first war, "revue" was understood,' Veronica Kelly writes, 'as the newest new thing, epitomising cosmopolitan and revolutionary modernity in both mode and content.... As ragtime internationalised [through revue], its composers could be black or white, American or not.'[69] Bailey observes that during the run of *Hullo, Ragtime!* there were

> 130 American ragtime groups reported touring Britain's music halls together with countless British imitators ... In its immediate and extensive take-up as popular song and dance beyond the stage, American ragtime demonstrated the appeal of its greater expressive freedoms, somatically, sexually and colloquially, features happily appropriated to the more performative style of a lived popular modernism in big-city Britain, embodied in the pelvically driven modern couple.[70]

Ragtime and dancing to it were sensationalized by some in Britain as American decadence, in large part because of its emergence from African-American musical and dance cultures. In a scathing essay 'Ragtime: The New Tarantism', published in the *English Review*, Francis Toye, for instance, urged readers to 'beg' their local parliamentarians 'to persuade parliament to deport Messrs. Hirsch and Melville Gideon and their various satellites, both male and female, as highly undesirable aliens, before this unhappy country should be converted into an even larger lunatic asylum than it is at present'. He urged that syncopated rhythm with 'accents falling in unexpected places' was 'unhealthy', that ragtime dances were 'of a lascivious or merely ridiculous kind', 'a direct encouragement to hysteria', and that 'since the introduction of rag-time people are much more given to excitement and drink – and that not only when they are dancing'.[71]

Both Toye's construction of ragtime as monstrous and Bailey's sexually libertarian characterization of it draw out what Ronald Radano has described as the constructed 'animated properties of slave sound', 'qualities of racialized fleshliness'. In the ragtime craze '[r]acialized, animated, fleshly sound'[72] took on a commercial value, and the sound crossed over to non-African-American players in the international music industry and to white audiences. Like jazz in the 1920s, ragtime 'promised a sensual and experimental way of living in the present as well as creating a future'.[73] In Anna's Dominican memories, white colonial respectability would bar her from dancing in the streets at Masquerade in time to African-Caribbean music. Rhys juxtaposes the scene of colonial prohibition with the resonances of British consumption of ragtime.

The most overt allusions to artistic decadence in *Voyage in the Dark* are in Part Three, chapter 6, in which Anna recalls visiting the flat of d'Adhémar with her friend Laurie, after d'Adhémar, whom Laurie thinks is 'slightly potty, but an awfully sweet old thing', had promised to show Laurie 'a marvellous book of dirty pictures'.[74] Perfume-wearing d'Adhemar recites French decadent poet Jean Richepin's 'Les Philistins', a poem which vaunts cross-generational rebellion against paternal bourgeois values, with children becoming not 'Clean shaven, stoutly built / Lawyers' but 'most hairy / Poets'.[75] Laurie, who at this point in the narrative is supporting herself on the gifts of casual sexual partners rather than as a chorus girl, is '[v]ery disappointed' by the Aubrey Beardsley drawings, commenting, 'I don't call that hot stuff. Is that book really worth a lot of money? All I can say is, some people don't know what to do with their money.'[76] The Beardsley book, the recitation and the perfume mark d'Adhemar's self-fashioning and posturing as inspired by English and French decadent art and literature. Laurie's dismissal of the value of Beardsley's work draws attention to the fact that 'for all their obsession with being "new" and their supposedly "immoral" approach to art and culture, the Victorian Decadents were in fact a "deeply conservative avant-garde" … Although often outrageously iconoclastic and ostentatiously eccentric, they were also surprisingly bourgeois in their own personal tastes and habits'.[77] For d'Adhémar, Laurie is a metonym of his sexual frustration that he self-absorbedly projects on to the 'dead streets' around his 'flat'. '[F]rustration', he tells Laurie and Anna, 'can become something homely, desirable and warm'; Laurie responds, 'Go on, Daddy … don't drivel'.[78] Daddy is a diminutive of d'Adhémar which draws out their age difference, but also a term for a lover in the African-American musical cultures from which ragtime, a music associated with Anna spending time with Laurie, Carl and Joe, emerged.[79]

*Voyage in the Dark* is punctuated by crucial shifts in modes of representation that associate and arrange scenes that instantiate in dream and delirium the accumulation of Atlantic and circum-Atlantic history, including aesthetic history, in the present. When Anna fears she may be pregnant by one of a number of nameless men with whom she has sex after Carl abandons her, she begins to dream about the sea, the Atlantic Ocean. For the pregnant subject, maternal subjectivity constitutes what Drucilla Cornell terms 'the future anterior', anticipation of a future self's 'continuity and bodily integrity'.[80] I would extend this to include anticipation of moral integrity. Anna can project a future anterior of maternal subjectivity to a point of dread maternal recognition of the baby at birth. In a state of panic and the sense of muddle integral to depression, she tries to think through the medical implications for the baby of the abortifacients she has been taking:

> And all the time thinking round and round in a circle that is there inside me, and about all the things I had taken so that if I had it, it would be a monster. The Abbé Sebastian's Pills, primrose label, one guinea a box, daffodil label, two guineas, orange label, three guineas. No eyes, perhaps.... No arms, perhaps.... Pull yourself together.

She quickly decides, 'I want not to have it.' The baby is objectified as 'it'. In her mind the pregnancy is a dread, unnameable 'that' or 'it': 'Like seasickness, only worse, and everything heaving up and down. And vomiting. And thinking, "It can't be that, it can't be that. Oh, it can't be that. Pull yourself together; it can't be that. Didn't I always.... And besides it's never happened before. Why should it happen now?"'[81] The language of objectification marks a terror of inhabiting the subjectivity of a pregnant woman. Her acute anxiety about the prospect of pregnancy signals 'the difficulties of filiation' with the foetus and the English.[82] The segue to the dreams of the sea are the voices of the respectable she projects on their 'eternal grimace of disapproval' at the conduct of young women like her. The last voice is, 'Why didn't you bloody well make a hole in the water?'[83]

This references a standard scenario of the seduced and abandoned woman: suicide by drowning. L. J. Nicoletti notes that the scenario is 'omnipresent in Victorian London's visual culture' often with a representation of a church in the background to register the woman's sinfulness. In representing seduced and abandoned women, 'Victorian writers and artists transformed their subject's corrupt life and violent death into a peaceful martyrdom. They left the woman's body unscathed because Victorian art and literature constructed suicide as a redemptive act for unchaste women.'[84] The representation of the death of Sibyl Vane, chaste, but spurned after she has fallen from grace in Dorian's eyes, becoming merely a 'third-rate actress with a pretty face', also draws on the aesthetic tradition of constructing female suicides as redemptive. In talking earlier to Lord Henry of his love for Sibyl, Dorian had described her in religious language as a 'sacred' object of his devotion.[85] The pun on 'bloody well' in *Voyage in the Dark*, by contrast, draws out the violent impact of suicide on the body. The allusions in Anna's dream suggest a pun on hole and the question of why Anna could not make a whole of herself through migration and maturation. In the dream, Anna is 'on a ship' and is unable to reach the shore of her home island, as 'the deck of the ship expanded. Somebody had fallen overboard.'[86] '[F]allen' and the syllable 'board', with its pun on bawd, suggest the ways she will be positioned as a single pregnant woman in the eyes of society. The formulation 'somebody had fallen overboard' equivocates over agency, over whether the fall was a suicide, an accident or an act of violence against the person who fell. Overboard has a range of meanings which resonate with Anna's sense of her predicament: 'over the side of a ship … ; out of, off, or from a ship into the water'; '*to throw* (also *cast, fling*, etc.) *overboard*: to cast aside, discard, reject, renounce'; '*to go overboard*: to behave immoderately; to go too far; to display excessive enthusiasm'.[87]

Anna's dream of the sea features a symbol of the church, a seeming boy bishop in a coffin, who metamorphoses into a figure of experience rather than innocence, a 'little dwarf' supported physically like a puppet by a sailor.[88] The bishop, identified by Maslen as a 'malicious, inhuman symbol of paternal law and male privilege',[89] has 'large, light eyes in a narrow, cruel face' that 'rolled like a doll's as you lean it from one side to the other'.[90] In the early modern period, boy bishops were elected to preside over the feast of the Holy Innocents, the Christian festival that commemorated the Massacre of the Innocents, the mass infanticide of male children aged two and under ruthlessly ordered by the biblical Herod, about which an angel warned Jesus's father Joseph, urging him to flee to Egypt with his family to escape persecution. The massacre is related in Matthew 2, where its affect is represented as fulfilling Jeremiah's prophecy that 'a voice was heard, lamentation, and weeping, and great mourning, Rachel weeping *for* her children, and would not be comforted, because they are not'.[91] The dream condenses Anna's ambivalence around the prospect of an abortion.

Rhys draws out Anna's and her white Creole family's sense of financial dispossession as a reason for Anna's inability to make a whole of herself. After the death of her father, her English stepmother Hester sold the estate Morgan's Rest, which her husband had bequeathed to her, though her Uncle Bo suggests that he had intended it should 'eventually be his daughter's property'. Hester invested the proceeds along with her own monies to help generate an income of 'under three hundred a year' to keep herself as a lady, representing herself as generously supporting Anna through gifts: 'passage to England', outfitting her for school and paying her 'expenses for a term', fully realizing that this was not a 'sort of decent education', and meeting a medical and a dental bill while Anna was on tour as a chorus girl.[92] In selling up in Dominica, Hester has determined to distance herself from what she sees as the contaminating proximity of black people and African Dominican culture and the degeneracy of Anna's Creole family (epitomized for her by Uncle Bo), views which accord with the discourse of tropicality and stock English stereotypes of the impurity of the white Creole.

Associated with tropicality, Anna's Creoleness places her in the eyes of other English characters as racially liminal, her sister chorus girls even nicknaming her 'Hottentot' and Walter pathologizing the tropics and conflating Anna with the tropical landscape as 'altogether too lush'.[93] When Anna lunches with Hester, the words of an advertising slogan for Bourne's Cocoa – 'What is Purity?' – keep running through her mind.[94] Cacao beans, like sugar cane, were a plantation crop of the Americas; indeed as a species the cacao tree is native to tropical South America. As Marshik points out, the slogan 'immediately evokes sexual purity because of its context' and 'frames purity as an expensive commodity only available to the English; women like Anna, doubly impure by virtue of class and colonial identity, can never meet its price'.[95]

With the condensation characteristic of dreams, 'somebody had fallen overboard' resonates with the history of enslaved people being thrown overboard from slaving ships, most infamously from the *Zong* in 1781, when 132 enslaved people were killed or pressed to suicide so that the shipowners could claim their insurance value of £30 each. James Walvin notes, 'The very name – the *Zong* – quickly entered the demonology of Atlantic slavery and came to represent the depravity and heartless violence of the entire slave system.'[96] As such, it is integral to the historical consciousness or unconscious of Caribbean people. In *Voyage in the Dark* the condensation is haunted by and engages with the aesthetic sedimentation of its allusions to falling. With the question '"What's overboard?"' Rhys challenges her readers to look in the hold, over the side of the deck and under the water that at the opening of the dream is 'transparent as glass'. In dream at this point Anna does not see the ship's hold or what is in the water, but 'confused figures' on deck:

> I was still trying to walk up the deck and get ashore. I took huge, climbing, flying strides among confused figures. I was powerless and very tired, but I had to go on. And the dream rose into a climax of meaninglessness, fatigue and powerlessness, and the deck was heaving up and down, and when I woke up everything was still heaving up and down.
>
> It was funny how, after that, I kept on dreaming about the sea.[97]

The word 'figures' suggests commodification in flows of capital and, with reference to the *Zong* massacre and similar incidents, hints at calculation about what and who might be pressed or thrown 'overboard', cast aside. '[C]onfused figures' emphasize the history of racialized terror and violence of an Atlantic abyss as elucidated by Edouard Glissant: 'deportation' of African people in the holds of slave ships; human 'cargo' thrown 'overboard'; and the wrenching of African people towards an unfamiliar material and spiritual diasporic futurity in a 'new land'.[98] In the first version of the novel's ending – which the publisher Constable insisted Rhys revise – Uncle Bo suggests to Hester in Anna's delirium that she is confused about the 'figures' voted by the British parliament as compensation for the abolition of slavery: 'Oh yes it may have been voted all right but we never got it it all stayed in the good old home coop and if you like to come and have a look at things I can prove that to you easily enough if you'd like to come and have a look.'[99] Caught up among the 'confused figures', Anna in dream is unable to step home to a plantation culture in decay, a displacement which suggests the affective subconscious reach of Atlantic history – 'that awful dropping of the heart', 'meaninglessness, fatigue and powerlessness', a mourning seasickness that segues into morning sickness – in the production of her sense of homelessness. Anna's subsequent recurring 'dreaming about the sea' suggests that the futurity she is haunted by is the inescapable question '"What's overboard?"' and the historical acknowledgements of the incommensurability of the black Atlantic abyss that lie outside her range of vision in the first dream.[100]

The words that haunt Anna's delirium while suffering from post-abortion haemhorrhage are 'ought', 'stop', 'ought to be stopped' and 'fall' and there are condensed associative links between the iterations.[101] The subject implied by the repetition of the passive infinitive is the 'huge machine of law, order, respectability', an image here of the feeding of moral panic.[102] The memories compress, at times to the point of ellipsis, awareness of the sexual dangers for white women in laying claim to freedoms outside a middle-class propriety that screens them from the life of the street: sexual fall; the 'eternal grimace of disapproval' in the face of society;[103] loss of respectability and racial caste; syphilis.[104] Anna's delirious memories of growing up in Dominica and her sexual experiences in England are intercut with the censorious voices of the landlady Mrs Polo and the doctor who eventually attends her, and the voice of the worldly Laurie, called to the scene by Mrs Polo.

There are two extant versions of the final section of *Voyage in the Dark*: the version published in 1934 and the version submitted to Constable. Linking editorial suppression and abortion through the figure of mutilation, Rhys tells the story in letters and her autobiography of having to capitulate to the demands by Michael Sadlier, of Constable, that she change her original ending to *Voyage in the Dark*.[105] Mervyn Morris notes that, in the story, Sadlier 'represents commercial instinct and genial male patronage'.[106] Reading Part IV reductively as culminating in Anna's death from the abortion, Sadlier, in Rhys's account, insisted that she revise Part IV to provide a more optimistic ending by giving Anna a 'chance' at a happier life by having her 'recover and meet a rich man' or a 'poor, good-natured man'.[107] Jonathan Cape had already withdrawn from its contract to publish the book because of a 'dispute about the end' and Hamish Hamilton had also insisted on 'severe cuts'.[108] That Rhys was ultimately satisfied with her revision is suggested by her telling Peter Wolfe in 1974 that she thought it her finest book.[109]

In the first version the ticking clock in the room as Anna lies bleeding on the bed leads her to remember clocks and clock time marking her sexual encounters. At 'nearly four o'clock' partners say 'perhaps you ought to be', 'perhaps you ought to be going', a practice that allows her partners to maintain a semblance of respectability.[110] The sedimentation of the practice in cultures of sexual dissidence is suggested by the fact that in cross-examination at his first trial Wilde was asked about young men who would 'come' to his hotel room 'late at night – twelve or one o'clock – and stay until four in the morning'.[111] In three of the scenes or one scene remembered three times a man refuses to act on Anna's withdrawal of consent to sex; the juxtaposition of censorious voices with the scene(s) of rape highlights the limits of what the respectable do and do not see and speak up about. The fullest of these memories is: 'And I kept saying stop stop stop please stop will you stop   and he said I thought you'd say that and he laughed and it sounded funny and his face was very white and his nostrils going in and out.'[112] This may be a resurfacing of a memory of what happened with 'the man at that supper-party at the Greyhound, Croydon' who 'told' her, '"You don't know how to kiss. I'll show you how to kiss. This is what you do."' An earlier memory of the incident when Walter started to kiss her with the intent of having sex with her for the first time made her feel 'giddy'.[113] In the 1934 published version of the ending of *Voyage in the Dark* there are two memories of a man refusing to 'stop' when Anna 'tried to hang back'.[114] Anna tells Mrs Polo three times that she feels 'giddy'. The voices of white onlookers to Dominican Masquerade, some named, others not, indoors, uphold the 'decent' and 'respectable' in relation to the things they insist 'ought to be stopped': in the published version of Part IV, Masquerade; and in the first version, Masquerade, the near nakedness of male masqueraders and 'all these Roman Catholic priests and nuns in an English island', a legacy of French imperial rule of and influence on Dominica. Repressive Englishwoman Hester protests about the near nudity and Catholicism.[115] Mrs Polo worries about bloodied sheets and mattress and scandal attaching itself to her boarding house, concerns expressed more obliquely in the published version. In the first version of the ending Anna thinks while riding a horse, an image which condenses her sexual experiences in England, 'I'm going to fall nothing can save me now but still I clung desperately with my knees feeling very sick and the waves of pain going through me like the sea I always knew it was like waves and like the sea I always knew it was like waves and like the sea.'[116]

In addressing the temporalities of decadence in *Voyage in the Dark* (British, Irish, US, French and Caribbean), Rhys pieces together intertextual and intermedial resonances and counterpoint that chart the particularities and the political and aesthetic reach of her representation of Anna Morgan and of the cultures of sexual dissidence of which she becomes part. Rhys's treatment of these temporalities, including the transcultural seriality of moral panics, has resisted absorption into standard literary historiographies of modernism and recent New Modernist scholarship on decadence.[117] The sheets bloodied by post-abortion haemorrhage and hinted-at loss of virginity through rape test the limits of the representability of Anna's experience on the pages (sheets) of the book. In Chapter 6, I return to *Voyage in the Dark*, layering into the argument of *Jean Rhys's Modernist Bearings and Experimental Aesthetics* an analysis of the novel's narrative arc around the *doudou*.

# Notes

1. Rhys, letter to Evelyn Scott, 18 February 1934, in *Letters 1931–1966*, 24.
2. Rhys, *Voyage in the Dark*, 7, 158.
3. Quoted in Simon Watney, *Policing Desire: Pornography, Aids and the Media*, 3rd ed. (London: Cassell, 1997), 39.
4. Watney, *Policing Desire*, 43, his emphasis.
5. Rhys, *Voyage in the Dark*, 19.
6. Ibid., 7, 15.
7. Wilde, *The Picture of Dorian Gray*, ed. Peter Ackroyd (Harmondsworth: Penguin, 1985), 73, 86, 115, 130, 131, 132.
8. Katherine Mansfield, 'A Little Episode', in *The Collected Fiction of Katherine Mansfield, 1898–1915*, ed. Gerri Kimber and Vincent O'Sullivan (Edinburgh: Edinburgh University Press, 2012), 538–44.
9. Rhys, *Voyage in the Dark*, 64.
10. Wilde, *The Picture of Dorian Gray*, 139, 138.
11. Oscar Wilde, *Poems and Essays* (London: Dent, 1956), 336.
12. Esty, *Unseasonable Youth*, 106.
13. Wilde, *The Picture of Dorian Gray*, 23.

14 Phyllis Weliver, 'Oscar Wilde, Music, and the "Opium-tainted Cigarette": Disinterested Dandies and Critical Play', *Journal of Victorian Culture* 13, no. 3 (2010): 325.
15 Esty, *Unseasonable Youth*, 105.
16 Rhys, *Voyage in the Dark*, 7–8.
17 Ibid., 15.
18 Ibid., 7–8.
19 Joseph Conrad, *Heart of Darkness*, ed. Richard Kimbrough, Norton Critical Edition, 3rd ed. (New York: W. W. Norton, 1988), 15.
20 Rhys, *Voyage in the Dark*, 12.
21 Ibid., 9.
22 Ibid., 15–16.
23 Wilde, *The Picture of Dorian Gray*, 163.
24 Rhys, *Voyage in the Dark*, 8.
25 Erica L. Johnson, 'Haunted: Affective Memory in Jean Rhys's *Good Morning, Midnight*', *Affirmations: Of the Modern* 1, no. 2 (2014): 16.
26 Rhys, *Voyage in the Dark*, 26, 120, 126.
27 Ibid., 147.
28 Ibid., 15, 17.
29 Thomas, *The Worlding of Jean Rhys*, 67–8.
30 Rhys, *Voyage in the Dark*, 10.
31 Ibid., 80.
32 Susan Manning and Andrew Taylor, 'Introduction: What Is Transatlantic Literary Studies', in *Transatlantic Literary Studies: A Reader*, ed. Manning and Taylor (Baltimore, MD: Johns Hopkins University Press, 2007), 5.
33 Rhys, *Voyage in the Dark*, 100, 135.
34 Sean X. Goudie, *Creole America: The West Indies and the Formation of Literature and Culture in the New Republic* (Philadelphia: University of Pennsylvania Press, 2006), 203.
35 Ibid., 9.
36 Wilde, *The Picture of Dorian Gray*, 155–7.
37 Rhys, *Voyage in the Dark*, 9.
38 Émile Zola, *Nana*, introduced by Burton Rascoe (New York: Alfred A. Knopf, 1925), 287–8.
39 Rhys, *Voyage in the Dark*, 9.
40 Laura Deal, 'Zola in England: Controversy and Change in the 1890s', Hons. diss., American University, Washington DC, 2008.
41 Wilde, *The Picture of Dorian Gray*, 162, 163, 220.
42 Curtis Marez, 'The Other Addict: Reflections on Colonialism and Oscar Wilde's Opium Smoke Screen', *English Literary History* 64, no. 1 (1997): 257, 275.

43 Edouard Roditi, 'From "Fiction as Allegory"', in Oscar Wilde, *The Picture of Dorian Gray*, ed. Donald L. Lawler, Norton Critical Edition (New York: W. W. Norton, 1988), 369–70.
44 Rhys, *Voyage in the Dark*, 44–5.
45 Hugh Barty-King and Anton Messel, *Rum: Yesterday and Today* (London: Heinemann, 1983).
46 *Oxford English Dictionary Online*.
47 Rhys, *Voyage in the Dark*, 48.
48 Ibid., 9.
49 Ibid., 131.
50 Richard Lawrence Miller, *The Encyclopedia of Addictive Drugs* (Westport, CT: Greenwood Press, 2002), 153, his emphasis. Jane Nardin points out that the standard 'modernist drunk narrative' is 'the story of a sensitive, artistic male who heroically and freely chooses alcohol for its power both to affirm his cosmic despair and to render it bearable'. She argues that Rhys 'avoids representing alcoholism as a disease of the will. The novel does, however, represent it as a disease of modernity'. '"As Soon As I Sober Up I Will Start Again": Alcohol and the Will in Jean Rhys's Pre-War Novels', *Papers on Language and Literature* 42, no. 1 (2006): 46, 57.
51 Thacker, 'The Idea of a Critical Literary Geography', 69.
52 Judith R. Walkowitz, *Nights Out: Life in Cosmopolitan London* (New Haven, CT: Yale University Press, 2012), 36.
53 Marc Matera, *Black London: The Imperial Metropolis and Decolonization in the Twentieth Century* (Berkeley: University of California Press, 2015), chapter 4.
54 'Overdoing Ragtime in England May Be Its Death, Says Butt', *Variety*, 10 January 1913, 1.
55 '£7,000 a Year as a Pianist', *Manchester Courier and Lancashire General Advertiser*, 31 December 1913, 3. Gideon also gained notoriety for his conduct of an affair after his evening performances at Oddendino's with a former chorus girl, Lilian Enid Borrows, who had in 1908 married David Wellesley Bell, an heir to an estate worth £100,000. The divorce proceedings were reported around the world. 'Gaiety Girl's Confession', *New Zealand Herald*, 4 July 1914, 2; 'An Actress's Divorce', *Times* (London), 20 May 1914, 4.
56 Walkowitz, *Nights Out*, 96.
57 Ross Laird, *Tantalizing Tingles: A Discography of Early Ragtime, Jazz, and Novelty Syncopated Piano Recordings, 1889–1934* (Westport, CT: Greenwood, 1995), 71. The song later became part of Al Jolson's blackface repertoire. This leads Emery to misread its provenance. She identifies it as one of the 'minstrel songs' Anna remembers, reading them simply as evoking 'plantation nostalgia' in the present time of the novel. Emery, 'Caribbean Modernism', 49, 57, 58.
58 Oliver Sacks, *Musicophilia: Tales of Music and the Brain*, Kindle Edition, location 3856.

59  Peter Bailey, '"*Hullo, Ragtime?*" West End Revue and the Americanisation of Popular Culture in Pre-1914 London', in *Popular Musical Theatre in London and Berlin 1890–1939*, ed. Len Platt, Tobias Becker and David Linton (Cambridge: Cambridge University Press, 2014), 146-7. The original painting is now lost. The vibrancy and carnivalesque of the original might be hinted at in a contemporaneous painting of his, *Dance Hall Scene* (*c*. 1913–14), heavily influenced by futurist Gino Severini's *The Dance of the 'Pan-Pan' at the Monico* (1909–11).
60  Michael Slater, *The Great Charles Dickens Scandal* (New Haven, CT: Yale University Press, 2012), 71.
61  Douglas O. Linder, ed. 'Famous World Trials. The Trials of Oscar Wilde. 1895', School of Law, University of Missouri-Kansas City, 2015, http://law2.umkc.edu/faculty/projects/ftrials/wilde/wilde.htm, accessed 21 August 2015.
62  Linder, ed. 'Famous World Trials. The Trials of Oscar Wilde'.
63  Rhys, *Voyage in the Dark*, 98–9.
64  Ibid., 100.
65  Ibid., 69.
66  Ibid., 106.
67  Ibid., 132.
68  'camp, *adj.* and *n*.$^5$ A.', *Oxford English Dictionary Online*.
69  Veronica Kelly, 'Come Over Here! The Local Hybridisation of International "Ragtime Revues" in Australia', *Popular Entertainment Studies* 4, no. 1 (2013): 27, 39.
70  Bailey, '"*Hullo, Ragtime?*"' 144, 148.
71  Frances Toye, 'Ragtime: The New Tarantism', *English Review*, March 1913, 658, 656, 654.
72  Radano, 'Black Music Labor and the Animated Properties of Slave Sound', 195, 199, 206.
73  Donald, *Some of These Days*, 7.
74  Rhys, *Voyage in the Dark*, 145.
75  Jean Richepin, 'Philistines', trans. unknown, http://wulfshead.blogspot.com.au/2013/04/philistines.html, accessed 19 August 2014.
76  Rhys, *Voyage in the Dark*, 145.
77  Chris Snodgrass, *Aubrey Beardsley: Dandy of the Grotesque* (New York: Oxford University Press, 1995), 5.
78  Rhys, *Voyage in the Dark*, 145.
79  *Oxford English Dictionary Online*.
80  Drucilla Cornell, *The Imaginary Domain: Abortion, Pornography & Sexual Harassment* (New York & London: Routledge, 1995), 43.
81  Rhys, *Voyage in the Dark*, 143, 146, 138.
82  Edward Said, *The World, the Text and the Critic* (Cambridge, MA: Harvard University Press, 1983), 17.
83  Rhys, *Voyage in the Dark*, 140.

84 L. J. Nicoletti, 'Downward Mobility: Victorian Women, Suicide, and London's "Bridge of Sighs"', *Literary London: Interdisciplinary Studies in the Representation of London* 2, no. 1 (March 2004), para. 6, para. 19, http://www.literarylondon.org/london-journal/march2004/nicoletti.html, accessed 29 July 2015.
85 Wilde, *The Picture of Dorian Gray*, 116, 77.
86 Rhys, *Voyage in the Dark*, 140.
87 'overboard, *adv.*,1.a, 2.a., 2.b.', *Oxford English Dictionary Online*.
88 Rhys, *Voyage in the Dark*, 140.
89 Maslen, *Ferocious Things*, 178.
90 Rhys, *Voyage in the Dark*, 141.
91 Mt. 2.18, *King James Bible*.
92 Rhys, *Voyage in the Dark*, 52, 54.
93 Ibid., 12, 46. Joseph Clarke reads the tropicality identified by Rhys in the English naming of Anna as Hottentot as Rhys's use of a 'representational grammar of blackness as pollution ... to elicit ... a *racialized* affective coherence in the reader'. 'Caribbean Modernism and the Postcolonial Social Contract in *Voyage in the Dark*', *Journal of Caribbean Literatures* 3, no. 3 (Summer 2003): 5.
94 Rhys, *Voyage in the Dark*, 50.
95 Marshik, *British Modernism and Censorship*, 179.
96 James Walvin, *The Zong: A Massacre, the Law and the End of Slavery* (New Haven, CT: Yale University Press, 2011), 2.
97 Rhys, *Voyage in the Dark*, 140, 141.
98 Edouard Glissant, *Poetics of Relation*, trans. Betsy Wing (Ann Arbor: University of Michigan Press, 1997), 5–7.
99 Rhys, '*Voyage in the Dark*. Part IV (Original Version)', 386.
100 The historicity of the dream, including its referencing of aesthetic history, complicates more sanguine readings of this passage. Maslen, for instance, argues: 'Dreaming of the sea alone, bereft of the comforting, quotidian or homely motifs of ships and islands discloses that in place of a comforting nostalgia of home, Anna has succumbed to a despairing desire for the ocean itself, as a sublime, featureless infinite – in other words, for the ocean as death' (*Ferocious Things*, 178). Joseph Clarke has drawn attention to a different moment in *Voyage in the Dark* in which in delirium Anna 'seems to move toward some acknowledgment' of African Caribbean 'bodies and ... experiences' only to have the prospect of '[i]nsight ... withdrawn' as she thinks in Part IV she is about to fall from the horse she has been riding. Clarke, 'Caribbean Modernism', 11.
101 In the first version of the ending (Rhys, '*Voyage in the Dark*. Part IV [Original Version])', 384–9, and in the published version (Rhys, *Voyage in the Dark*), 155–8.
102 Rhys, 'Vienne', 241.
103 Rhys, *Voyage in the Dark*, 140.

104 For a discussion of the ways in which Anna's sighting of a female duppy with yaws plays out fears of syphilis, see Thomas, *The Worlding of Jean Rhys*, 108–9.
105 Rhys, letter to Evelyn Scott, 10 June 1934, *Letters 1931–1966*, 33.
106 Mervyn Morris, 'Oh, Give the Girl a Chance: Jean Rhys and *Voyage in the Dark*', *Journal of West Indian Literature* 3, no. 22 (Sept. 1989): 3.
107 Rhys, *Smile Please*, 127. In a letter to Evelyn Scott about Sadleir's demand for cuts, Rhys writes: 'I'm afraid it will make it meaningless. The worst is that it is precisely the last part which I am most certain of that will have to be mutilated.' Rhys, letter to Evelyn Scott, 10 June 1934, *Letters 1931–1966*, 33. For Constable Rhys did cut 2,400 words from Part IV, remove Anna's imagining of the foetus during an instrumental abortion, change the improvisational style of Anna's delirium after her abortion, and shift sentiments of the female abortionist to the male doctor who attends Anna. She cut detail of Masquerade that would fit the aesthetic category of the 'very picturesque' ('*Voyage in the Dark*. Part IV [Original Version]', 385), a newly introduced character (Aunt Jane) and newly introduced themes (Anna's relationship with her mother, defiance of Hester through singing local songs and compensation to slaveowners in the 1830s for freeing bondspeople). She also followed the writerly dictum 'show, don't tell' by dropping the comment that black Masqueraders 'were laughing at the idea that anybody black would want to be white' ('*Voyage in the Dark*. Part IV [Original Version]', 387).
108 Nancy Hemond Brown, 'Jean Rhys and *Voyage in the Dark*', *London Magazine* 25, nos. 1 & 2 (April/May 1985): 41.
109 Jean Rhys, letter to Peter Wolfe, 12 July 1974, Jean Rhys Papers.
110 Rhys, '*Voyage in the Dark*. Part IV (Original Version)', 383, 384, 387.
111 Linder, ed. 'Famous World Trials. The Trials of Oscar Wilde'.
112 Rhys, '*Voyage in the Dark*. Part IV (Original Version)', 385. The extra spacing between some words is Rhys's.
113 Rhys, *Voyage in the Dark*, 20. There was a Greyhound Hotel in Croydon.
114 Ibid., 156, 158, 157.
115 Rhys, '*Voyage in the Dark*. Part IV (Original Version)', 386.
116 Ibid., 388.
117 Vincent Sherry, *Modernism and the Reinvention of Decadence* (New York: Cambridge University Press, 2015); Kristin Mahoney, *Literature and the Politics of Post-Victorian Decadence* (Cambridge: Cambridge University Press, 2015); Kate Hext and Alex Murray, ed. *Decadence in the Age of Modernism* (Baltimore, MD: Johns Hopkins University Press, 2019).

# 4

# Depressive time and jazz modernism in *Good Morning, Midnight*

In *Good Morning, Midnight*, protagonist Sasha Jansen revisits Paris during the 1937 International Exposition of Arts and Technics in Modern Life, which aimed to showcase evidence of material and moral reconstruction after the Great Depression and of 'technical progress in science and in art'.[1] *Good Morning, Midnight* evinces technical experiment in Rhys's aesthetics of time, registering, often ironically, the ways in which time accumulates in familiar places (the modern city's hotel rooms, restaurants, bars, female toilets, studios and streets), in the routines of everyday living, in music, in the use of clichés, in stereotyping and in images of women drawn from sexology, literature, art and vernacular cultures: the female outcast, the drowning woman, the weeping woman, the *doudou* of the French imperial imaginary, the intellectual woman and the dreaming woman. Having dealt at some length with the intellectual woman and the dreaming woman in *The Worlding of Jean Rhys*, and their resonances in Sasha's relationships with René and the man known only as the *commis voyageur*, in this chapter I focus on Rhys's interest in the drowning woman, the crying woman and female outcast; in Chapter 6, I trace the genealogy of Rhys's interest in the *doudou*. Sasha images her at times suicidal despair as 'drowning', 'sink[ing] to the accompaniment of loud laughter'. Her 'deep, dark river' is grief over the death of a baby son and the failure of her marriage to Enno and the dreams of a better life outside England that were part of the romance of and sustained the marriage.[2] Memory acts as a vortex, drawing Sasha back to depressive immersion in the post–First World War past, a process she compares to the action of an earworm, 'cheap gramophone records starting up in your head', '"Here this happened, here that happened."'[3] In the 1919 of the novel, popular musical time is characterized by the tango, English music hall, French cabaret and the hit 'For tonight, for tonight, Let me dream out my dream of delight' from Edward German's opera of *Tom Jones* (1907). The music of the novel's present in 1937 is swing, biguine and hotcha, all part of an international commercialized pleasure industry rather than just a black Atlantic musical reach. Rhys's most persistent musical allusion in the novel is to the song 'Swing High, Swing Low', first recorded by various artists in 1937. The sentiments of the song are folk advice drawing on the idea of life as a dance. The song, a dance tune, prescribes for the 'lonely and blue' a way of living in the tempo of swing (rather than progress), in a playful 'rhythmical campaign' that 'can do more than champagne' to cheer them up or help them cope.[4] Rhys represents jazz modernism as a commodity culture of the good time. James Donald writes of 'jazz modernism' as a 'style for living assertively in the present'; 'jazz, as a cultural phenomenon even more than as music, served as a symbol and symptom of a modernist attitude, or mentality: … a new emphasis on interiority, a new sense of the body and sexuality, and modernity experienced, viscerally, as rhythm'.[5] I highlight the temporal condensation in the image of red lights in the main memory sequence of Part 3 as a suggestive obscuring of traumatic reaches of memory. The section beginning '[n]ow the lights are red, dusky red, haggard red, cruel red' is followed by a centred asterisk and then the memory of Sasha's first improvisation around 'Swing high, swing low'. Rhys sets her treatment of a surface–depth dichotomy in Sasha's sense of her world alongside the handling of dimensionality by Oscar Wilde and Pablo Picasso.

Rhys exposes the internationalist framing of the Exhibition as a paean to progress – announced even in its name – as a façade in a predatory, market-driven world in which 'homo homini lupus' (man is wolf to man).[6] René comments to Sasha that the Star of Peace at the Exhibition is shabby. In the novel the international is riven by nationalist and imperialist conflict and inequalities based on gender, race, class and religion. Rhys structures Part 3 of *Good Morning, Midnight* as an 'ordered, undulating procession' of memories on Sasha's part organized by lodgings and their surrounding streets which chart her journey to becoming depressed and lachrymose.[7] An overarching undulation of Part 3 is from the prospect of peace after the First World War in The Hague, a city even then associated with international justice and law, to the fact and prospect of war in 1937: the French armed suppression of the Moroccan nationalist Comité d'Action Marocaine (in which René claims to have fought as a Foreign Legionnaire), the Spanish Civil War and international tension expressed in the architectural confrontation between Nazi German and Communist Russian pavilions at the Exhibition, on which so much has been written.[8] Resonating with this ideological confrontation, Sasha's dream about 'the Exhibition' features 'passages to the right and passages to the left, but no exit sign' when she 'want[s] the way out', projecting the contemporary world not as morally reconstructed or reconstructing, but rather as a nightmare.⁹ The gramophone records 'I Do Like a S'Nice, S'Mince, S'pie' and 'There's One More River to Cross' are part of a complexly allusive paragraph which is a segue between the memories of Sasha's return to her censorious family in England and one of the more famous passages in the novel, in which self is defined by negativity: 'I have no pride – no pride, no name, no face, no country. I don't belong anywhere. Too sad, too sad.' Sasha voluntarily imagines '[s]inging defiantly' in the streets songs from different musical traditions that are not part of the temporality of the 'extremely respectable'.¹⁰ The lyrics of the first song are from English music hall performer Jay Laurier's 'I Do Like a S'Nice, S'Mince, S'pie' (1914) and the second are from Paul Tremaine and His Orchestra's 'There's One More River to Cross' (1930), a fox trot arrangement of a traditional song.¹¹ The food mentioned in Laurier's song – 'lamb, ham', 'jam', 'roly-poly' pudding and 'mince pie' – is English fare. 'There's One More River to Cross' is a comic song about Noah boarding animals on the ark and salvation after crossing the Jordan River. It plays on the comic incongruity between a biblical theme and fox trot tempo and is part of the rescue motif that runs through *Good Morning, Midnight*, including in 'Swing High, Swing Low'. Rhys's allusions to popular and comic contemporary songs demonstrate the world rescuing Sasha, catalysing a precarious composure, even if around a defiant negative.

As Katherine Streip, Elaine Savory and Laura Wainwright, among other critics, have noted, *Good Morning, Midnight* is Rhys's most grimly humorous novel.¹² Sasha remembers from an English lesson she gave in Paris in the mid-1920s some of Mrs Erlynne's lines from Oscar Wilde's serio-comedy *Lady Windermere's Fan*: 'The laughter, the horrible laughter of the world – a thing more tragic than all the tears the world has ever shed.'¹³ Mrs Erlynne, a type of the woman with a past – the adventuress – is railing against the scornful social treatment of the 'outcast' woman, 'fall[en] into the pit, to be despised, mocked, abandoned, sneered at'.¹⁴ Neil Sammells would position the outcast as a new posture of Mrs Erlynne in a play in which 'the stylization at work is the rapidity and emphatic theatricality with which the characters swap one posture, one surface, one signification for another'.¹⁵ Rhys connects the type of the outcast and the sacrificial prey to market forces. Reflecting on Mr Blank firing her from the fashion house, Sasha criticizes the view she imputes to him that she is 'an inefficient member of Society, slow in the uptake, uncertain, slightly damaged in the fray.... Some must cry so that others may be able to laugh the more heartily. Sacrifices are necessary.'¹⁶ Summarizing an argument of Alenka Zupancic, Lauren Berlant and Sianne Ngai posit 'that the *question* of what's living, what's mechanical, and who needs to know is what really haunts the comedic and makes it an uncanny scene of aesthetic, moral and political judgment'.[17] Sasha's self-conscious strategies of immersing herself in the present to avert being distressingly 'saturated' by memories,[18] strategies that repeatedly fail, pose the queries 'what's living' and 'what's mechanical'. Tim Armstrong points out that 'technology encouraged the tabulation of time, and its equation with productivity', one form of which was 'personal regimes that stressed its efficient use'.[19] Sasha thinks of her personal regime as a daily 'programme', and here Rhys is being ironic, drawing attention to the precariousness of Sasha's sense of control over the temporality of her life, 'not to leave anything to chance – no gaps'.[20]

The motif of a despairing woman drowning herself in a river recurs in each of Rhys's novels from *Quartet* through to *Good Morning, Midnight*.[21] In *Quartet* and *After Leaving Mr Mackenzie*, the motif is part of scenes of misrecognition of Marya and Julia as they stand in what could be visual frames of the female suicide popularized in nineteenth-century art.[22] As discussed in Chapter 3, in *Voyage in the Dark* the newly pregnant Anna attributes the sentiment '[w]hy didn't you bloody well make a hole in the water?' to social judgement of the fallen woman.[23] Anna projects the hackneyed interpellation of the fallen woman onto herself and starts dreaming of the sea in terms which resonate with transatlantic history. The 'deep, dark river' cited in Sasha's consciousness has different figurative and allusive resonances than sexual fall and the shame and anguish associated with the stereotypical icon of the female suicide. Nicoletti observes that the Victorian iconography of the drowned fallen woman does not feature 'rescues' and 'resuscitation', characteristically showing 'the middle class spectator ... as an appalled but helpless observer' and suggesting that the suicide 'was beyond social intervention and institutional reform'.[24] Thomas Hood represents the '[r]ashly importunate' female suicide as redeemed by death in his iconic poem 'The Bridge of Sighs' (1844). Hood invites readers to

> Think of her mournfully,
> Gently and humanly;
> Not of the stains of her,
> All that remains of her
> Now is pure womanly ... .
>
> Past all dishonour,
> Death has left on her
> Only the beautiful.

The female figure of the poem is represented stereotypically as 'of Eve's family', weak and 'evil'.[25] In Hood's projection, death makes her whole again. For Sasha, under the 'surface' current of the river 'there is always stagnant water, calm, indifferent – the bitter peace that is very near to death, to hate'. It is a 'heaven' of being 'dead to the world'.[26]

Sasha identifies the drowning woman as a cliché of the 'extremely respectable'. Their deeply ingrained formulaic styles of thinking are 'very proper', 'melodramatic', borrowed from 'a sentimental ballad': 'And that's what terrifies you about them. It isn't their cruelty, it isn't even their shrewdness – it's their extraordinary naiveté. Everything in their whole bloody world is a cliché.' Seeking help from her family that she has alienated by marrying a continental European man who abandoned her, Sasha remembers returning to London to be greeted by an 'old devil' with, '"Why didn't you drown yourself … in the Seine?" … "We consider you as dead. Why didn't you make a hole in the water?"'[27] The clichés close off the 'scope of empathy (both cognitive and affective)'; they are 'automated'.[28] For the 'old devil' the Seine is a metonym of the foreign shame and disgrace he projects onto Sasha. Through allusion to D. H. Lawrence's *Lady Chatterley's Lover*, Rhys suggests that Sasha's family and the English more broadly prostitute themselves to the 'bitch-goddess': 'Money. Success'.[29] While Sasha mordantly derides obsession with money and success, her experience of poverty in Europe underlines the psychological and economic need for a sustaining income. After Enno deserts her there are periods in which Sasha can barely afford to eat or relies on charity, eating at a convent 'where the nuns supply very cheap meals for destitute girls' during what the novel's retrospective timeframe suggests is the Great Depression.[30] Revisiting Paris, Sasha thinks:

> Saved, rescued, fished-up, half-drowned, out of the deep, dark river, dry clothes, hair shampooed and set. Nobody would know I had ever been in it. Except, of course, that there always remains something. Yes, there always remains something…. Never mind, here I am, sane and dry, with my place to hide in. What more do I want? … I'm a bit of an automaton, but sane, surely – dry, cold and sane.

Perhaps cynically playing to the sentiment of the family patriarch, Sasha represents financial gifts – an inheritance of £2 10s per week and her friend Sidonie's treat of a holiday in Paris – as being '[s]aved, rescued', given a 'place to hide in' and to live rather mechanically.[31] Her contracted life pointedly contrasts with the kind of expansive creative vision Virginia Woolf projects for the woman who has £500 a year and a room in which to write in *A Room of One's Own* (1929).[32]

Rhys's 'deep, dark river' resonates with Wilde's image of life for the disgraced woman as a 'fall into the pit' to withstand which she would need the resilience afforded by 'wit', 'courage', and the capacity to weather 'dishonour'.[33] What 'always remains' for Sasha – she is '[s]aved, rescued, but not quite so good as new' – are teariness, a grim wit and affect represented as an animal familiar, a 'fierce wolf' which will strike her tormentors at some time in the future. The wit animates Sasha, cutting across her sense of herself as having 'been made very cold and very sane ... very passive'.[34] The profanity and desolation of Sasha's world are underlined by the repeated use of the word 'damned'. The word clusters particularly in her memories of working at and being fired from the fashion house managed by Mr Blank and of her return to her hotel room at the end of the novel, and is emphasized in the closing scenes of Part 1, with 'shut the damned world out' being repeated, and of Part 2, with '[t]his damned room – it's saturated with the past' opening the final paragraph.[35] Wilde's Mrs Erlynne characterizes the condition of the female outcast as being '[t]o find the door shut against one, to have to creep in hideous byways, afraid every moment lest the mask should be stripped from one's face'.[36] Rhys draws from Mrs Erlynne's dialogue about the female outcast four motifs for *Good Morning, Midnight* – the laughter of the world, the pit, the shut door and the social mask – though Rhys's protagonists live on a very different social plane than Wilde's.

Rhys focuses on drowning (understood, like crying, as a metaphor of saturation in grief and trauma) and Sasha's precarious balancing between memory and coping. Sasha, perhaps pointedly on Rhys's part, positions her drowning as being without 'willing and eager friends on the bank waiting to pull you out at the first sign of distress', the only witness being her subjective sense of 'the accompaniment of loud laughter' as she sinks.[37] Rhys plays a variation on the good Samaritan motif in *Quartet*. Such 'willing and eager' friends feature, by contrast, in a series of Pablo Picasso's artworks from late 1932 and early 1933 on the theme of the rescue of a drowning, possibly drowned woman across a number of genres (drawing, painting and etching). Several are titled *Le sauvetage* (the rescue). Rhys could have seen images of works in the series in articles in *Minotaure* and *Cahiers d'art*, both stocked by Zwemmer's bookshop, which specialized in modern art and was located in Charing Cross Road in London (close to where Rhys was living in the late 1930s).[38] The series has been interpreted as a '"diary"' of a phase of Picasso's affair with Marie-Thérèse Walter, a strong swimmer, who had 'fall[en] victim to spirochetosis, a sometimes fatal disease that she contracted after swimming in the sewage-polluted waters of the river Marne [a tributary of the Seine] where she went rowing'.[39] Picasso focuses on the act of rescue, of being pulled and pulling from water. The nudity of the figures represents this as an intimate gesture. Indeed, John Richardson finds the rescued women 'voluptuously inert'.[40] To use the diary analogy, some entries in the series represent the woman being rescued from water as a muse of a bearded artist figure, some explore the fulcrum of balance between the woman and her rescuer(s). In some the woman is rescued by women who resemble her physically, perhaps projecting a balancing between threatened life and a will to live. The rescuing women are on the bank or land and occasionally one helps lift the drowned/drowning woman from the water. In one the woman and the rescuer are abstract, ungendered and metallic and the figure rescued seems to have been hoisted fully to the surface of the water where it balances. It is one of the few entries in which both figures are three-dimensional; the rescuer usually has more depth. By examining her grandfather's potential allusions to canonical depictions of the death of Jesus, art critic and curator Diana Widmaier Picasso argues that Picasso's rescue series offers 'existential reflection on life and death, joy and gravity, beauty and horror, possession and loss. The artist makes the link between a real event (Marie-Thérèse's illness), a religious subject (the Crucifixion, Pietà and Resurrection) and the universal themes of suffering and death.'[41] Rhys's mother and child are Sasha and her dead son. The allusion to Picasso's art places Rhys's command of narrative techniques – interior monologue and temporal and structural improvisation with jazz form – beside Picasso's modernist artistic innovation. Sasha's jazz improvisations salvage some agency over her memories.

Picasso's *Guernica* was the centrepiece of the Spanish Pavilion at the Exhibition. Paintings from Picasso's 1930s series of weeping women were exhibited in *Picasso's 'Guernica' with 67 Preparatory Paintings, Sketches and Studies* held at the New Burlington Gallery in London in October 1938 and at the Whitechapel Art Gallery in January 1939. *Weeping Woman* (1937) was exhibited at the Cheltenham Museum and Gallery from 28 July to 1 September 1937 and The Guildhall, Gloucester from 28 May to 26 June 1938.[42] Picasso's *Weeping Woman* (Tate Gallery) is, a major Picasso website notes, 'regarded as a thematic continuation of the tragedy depicted in … *Guernica*. In focusing on the image of a woman crying, the artist was no longer painting the effects of the Spanish Civil War directly, but rather referring to a singular universal image of suffering.' It suggests that the painting demands that viewers 'imagine' themselves 'into the excoriated face of this woman, into her dark eyes', linking the 'solid'-looking tears to Spanish images of the 'Mater Dolorosa, the weeping Virgin'. Picasso comments on the series, 'women are suffering machines', and on the model Dora Maar, 'I've painted her in tortured forms, not through sadism, and not with pleasure; just obeying a vision that forced itself on me.'[43]

'In order to emphasize the two-dimensional nature of the work, Picasso makes no attempt to create "depth" in the painting by the use of linear perspective or any type of modelling/shading like chiaroscuro',[44] the *Art Encyclopedia* observes. When Sasha bursts into tears in public, she is acutely conscious not of sanctity but of the spectacle she makes of her suffering. Focalizing the novel through Sasha's interior monologue and an embedded third-person narrative about a Martinican woman (which I discuss in Chapter 6), Rhys gives depth and personality to the experience of crying women. Sasha's apocalyptic image close to the end of the novel is of a machine with undulating white steel arms, some with lights at their ends and others with heavily mascaraed eyes. As Emery notes, a 'formal process of dream logic and metaphor creates this vision through a movement of condensation and unification',[45] drawing together elements of memory and nightmare: popular music, the machine, steel arms, lights, eyes. Heavily mascaraed eyes are a feature of Picasso's *Weeping Woman* (1937), held at the Tate Gallery, and *Weeping Woman* (1937), held at the National Gallery of Victoria, both of figures with mask-like faces painted in cubist style.

Sasha's procession of memories in Part 3 begins in post–First World War The Hague with the promise of 'No more war', 'a good time', escape from London to 'the good life' in Europe, marriage to Enno and the romance of travelling to Paris.[46] Sasha and Enno's relationship has no solid financial foundation; they usually live by borrowing money and 'luck'. Sasha does have some good times in Paris: 'I've never been so happy in my life. I'm alive, eating ravioli and drinking wine. I've escaped. A door has opened and let me out into the sun. What more do I want? Anything might happen.'[47] The metaphor of '[s]unshine' as a 'sweet place' resonates with the Emily Dickinson poem Rhys uses as the novel's epigraph.[48] Enno seems to abandon Sasha, though, during the pregnancy. 'What's going to happen?' she thinks, before he returns unexpectedly. The memory sequence – which Sasha ironically dubs her 'golden days' – has rhythmical patterns: rooms, sometimes with addresses, as subtitles of sections or identified in the first sentence of a section; desire for Paris in the repetition '*When – we – get – to – Paris*' and train wheels sounding out 'Paris, Paris, Paris, Paris';[49] fluctuations in Sasha and Enno's fortunes and the quality of their lodgings and relationship; open and shut doors; repetition of 'luck' and 'lucky', of 'money', and of 'laugh', 'laughing' or 'laughter'.[50] Intense moments of Sasha's mourning of her son, who died at five weeks in a charity hospital, and a subsequent marriage disintegration are condensed temporally in an image of 'red, dusky red, haggard red, cruel red' 'lights'.[51]

Edward Said has pointed to the ways in which 'difficulties of filiation' are projected in modernist literature through figures of 'childless couples, orphaned children, aborted childbirths, and unregenerately celibate men and women' and draws attention to the possibility of historically contingent 'compensatory order[s]' of affiliation providing alternative 'form[s] of relationship'.[52] The death of Sasha's child instances the 'human poignancy' of the impact of poverty on ties of filiation.[53] During labour the midwife at the charity hospital urges, 'Courage, courage', while birthing mothers cry out, 'Jesus, Jesus', 'Mother, Mother', and Sasha, 'Chloroform, chloroform', the last, she realizes, not for the 'poor'; Sasha is tormented by awareness of the need for 'money, money' to support the future of the child. Anxiety causes her breast milk to dry up and the unnamed boy is fed 'Nestlé's milk'. The midwife, who recommends a 'tisane of orange-flower water' for the nerves of impoverished mothers and calls Sasha's worry 'nothing at all', wraps Sasha's abdomen so that childbirth will leave 'no trace, no mark, nothing'.[54] Sasha's abject thought of the mouldering body of the child makes '[e]verything all spoiled'. Religious faith, a form of filiation, provides Sasha no consolation: she thinks 'God is very cruel'.[55]

The sense of cruelty, what Maslen calls 'cosmic hopelessness',[56] is exacerbated when her and Enno's financial 'luck' improves after their son's death, a mortifying sign of the 'horrible laughter of the world'; now, for Sasha, 'the lights are red'. The section describing the change of fortune focuses primarily on memories of an acquaintance who tells Sasha stories he thinks are 'droll', trying to cheer her up: 'You mustn't be sad; you must laugh, you must dance….' The stories with their mockery of the human distress of others and related while drinking champagne are, however, more signs of the 'laughter of the world'. The 'dusky red, haggard red, cruel red' lights signal warning, danger, stop, '[n]ot to think', anger, passion, impasse and the adjectives catch up affects of gloom, melancholy, anxiety, fatigue, terror, privation, torment, the world's indifference to or pleasure in Sasha's suffering.[57] Red lights also signal prostitution. While there is no suggestion in the novel that Sasha has earned a living as a professional prostitute, that she recognizes the gigolo René's pick up manouevres and has agreed to go to the flat of an unnamed man from Lille for a drink during a time when she has been struggling to make enough money to eat, remembering him as a man 'determined to get people on the cheap', opens the possibility of amateur prostitution.[58] He dashes off in a taxi after she hints to him how impoverished she is. For Maslen, Sasha's despair is 'hyperbolic', forestalling 'acknowledgement of the "real," inaccessible, unspeakable trauma', 'an abyssal loss'.[59] The red lights would represent an impassable threshold to this trauma. Lines from Paul

Robeson's version of 'Gloomy Sunday' – Rhys alludes to the song on the first page of the novel – might frame Sasha's experience:

> I waited 'til dreams, like my heart, were all broken
> The flowers were all dead and the words were unspoken
> The grief that I knew was beyond all consoling[.][60]

Maslen suggests:

> [T]he 'enormous machine' of commodity capitalism has indeed displaced the God whom Sasha accuses in her desolation. Or, to put it differently, Rhys's social critique in this novel is facilitated by Sasha's sense of the ethical impoverishment of capitalism and commodity culture, but since the culture is apprehended through conventional and apolitical melancholic imagery, her perception of political and social injustice tends to masquerade as metaphysical 'angst'.[61]

In the context of Sasha's cynicism about the bourgeoisie in her memories of Paris, the image of red lights, though, also links the 'melancholic' impasse with ambivalent leftist political inclinations.[62] Part 3, the most linear exposition of Sasha's back story, is reprised as

> A room? A nice room? A beautiful room? A beautiful room with bath? Swing high, swing low, swing to and fro.... This happened and that happened....
>     And then the days came when I was alone.[63]

The allusion to 'Swing High, Swing Low' ('Swing high, swing low, swing to and fro') suggests that a 'little swing', a metonym for jazz modernism, has not been able to rescue the money-troubled marriage.[64]

This is the third time that Sasha hears what might at first appear to be just a musical mind pop; the second time it is part of rhymical verbal improvisation on the theme of the social planes of hotel rooms, caught up again here in the list of room types. The return to the earlier improvisation positions Part 3 as an extended improvisation on the earlier improvisation, initiated by the opening words of the Part ' ... *The room at the Steens*', a sequence of voluntary rather than involuntary memories set to jazz form.[65] The segue at the end of Part 2 – 'Rooms, streets, streets, rooms....' – sets up the improvisation.[66] The improvisations are little songs ('die kleinen Lieder') she makes out of her great sorrows ('grossen Schmerzen'), lines remembered from Heinrich Heine's 'Lyrical Intermezzo' and improvised on with 'homo homini lupus' as she recollects her encounter with Mr Blank.[67] Tim I. Williams points to research showing that musical 'mind pops indicate activation of semantic networks of related concepts'.[68] The fuller song lyrics of 'Swing High, Swing Low' reveal the semantic networks of the musical mind pop in the novel: you will never be rejected 'if your swinging is up to date'; for the dejected, dancing, as a style of rhythmic movement and living, can lift the spirits. Swing dancing is not sinful.[69] In context the 'rhythmical campaign' may encompass but also extends beyond sexual innuendo. When Sasha overhears the hotel patronne talking with a potential customer about the availability of classes of rooms, she begins improvising, 'A room. A nice room. A beautiful room. A beautiful room with bath. A very beautiful room with bath.' She hears, 'Swing high. …' The gap indicated by the ellipsis gives her time to improvise on the third line of the song's chorus, 'Not fast, not slow', with 'Now, slowly down'. 'A beautiful room with bath. A room with bath. A nice room. A room … '[70] The effect of such repetition is comic commentary on sales jargon and ironic commentary on the relation of hotel rooms to social planes, a cause of anxiety for Sasha, who is concerned about which plane her friend Sidonie, who booked and paid for her room, has placed her on. The semantic network is the fluctuation of social standing and room tariffs. Embedded in a memory of her anxious playfulness around this fluctuation, the third surfacing of 'Swing High, Swing Low' acts as a segue to her memory of being 'alone' after the marital breakdown through the unarticulated lyrics about being 'lonely and blue' covered over by ellipsis. The song has become part of the 'affective fabric' of her life.[71] In 'Songs My Mother Didn't Teach Me' Rhys alludes to Florizel's praise of Perdita in Shakespeare's *The Winter's Tale* to describe music and lyrics that become earworms: 'and for the ord'ring your affairs, / To sing them too'.[72] Sasha bookends her marriage to Enno with a high and low: the excitement of travelling to Paris by train, caught up again in the prelude to her apocalyptic vision of the future, and a stock cinematic scene, with her 'film-mind' framing the breakdown visually as a couple parting at a railway station, with one 'leaning out of the carriage window'. In her next hotel room she kills a fly, remembering thinking of it, 'You won't dance again', a comment that mordantly juxtaposes herself with the insect.[73] Katherine Mansfield's story 'The Fly', known to Rhys, also juxtaposes a character, a comfortably-off boss in the City of London struggling to mourn the death of a son, and a fly killed by the character.[74] The man's soldier son has died in the First World War. Rhys's intertextual reach to Mansfield's narrative draws out the gender and class differences between Sasha and the boss. Sasha contemplates the mouldering body of her infant son; the boss cannot bear to think of his son's body as anything but 'unblemished in his uniform'.[75]

Sasha's improvisation, which demonstrates formal control over the memories arranged in Part 3, brings the past into being in the present moment and present tempos of improvisation. As such it challenges Erica L. Johnson's reading of the way Sasha's 'past' 'restructures memory as haunting', in which she crucially confers 'agency' and 'autonomy' on the past, arguing that Part 3 'exemplifies the novel's dynamic of haunting' and is 'something of a meta-example of affective memory'. She represents Sasha's past as '"stalk[ing]"' and 'predatory'; it 'lurks in her unconscious or preconscious and brushes up against or erupts into her consciousness through its own agency'.[76] Rhys, though, carefully positions the memory sequence of Part 3 as an 'ordered, undulating procession' and signals Sasha's variations on themes through structural and verbal echoes and repetitions.[77]

Lyrics from 'Swing High, Swing Low' first surface in Sasha's mind after her memory of being fired by Mr Blank about ten years before her return visit to Paris, abruptly shifting the mood and the tempo of the scene and bringing her back to her more immediate surroundings in the present. In the nonlinear chronology of Sasha's memories in the novel, this particular memory takes her back to the period after the death of her son and most probably after her parting with Enno. Mr Blank has tested and humiliated Sasha, her distress at not being able to find the cashier's office registered in memories of a labyrinth in which 'all the doors are shut'. 'The passages will never lead anywhere, the doors will always be shut,' Sasha reflects. She distinguishes herself from those with 'money and friends', who are 'quite secure' and with 'roots … well struck in'. For people like her she thinks there are '[n]o hospitable doors' that open. Sasha remembers that after she was fired, she walked from the fashion house onto the Avenue Marigny on a fine autumn day, and the musical mind pop surfaces involuntarily. Then there is an ellipsis and a line gap before the next section of Part 1, which begins, '[t]hinking of my jobs … ' and leads into voluntary memory of her failures to hold down employment in Paris.[78] The first ellipsis and line gap mark a rupture, a suspension in consciousness, temporary silence, a gap. 'Imagined music replays over time', Hyman, et al. note, 'includes pitch and melody … ; evokes emotion … ; and reactivates the brains [sic] areas involved in listening to music.'[79] To pick up the tempo, pitch and melody of the imagined music, the reader of an allusion to a musical mind pop or earworm would need to be part of what William Howland Kenney terms a circle of resonance, a listening community of the music.[80] Readers who hear the allusion musically will experience a marked shift in the tempo of reading. In retrospect only, Sasha imagines dressing down Mr Blank as a representative of 'Society', so the musical mind pop may be connected with her contemporary negotiation of 'tensions … around questions of authority and submission', which Kenney suggests was a common affective factor in the development of a taste for jazz in the period.[81]

Rhys's allusion to 'Swing High, Swing Low', a signature song of 1937, cannot be traced to a particular recording or performer, its provenance in the novel being more its popular contemporaneity, the mechanics of its commercial dissemination and consumption, and its transatlantic circle of resonance for Sasha. The song was written by Ralph Freed and Burton Lane and recorded in 1937 by Tempo King and His Kings of Tempo, Phil Harris and His Orchestra, Ruby Newman and His Rainbow Room Orchestra featuring Ray Heatherton, Vincent Lopez and His Orchestra, The Ink Spots, Glen Gray and the Casa Loma Orchestra, Music in the Russ Morgan Manner and Dorothy Lamour.[82] Two choruses of the song were played as part of the opening credits of the 1937 film of the same title, an adaptation of George Manker Watters and Arthur Hopkins's play *Burlesque* (1927), which had already been adapted for film as *The Dance of Life* (1929).[83] The recording of 'Swing High, Swing Low' by Tempo King and His Kings of Tempo, who modelled their style closely on Fats Waller's,[84] predates the release of the film. The version by the Ink Spots features scat, the group's harmonies being a precursor of doo wop. The film *Swing High, Swing Low* is set in and on the border of the Panama Canal Zone, then an unincorporated territory of the United States, and in New York, and includes many tropicalist tropes: the threat of illness in the tropics; a production song titled 'Panamania'; a beach with palm trees; alcohol aplenty; and stereotypical non-white characters.[85] Trumpeter Skid Johnson (played by Fred McMurray) hones his musicianship in an Afro-Latin contact zone between cultures in Panama City after a tour of duty as a soldier in the Canal Zone; his style makes him a star on his return to New York. U.S. singer Maggie King (played by Carole Lombard), whom he first met in the Canal Zone, becomes a wholesome figure in his life, rescuing him from alcoholism and gambling, and they marry, though the marriage goes through a rough patch. Dorothy Lamour, who recorded the theme song, had a supporting role in the film as Maggie's foil Anita Alvarez. 'Panamania' celebrates a 'new dance' craze ('fever') originating in the Canal Zone, 'Hot fiery gal zone'.[86] Kenney points to the important role of the 'jukebox', 'radio broadcasts and movie sound tracks' in popularizing swing music and of swing as a 'promotional term used in defining dance music aimed at the youth market'.[87] Through these media and records, in 1939 many of the novel's readers would have been familiar enough with 'Swing High, Swing Low' to be able to pick up the shift in tempo with Sasha's improvisations, albeit in a variety of commodified musical arrangements.

In Sasha's apocalyptic drunken visual and aural hallucination after Réne leaves her room, she sees 'an enormous machine, made of white steel', an emblem of a world with no prospect of redemption or redemptive progress: 'Venus is dead;

Apollo is dead; even Jesus is dead.' Against a 'grey sky' redolent of England that 'terrifies' Sasha, the machine's 'flexible arms' dance, 'wave to an accompaniment of music and of song. Like this: "Hotcha – hotcha – hotcha...."'[88] Hotcha is jazz 'marked by a strong rhythm' and a cry of 'enthusiastic approval or delight'.[89] It was a signature cry in the performances of Fats Waller, one of the leading celebrity 'proselytizers of the good time, a perennial element in the popular aesthetic yet historically and culturally specific'.[90] The terrifying grey sky catches up a memory of Calais: 'a grey day. It was like walking in London'.[91] Sasha's capacity to respond instantly to the jazz tune by singing the lyrics demonstrates a mechanization of her auditory consciousness that is integral to the terror of the vision. In Henri Bergson's theory of humour, comedy derives from the mechanical being encrusted on the living. In Sasha's vision, living, by contrast, is mechanical. For Emery, it 'exposes her songs as the dance-hall rhythms of mass culture, not the poetry she might have hoped for', forcing a recognition of 'herself as part of a feminized mass culture that she dreads for its mechanical artificiality'.[92] Rhys's treatment of Sasha's interest in jazz, though, is, as I have shown, far more ambivalent than Emery suggests. Sasha has a command of jazz as a form apparent in a narrative dexterity, a wit in inner speech and consciousness which – at times – may, as part of a rhythmical campaign, rescue her from more uncontrollable depths of depressive grief. Rhys's musical allusions distinguish the authorial and narrative voices of the text. Rhys uses allusive juxtaposition – of Sasha and Mrs Erlynne as outcast, Sasha and the Victorian icon of the female suicide and Sasha with images in Picasso's rescue and weeping women series of the 1930s – to draw out her aesthetic flair in fleshing out the experience, inner lives and personality of female types drawn intermedially from theatre, popular culture, poetry, art and music.

## Notes

1  'The 1937 International Exhibition, Paris: An International Exposition of Arts and Techniques Applied to Modern Life', *Architectural Record*, October 1937, 82, in *World's Fairs: A Global History of Expositions* (Marlborough: Adam Matthew Digital, n.d.), http://www.worldsfairs.amdigital.co.uk.ez.library.latrobe.edu.au/Documents/Details/HMLSC_upam_BX22_AMD587, accessed 29 September 2019.
2  Rhys, *Good Morning, Midnight*, 4.
3  Ibid., 8.
4  'Swing High Swing Low Lyrics', https://genius.com/The-ink-spots-swing-high-swing-low-lyrics, accessed 17 June 2018.

5   Donald, *Some of These Days*, 1, 18.
6   Rhys, *Good Morning, Midnight*, 16.
7   Ibid., 89.
8   For a recent overview with new scholarship, see Danilo Udovicki-Selb, 'Facing Hitler's Pavilion: The Uses of Modernity in the Soviet Pavilion at the 1937 Paris International Exhibition', *Journal of Contemporary History* 47, no. 1 (2012): 13–47. In Rhys criticism, see Emery, *Jean Rhys at 'World's End'*, 144–72; Christina Britzolakis, '"This Way to the Exhibition": Genealogies of Urban Spectacle in Jean Rhys's Interwar Fiction', *Textual Practice* 21, no. 3 (2007): 457–82; and Camarasana, 'Exhibitions and Repetitions'.
9   Rhys, *Good Morning, Midnight*, 6.
10  Ibid., 33, 126.
11  Jay Laurier, 'I Do Like a S'Nice, S'Mince, S'Pie', https://monologues.co.uk/musichall/Songs-I/I-Do-Like-A-Snice-Spince-Spie.htm, accessed 4 October 2018; Paul Tremaine and His Orchestra, 'There's One More River to Cross' (1930), *YouTube*, https://www.youtube.com/watch?v=QAjn-XOiO1A, accessed 27 September 2019. The lyrics of both are slightly, but not substantively misremembered, which suggests that Rhys is keeping to the narrator's potentially fallible memory of the songs. Jay Laurier was an English music hall performer with a very mobile comic face; after the advent of screen sound some of his music hall songs were recorded and shown as shorts in cinema programmes, so the allusion could be both musical and visual.
12  Katharine Streip, '"Just a Cérébrale": Jean Rhys, Women's Humour, and Ressentiment', *Representations* 45 (1994): 117–44; Savory, *Jean Rhys*, 109–32; and Laura Wainwright, '"Doesn't That Make You Laugh?": Modernist Comedy in Jean Rhys's *After Leaving Mr Mackenzie* and *Good Morning, Midnight*', *Journal of International Women's Studies* 10, no. 3 (2009): 348–57.
13  Rhys, *Good Morning, Midnight*, 113–14.
14  Oscar Wilde, *Lady Windermere's Fan*, in *Five Plays*, by Oscar Wilde (New York: Bantam, 1961), 37.
15  Neil Sammells, *Wilde Style: The Plays and Prose of Oscar Wilde* (2000; repr., London: Routledge, 2014), 88.
16  Rhys, *Good Morning, Midnight*, 20.
17  Lauren Berlant and Sianne Ngai, 'Comedy Has Issues', *Critical Inquiry* 43, no. 2 (2017): 234, their emphasis.
18  Rhys, *Good Morning, Midnight*, 89.
19  Tim Armstrong, 'Modernist Temporality: The Science and Philosophy and Aesthetics of Temporality from 1880', in *The Cambridge History of Modernism*, ed. Vincent Sherry (Cambridge: Cambridge University Press, 2016), 33.
20  Rhys, *Good Morning, Midnight*, 8.

21  When Francis Wyndham tried to locate Rhys in the 1940s, he was, Diana Athill reports, 'told by one person that she had drowned herself in the Seine, by another that she had drunk herself to death. People expected that kind of fate for her.' *Stet* (London: Granta, 2000), 152. The image of being 'rescued' from the 'deep, dark river' resonated with Rhys at a personal level; in correspondence with Selma Vaz Dias in 1960, Rhys alludes to it to describe Vaz Dias's discovery of her whereabouts in 1949 over a radio adaptation of *Good Morning, Midnight*. Letter to Vaz Dias, 21 January 1960, Jean Rhys Papers.

22  After Marya leaves the Palais de Justice, where she had enquired after the recently arrested Stephan, she stands on the 'peaceful' Quai des Orfèvres watching the play of lights on the water. A young man 'call[s]' to her, '"Hé, little one. Is it for tonight the suicide?"' She is more conscious of the 'beautiful muddle' which she is 'in' (Rhys, *Quartet*, 25). Listening to a violinist play what Stephan identifies as a 'Russian song … called in French *Par Pitié*', Marya thinks of 'fate' as a 'dark river that swept you on you didn't know where – nobody knew where' (112). In Part 3 of *After Leaving Mr Mackenzie*, as Julia stands on the banks of the Seine watching the 'danc[ing]' 'shadows' of 'branches' and 'smoke' on the water a policeman asks, 'There's something that doesn't go', and Julia, recognizing a visual field in which he might have placed her, responds 'cold[ly]': '"I haven't the slightest intention of committing suicide, I assure you"' (Rhys, *After Leaving Mr Mackenzie*, 132). The idea, though, prompts her to see the 'shadows' of what the policeman suggests is the limb of a tree, as not 'be[ing] on the surface' but 'struggling, wriggling upwards from the depths of the water' (133). Julia's Uncle Griffiths has behaved like the censorious patriarch of *Good Morning, Midnight*. To himself he thinks 'she had made a mess of things and was trying to get hold of some money' (59); to her he says that her husband was a 'damned bad lot' and '"You deserted your family. And now you can't expect to walk back and be received with open arms"' (59, 61).

23  Rhys, *Voyage in the Dark*, 140.

24  Nicoletti, 'Downward Mobility', para. 18, para. 17.

25  Thomas Hood, 'The Bridge of Sighs', *PoemHunter.com*, https://www.poemhunter.com/poem/the-bridge-of-sighs, accessed 15 September 2018.

26  Rhys, *Good Morning, Midnight*, 126, 74.

27  Ibid., 31.

28  Craig Jordan-Baker, 'On Cliché: Expression, Cognition and Understanding', *Journal of Creative Writing Studies* 2, no. 2 (2016): 9.

29  D. H. Lawrence, *Lady Chatterley's Lover* (1920; Harmondsworth: Penguin, 1960). The term 'bitch-goddess' is usually traced to William James, describing 'U.S. civilization' in a 1906 letter to H. G. Wells. *Word Histories*, https://wordhistories.net/2019/01/17/bitch-goddess/, accessed 10 May 2019. Lawrence applies the term to the English. Sir Clifford Chatterley's 'prostitut[ing]' of himself to the bitch-goddess leaves his wife Connie experiencing a 'fear of nothingness in her life' (53, 64). In

developing the dreaming woman motif in *Good Morning, Midnight*, Rhys alludes to Lawrence's *The Trespasser*. See Thomas, *The Worlding of Jean Rhys*, 132–5.
30  Rhys, *Good Morning, Midnight*, 73, 117.
31  Ibid., 4, 32.
32  Virginia Woolf, *A Room of One's Own* (1929; repr., London: Grafton, 1978).
33  Wilde, *Lady Windermere's Fan*, 37.
34  Rhys, *Good Morning, Midnight*, 76, 40, 5.
35  Ibid., 65, 89.
36  Wilde, *Lady Windermere's Fan*, 37.
37  Rhys, *Good Morning, Midnight*, 4.
38  Images of *Le sauvetage* featured in André Breton's 'Picasso dans son élément' in *Minotaure* in 1933, no. 1: 12–13 and in *Cahiers d'Art* in 1935, no. 7/10: 27. They were not included in *A Collection of Fifty Drawings by Picasso* held at the Zwemmer Gallery in 1937. Zwemmer's 'stock[ed] foreign books and magazines, and partly through the Zwemmer Gallery, opened in 1929, … became associated not simply with the subject of art in general, and the academic or lay study of it, but with modern art in particular. It quickly became known as one of the few places in London where those interested in modern European art could find out about it in the latest books and magazines.' Nigel Vaux Halliday, *More Than a Bookshop: Zwemmer's and Art in the Twentieth Century* (London: Philip Wilson Publishers, 1991), 44.
39  Diana Widmaier Picasso, 'Rescue: The End of a Year', in *The EY Exhibition. Picasso 1932: Love Fame Tragedy*, ed. Achim Borchardt-Hume and Nancy Ireson (London: Tate Publishing, 2018), 210.
40  John Richardson, 'L'amour fou', *New York Review of Books*, 19 December 1985.
41  Widmaier Picasso, 'Rescue', 213.
42  Helen Little, 'Picasso and Britain: A Selected Chronology of Exhibitions and Acquisitions 1900–1960', in *Picasso & Modern British Art*, ed. James Beechey and Chris Stephens (London: Tate Publishing, 2012), 222–5.
43  Pablo Picasso: Paintings, Quotes and Biography, https://www.pablopicasso.org/the-weeping-woman.jsp., accessed 27 June 2019.
44  'Weeping Woman' (1937), *Art Encyclopedia*, http://www.visual-arts-cork.com/paintings-analysis/weeping-woman.htm, accessed 27 June 2019.
45  Emery, *Jean Rhys at 'World's End'*, 167.
46  Rhys, *Good Morning, Midnight*, 94.
47  Ibid., 100, 102.
48  Ibid., [v].
49  Ibid., 106, 118, 96, 101.
50  'luck' and 'lucky': ibid., 98, 110, 112, 114, 115; 'money': 94, 96, 97, 101, 103, 106, 115, 116, 117, 118; 'laugh', 'laughing' or 'laughter': 99, 105, 110, 111, 113, 116.
51  Ibid., 115.
52  Said, *The World, the Text and the Critic*, 17, 19.

53 Maslen, *Ferocious Things*, 148.
54 Rhys, *Good Morning, Midnight*, 45–6, 47, 46–7.
55 Ibid., 115.
56 Maslen, *Ferocious Things*, 127.
57 Rhys, *Good Morning, Midnight*, 115, 116, 115.
58 Ibid., 41. The man positions an earlier girlfriend of his as a prostitute by suggesting, after she asks him for money for new shoes, that she has a pimp on the side (ibid., 72).
59 Maslen, *Ferocious Things*, 125.
60 Gloomy Sunday Lyrics, https://genius.com/Paul-robeson-gloomy-sunday-lyrics, accessed 17 June 2018. Written in Hungarian by Hungarian expatriate Rezsö Seress in 1932 in Paris, it has been dubbed the Hungarian Suicide Song. 'Gloomy Sunday' was recorded in different English translations and arrangements in 1936 by Hal Kemp, Paul Robeson, Vincent Lopez and His Orchestra, Henry King and His Orchestra, Paul Whiteman and His Orchestra and The Albert Sandler Trio with Hildegarde. 'Gloomy Sunday', phespirit.info, http://www.phespirit.info/gloomysunday/recordings.htm, accessed 17 June 2018. Later Sasha hears or remembers 'Sombre Dimanche', a French version of the song, first recorded by Damia (Louise Marie Damien), a renowned singer of *chansons réalistes*, in 1936.
61 Maslen, *Ferocious Things*, 126.
62 In reflecting on her failure of empathy for a kitchen hand in a tabac she visits, Sasha equivocally alludes to 'Les Mains de Jean-Marie', Arthur Rimbaud's poem about the part of working-class women in the revolutionary Paris Commune of 1871, asking, 'When the revolution comes, won't those be the hands to be kissed?' (Rhys, *Good Morning, Midnight*, 86). In the novel Russia is associated with political and religious repression, from Sasha's Russian student of English telling the story of the female 'revolutionary' killed brutally in the notorious Peter and Paul Fortress before the Bolsheviks came to power, his other stories about 'pain and torture', and the student's wealthy family fleeing Bolshevik rule (114), to Serge Rubin's exile as a person of Russian Jewish ancestry.
63 Rhys, *Good Morning, Midnight*, 117.
64 'Swing High, Swing Low' [lyrics].
65 Rhys, *Good Morning, Midnight*, 93, her italics.
66 Ibid., 89.
67 Ibid., 16.
68 Williams, 'The Classification of Involuntary Musical Imagery', 10.
69 'Swing High, Swing Low' [lyrics].
70 Rhys, *Good Morning, Midnight*, 24.
71 Sam Halliday, *Sonic Modernity: Representing Sound in Literature, Culture and the Arts* (Edinburgh: Edinburgh University Press, 2013), 72.

72  William Shakespeare, *The Winter's Tale*, ed. Susan Snyder and Deborah T. Curren-Aquino (Cambridge: Cambridge University Press, 2007), Act 4, scene 4, 139–40. Quoted in Frattarola, *Modernist Soundscapes*, n.p.
73  Rhys, *Good Morning, Midnight*, 117.
74  Rhys, letter to Peggy Kirkaldy, 1949, *Letters 1931-1966*, 68.
75  Katherine Mansfield, 'The Fly', in *The Stories of Katherine Mansfield*, ed. Anthony Alpers (Auckland: Oxford University Press, 1984), 32. See Sue Thomas, 'Jean Rhys's Cardboard Doll's Houses', *Kunapipi* 26, no. 1 (2004): 39–53 for an analysis of the connections between Mansfield's story 'The Doll's House' and Rhys's manuscript story 'The Cardboard Dolls' House'. Mansfield's 'The Doll's House', 'Prelude', and 'At the Bay' form a suite of stories about the New Zealand Burnell family. In the late 1930s Rhys also seemed to be projecting a suite of stories about a colonial family, of which 'The Cardboard Dolls' House' is one.
76  Erica L. Johnson, 'Haunted', 15, 32, 16, 32, 33.
77  Rhys, *Good Morning, Midnight*, 89.
78  Ibid., 18, 22–3, 23, 21.
79  Ira E. Hyman, Jr., et al., 'Involuntary to Intrusive: Using Involuntary Musical Imagery to Explore Individual Differences and the Nature of Intrusive Thoughts', *Psychomusicology: Music, Mind and Brain* 25, no. 1 (2015): 24.
80  William Howland Kenney, *Recorded Music in American Life: The Phonograph and Popular Memory, 1890–1945* (New York: Oxford University Press, 1999), xv.
81  Ibid., 5, 19.
82  'Swing High, Swing Low', SecondHandSongs, https://secondhandsongs.com/work/169753/all, accessed 17 July 2019.
83  Frattarola places 'Swing High, Swing Low' only as theme music to the movie. *Modernist Soundscapes*, 135. She does not pick up the tropicality of the film.
84  Arwulf arwulf, 'Tempo King', *All Music*, https://www.allmusic.com/artist/tempo-kings-kings-of-rhythm-mn0001761671, accessed 30 August 2019.
85  Mitchell Leisen, dir. *Swing High, Swing Low*, Paramount Pictures, 1937. Available on *YouTube* at https://www.youtube.com/watch?v=7kfrc6wkm0I.
86  Ibid.
87  Kenney, *Recorded Music in American Life*, 180–1.
88  Rhys, *Good Morning, Midnight*, 155.
89  *Oxford English Dictionary Online*.
90  Bailey, 'Fats Waller Meets Harry Champion', *Cultural and Social History* 4, no. 4 (2007): 498–500.
91  Rhys, *Good Morning, Midnight*, 99.
92  Emery, *Jean Rhys at 'World's End'*, 168.

5

# Composing 'Till September Petronella' and 'Tigers Are Better-Looking'

The complex textual histories of and allusions in 'Till September Petronella' and 'Tigers Are Better-Looking' highlight the historically specific gendered, classed and racialized antagonisms and aggression that may be played out on the repressive grounds of taste and breeding. The intricate layers of allusion and thematic resonance developed in Rhys's revision process establish for readers of the early 1960s her provenance as a modern writer and her engagements with jazz modernist scenes, ragtime in 'Till September Petronella', set in 1914, and swing in 'Tigers Are Better-Looking', set in 1935. Rhys models the Appletree Club in 'Till September Petronella' on the Crabtree Club; in 'Tigers Are Better-Looking' the Jim-Jam Club in Wardour Street, Soho, is closely modelled on the Shim Sham Club, 'lauded in the entertainment press as a harbinger of London's new cosmopolitanism' in 1935.[1] Petronella Gray sings 'Ragtime Violin'; the 'Harlem-style' Shim Sham Club, which operated as a bottle party, specialized in hot swing music in the mid-1930s.[2] Topically for stories published in 1960 and 1962, both have gay characters, repressed in 'Till September Petronella', closeted in 'Tigers Are Better-Looking'. The Wolfenden Committee report had recommended in 1957 that homosexuality be decriminalized; in 1967 the Sexual Offences Act, which legalized homosexual acts between consenting adults over twenty-one in England and Wales, was passed. In 'Till September Petronella' Rhys assays the valency of gaiety and nothingness and in 'Tigers Are Better-Looking' of salvation and damnation. She limns different resonances of salvation and damnation than she had in *Good Morning, Midnight*. Countering Cecil Gray's cavalier dismissal of the possibility that women may experience 'rich melancholy', 'Till September Petronella' focuses on the 'aching affects and devalued words' of Petronella's consciousness, voicing through first-person narrative her 'grey nightmare' of depression.[3] Rhys's develops her representation of Petronella's depression beside Philip Heseltine's description of a depressive episode in 1915. These are silent intertexts.

In 1959, Rhys describes 'Till September Petronella' to Athill as 'Dated. But purposely'.⁴ In a decentring of British historical memory of the First World War, the precise date on which most of the action in 'Till September Petronella' takes place is 28 July 1914, the day on which Austria-Hungary declared war on Serbia. Britain declared war on Germany on 4 September 2014. The temporal setting introduced through revision gives Rhys scope to challenge characterizations of the club and salon scene in pre-war London as 'gay' and to ironize the promise of 'good times' for unmarried women solicited for sex.⁵ Douglas Goldring famously comments, 'The season of 1914 was a positive frenzy of gaiety.' He represents '[t]he period between 1907 and 1914' as 'witness[ing] the last wild orgie in which the dying Victorian world indulged before its downfall'.⁶ In her 1932 memoir *Laughing Torso*, Nina Hamnett describes the iconic modernist club the Cave of the Golden Calf as 'a really gay and cheerful place', a place for her to explore the 'spiritual freedom' proffered by her loss of virginity and bobbing of her hair.⁷ '"*Look gay*," they say. . . . ["]So can you wear something gay tomorrow afternoon?"' artist's model Petronella Gray, the first-person narrator, remembers. '"Not one of those drab affairs you usually clothe yourself in. Gay – do you know the meaning of the word? Think about it, it's very important."'⁸ Fragments of the memory of having been sexually objectified in sexually dissident contexts reverberate in the story, disrupting the linear narrative with an affective experience of depressive time. When Petronella tells the landlord of her Bloomsbury bed-sitting room that she is going away for a couple of weeks, he comments, 'So there's a good time coming for the ladies, is there – a good time coming for the girls?'⁹ The phrase 'good time', used again by a farmer propositioning Petronella for occasional sex in London, allows Rhys to pointedly engage with First and Second World War moral panics over the 'good-time girl'.¹⁰ The *Oxford English Dictionary Online* gives 1928 as the date of first published reference to a good-time girl. The term was popularized during the Second World War, although the term 'amateur' was still in use.¹¹

In 1915, Rhys, then working as an artist's model, was invited by the artist Adrian Allinson (1890–1959), then studying at the Slade School of Art in London, to holiday with him and friends in Gloucestershire. Philip Heseltine (1894–1930), who would become better known as composer Peter Warlock, and his then girlfriend Minnie Lucy (aka Puma) Channing, an artist's model, were among the holidaymakers. The first extant version of Rhys's and Adam's efforts to develop a narrative about the holiday is the Hebertson chapter of 'Triple

Sec' (1924). Here the story of the disastrous rural holiday has three thematic threads: the performance of gender in wartime; the highbrow gendering of mass culture by male aesthetes and its structuring of an alternative male heroic epic of conscientious objection; and the discrepancy between conscientious objection to war service and domestic aggression. The names of the holidaygoers are thinly disguised: Adrian Allinson as Adrian Hebertson, Philip Heseltine as Phil Forrester, A. K. Chanda as Chunder and Shahid Suhrawardy as Chira-wadi. Puma Channing is Billie. Allinson had introduced Heseltine and Channing to each other at the Café Royal, patrons of which would often frequent the Crabtree Club at 17 Greek Street after the café closed for the day. The Crabtree Club was founded by artist Augustus John in April 1914, after the Cave of the Golden Calf, a venue promoting itself as 'given up to gaiety, to a gaiety stimulating thought, rather than crushing it', went out of business.[12] Rhys and Allinson were habitués of the Crabtree Club. Augustus John refers only to the Café Royal and not the Crabtree Club in his Foreword to Cecil Gray's *Peter Warlock: A Memoir of Philip Heseltine*.[13] Heseltine and Channing were fictionalized as Julius Halliday and Minette Darrington (The Pussum) in D. H. Lawrence's *Women in Love* (1921); in *Antic Hay* (1923) Aldous Huxley based Coleman on Heseltine.

Both Heseltine and Rhys experienced depressive episodes over their lives. Heseltine's depressive episodes were so severe by May 1915 that he sought financial assistance to pay for medical treatment.[14] He died in 1930, with an inquest returning an open verdict on the possibility of suicide by 'coal-gas poisoning'.[15] In 1934 Heseltine's close friend Cecil Gray's *Peter Warlock: A Memoir of Philip Heseltine* (with contributions by Augustus John, Robert Nichols and Sir Richard Terry) was published. The holiday is introduced in Gray's memoir through a letter Heseltine sent his mentor Frederick Delius on 2 August 1915, in which he writes very movingly of the depressive episode he has been experiencing:

> [M]y outlook has daily become more confused and trance-like until the difficulty of collecting and writing down myself has been increased to its maximum point. My mind at the present moment is fitly comparable to the blurred humming of the distant peal of bells, whose slow, monotonous droning seems to blend with the grey, listless sky and the still trees, and the far-off, shadow-like hills, in an atmosphere of intolerable dejection and lifelessness on this late summer Sunday evening.... My head feels as though it were filled with a smoky vapour or a poisonous gas which kills all the finer impressions before they can penetrate to me, and stifles every thought, every idea, before it is born.[16]

The writing of the letter, he indicates, had been broken off 'by a nerve-shattering occurrence' which forced him to cut short his holiday.[17] Gray, who has very little understanding of depression, comments on the letter, after noting the female company:

> [N]o mood of depression is deeper or more real than that which comes as a reaction from the opposite extreme. The rich melancholy which exudes from this and many another letter of Philip's is often recognizably that which characterizes the morning after, or which the Greek physician Galen attributes to all living creatures except women and cocks at certain moments, which need not be specified.[18]

In Gray's reading of depression, women, lacking the phallus and the reaches of subjectivity he discerns in Heseltine – exceptionality, genius, individuality – are incapable of 'rich melancholy'. Gray thinks that Heseltine's adoration of Delius's music may have had a vitiating effect on his character, 'for its prevailing mood of tender melancholy and wistful resignation is the most subtle solvent that exists of all the civic and manly virtues, and even of the very will to live. It is the final and supreme expression of the desire for annihilation first voiced by Wagner in *Tristan und Isolde*.'[19] The opera *Tristan und Isolde* had become by the early twentieth century, John Daverio notes, 'a prime symbol of morbid desire, spiritual corruption, and feverish hedonism'.[20]

With ribald innuendo, Rhys and Channing are referred to by Gray as 'attractive young persons of the opposite sex who could not, even on the most charitable assumption, be considered to be the lawful and wedded wives of any of the inmates' of the house rented for the holiday.[21] Commenting on the repressive effect of contemporary biographical propriety, Nichols had complained to Gray that Heseltine 'can't be understood if the girls are indicated only in the most shadowy way'.[22] Details in the draft and published versions of 'Till September Petronella' suggest that Rhys had read Gray's book, particularly Heseltine's and Gray's accounts of the holiday and John's Preface. Barry Smith's 1994 biography of Warlock, in accord with changing biographical protocols concerning treatment of sex and sexuality, indicates his appalling misogyny.[23] John mentions his 'ribaldry and violence of language'.[24]

In 'Till September Petronella' Rhys puts in 'the girls' as more than innuendo in relation to other published accounts of the holiday available to her,[25] and implicitly insists through Petronella's narrative voicing of her depression that a woman, too, may experience 'rich melancholy'. She does not anticipate that her readers need recognize these bearings that have shaped her composition of the story. 'Till September Petronella' assays the depression of protagonist Petronella Gray and the place of Andy Marston and Julian Oakes in exacerbating it by aggressive, misogynistic repudiation of her vernacular modernist taste and breeding and degradation of her subjectivity, and thus humanity.

Rhys's Green Exercise Book of the later 1930s shows that at this time she was working on what could be a memoir of the holiday to supplement Heseltine's or Gray's account of it or a redevelopment of the diary record as contrapuntal fiction. The narrative voice in the Green Exercise Book fragment shifts between first- and third-person, and there are characters named Phil and Adrian. Billie is Phil's girlfriend and Gypsy is Adrian's. The material reworks a moment in 'Triple Sec' when Suzy accuses Phil of unmanliness because he has not enlisted in the armed services. Gypsy's accusation is uttered in the context of Phil's open declaration of his abhorrence of women. A fragment of material that may have been part of the 1940s novel or a much longer version of the 1960 story survives. It is largely a character study of Simone David, a French neighbour of the first-person narrator, whom she admires for her 'so cut-and-dried' attitude to life.[26] A letter from Rhys to Wyndham about the name of the narrator's boyfriend – Harmer – suggests that it dates from well before 1947.[27] The material is reworked into a couple of paragraphs in 'Till September Petronella' and Simone is renamed Estelle. Very fragmentary drafts of parts of the 1940s version of 'Till September Petronella' and of other stories which were in the projected collection *The Sound of the River* – 'Tigers Are Better-Looking', 'Outside the Machine', 'The Lotus', 'A Solid House', 'I Spy a Stranger' and 'Temps Perdi' – are in Rhys's Orange Notebook.[28] In cutting the narrative back from novel length to a short story Rhys might have taken up the challenge posed by Warlock's preference for 'smaller' musical 'forms' which 'concentrate' his creative 'powers', for 'first-rate small work' that 'is of infinitely greater value and significance than a second-rate large one', preference reported by Cecil Gray.[29]

The Crabtree Club features in a couple of the chapters of 'Triple Sec'; in 'Till September Petronella' Petronella brags that she was 'one of the first members' of a club she refers to as the Apple Tree, 'the singing and the gold'.[30] The name suggests temptation and sexual knowledge; 'the singing and the gold' alludes to lines from Gilbert Murray's 1902 translation of Euripides's play *Hippolytus* which describe the locale of the Daughters of the Sunset, 'The Apple-tree, the singing and the gold'.[31] The Daughters of the Sunset are the Hesperides of Greek mythology who tend a tree (or orchard in some stories) which bears golden apples, the eating of which confers eternal life.

The performative and self-mythologizing dimension of bohemian modernist identity-making has been drawn out in memoirs and recent studies of London's café, nightclub and cabaret scenes before the First World War.[32] In her 1929 memoir *Tiger Woman*, Betty May notes of Allinson's performance of the bohemian, for instance, that at the Café Royal he 'had no fear of the picturesque and dressed invariably in a velvet coat and a large stock. He used to play the piano marvelously with his long, sensitive fingers, and he had a wonderful white horse on which he would sometimes ride back to his house in the early hours of the morning. He was also said to possess a wonderful Chinese bed of incredible value.'[33] Gray reports that on the Gloucestershire holiday Heseltine was 'riding a motor-bicycle through the village streets at midnight at a speed of about sixty miles an hour, stark naked'.[34] Brooker notes that women 'brought a new daring to th[is] social scene with their boyish hairstyles [bobbed hair] and colourful fashions, by smoking in public, entering restaurants and walking London's streets unchaperoned, and in their freer sexual attitudes'.[35] While Nina Hamnett was frequenting the Cabaret Club at the Cave of the Golden Calf she 'wore in the daytime a clergyman's hat, a check coat, and a skirt with red facings, including the button-hole, which was faced with red too.... I wore white stockings and men's dancing pumps and was stared at in the Tottenham Court Road. One had to do something to celebrate one's freedom and escape from home.'[36] The prelude to Betty May's representation of her entry into London's artistic and writerly bohemias is an encounter with a 'well-dressed man'. Anticipating an 'adventure' by accompanying him to the West End in a taxi, she is taken aback when he forces himself on her sexually; rebuffed, he tells her of 'the advantages, the clothes, the dinners, the good times' he could offer her in exchange for sex. Further rebuffed, he 'push[es]' May 'down the stairs' of a nightclub, 'a new world containing no familiar figure' in which in freshly acquired 'flamboyant' clothes her 'personality burst suddenly forth in its full particularity'.[37]

In *London's Latin Quarter* (1926) Kenneth Hare represents the Crabtree Club as 'the first of the great Bohemian night clubs', a venue for

> *great talk*, mental unbending, and divine intellectual conversational orgies. 'Shop' talk, where no apology for 'shop' needs to be made, and verbal jousting such as may have burst of old on the entrance of Shakespeare and Ben Jonson under the roof of the Mermaid.... One could keep pace with modern movements in music and poetry by recitals, which were frequently instructive, if occasionally comic.... Augustus John; Epstein and Gaudier-Brzeska, the sculptors; Brodsky; Compton Mackenzie; Stelling ('Mr Gossip' of the *Sketch*); Gerald Cumberland, the author of *Set Down in Malice* – in fact, all the pick of Fleet Street were frequent visitors. Betty May, Billy Gordon, with many of the famous models of the day, and several famous actresses provided a feminine nucleus. The dancing stage was all that could be desired. Randall Cecil, son of Lord William Cecil,

represented aristocracy. The Slade and South Kensington [both art schools] sent contingents of young people brimming over with animal spirits.[38]

May recalls that 'everybody used to do *something* at the Crabtree. They danced or played or were amusing in one way or another. There used to be a stage there for small performances of one kind or another which we used to get up.'[39] Paul Nash disdainfully describes the Crabtree as '[a] place of utter coarseness and dull unrelieved monotony', with a clientele of 'only the very lowest city jews and the most pinched harlots'.[40] In *Smile Please*, Rhys mentions that published accounts of the club that she read 'seemed … rather false … perhaps a lot went on that I didn't know'. She identifies the clientele as 'mostly journalists or painters. If any writers came, I never met them.' 'It was at the Crabtree', she writes, 'that I first made up my mind that somehow I was going to leave England. I hadn't the least idea how I was going to do this, as I hadn't saved up enough money to pay the passage to anywhere, but I was quite determined that this was what I would do.'[41]

There are no scenes set at the Apple Tree in 'Till September Petronella'; for men in the story, the club is part of the sexual provenance of Petronella and Julian Oakes's girlfriend Frankie. Petronella has had her hair bobbed after starting to frequent the Apple Tree, and to Melville, the stranger she meets and has sex with in London, her talk of the Apple Tree, given its reputation, is enough to hint at sexual availability. Brooker points to the way in which bohemian women made 'a break from their own mothers and families, and indeed from the idea of family'.[42] Petronella acknowledges her break with family to herself after Marston queries whether her last name is indeed Gray: '"If you knew how bloody my home was you wouldn't be surprised that I wanted to change my name and forget all about it."'[43] Notably, the Dorian Gray motifs in the story are the othering of a female performer by male aesthetes, an image of a handsome young man – a 'plaster cast' of a head in classical Greek style – and a promise of immortality with the allusion to the grove of the Hesperides.[44]

Illicit heterosexual desire and sexual disgust are coded in 'Till September Petronella' through cross-breeding, crossing of species, and breeding. The adulterous men choose as their sexual objects women of a lower social class. The desire for illicit sex is represented as being in conflict with the sexually conservative, 'white, glaring' embodiments of the dominant rural ideal of Englishness of the Georgian period, a metonym drawn from weather and sky, 'ruddy' citizenship and reproductive sexuality.[45] The territorialism of this public ideal is realized in the hostility of the local people to the bohemianism of the house party. During the First World War, the sexism and classism which underpinned this territorialism would manifest itself in a moral panic around the amateur prostitute. That the public ideal may conflict with private desire is apparent when a farmer tries to recruit Petronella, after Julian's insults have driven her to leave the group, for secretive 'good time[s]' in London, promising her clothes, perfume and jewellery. The farmer propositions her with his 'eyes … fixed' on a portrait of Lady Emma Hamilton in a 'small, dark, stuffy room' of a pub.[46] Hamilton was renowned as the muse and model of artist George Romney and as Lord Horatio Nelson's mistress. Playing to the farmer's sexual and decadent objectification of her, Petronella entertains him by singing Irving Berlin's hit 'Ragtime Violin' (1911) in the car on the way to the railway station. The song celebrates Anna Lize's flirtatious rolling of her eyes with lust at Mr Brown's style of violin playing, a sign of his anticipated sexual prowess, making the instrument 'moan so beautiful'. Readers are left to recall the more sexually suggestive phrases and lines. Anna Lize, for instance, urges Mr Brown to make haste to 'Fid, fid, fid, fiddle the middle' of his violin.[47] (Julian has whistled the second act love duet from Richard Wagner's *Tristan und Isolde*. Frankie patronizes Petronella when she admits that she does not recognize the piece.)

The grey of English weather and skies is in Rhys's oeuvre her most consistent metonym for the cultural and moral disciplining of colonial and lower-class people in England. The association has a mordant edge, for grey is a customary mourning colour in the Caribbean.[48] For Petronella, grey becomes synonymous with depression and an abject, dreary Bloomsbury bed-sitting room. In Rhys's story 'I Spy a Stranger', which is set during the Second World War and a version of which was part of *The Sound of the River*, Laura collects examples of 'propaganda' against women in an exercise book and imagines books which might be written on the strength of it, titles like *Woman an Obstacle to the Insect Civilization?* and *Misogyny and British Humour*.[49] Laura's collection of material enables her both to deflect anxiety about the fates of her friends in Europe, where she had lived for many years, and to ground her critical voice-agency against English values in wartime. The Orange Notebook contains pages of what might be examples of the propaganda Laura collects and of comments on the situation of women in English culture. The phrase 'grey disease of sex hatred', collected by Rhys to name misogyny, is drawn from D. H. Lawrence's essay 'Pornography and Obscenity', published in *Phoenix: The Posthumous Papers of D. H. Lawrence* (1936). There grey is the colour of sexual puritanism, public guardianship of sexual morals, the 'lie of purity' and making 'a dirty little secret' of sex and masturbation.[50] In Petronella's imaginative geography of England the grey and white are menacing.

'Till September Petronella' commences with Petronella's memory of packing for the holiday; grieving after the departure of her French friend and neighbour Estelle for Paris, perhaps permanently, she anticipates the break will cheer her up. Estelle's company and continental sense of style have sustained Petronella in the absence of family. '[T]he thought came to me, like a revelation', Petronella remembers of her grief, 'that I could kill myself at any time I liked and so end it. After that I put a better face on things.' Estelle's 'cut-and-dried' attitude to life transforms the neighbouring Bloomsbury bed-sitting room she rents. The air of Estelle's room – 'alive … it grows in your head' – seems to be 'translated from [a] French or German or Hungarian' novel.[51] They would occasionally dine together on cheap continental fare in line with Estelle's dictum, '"You must have one good meal a day … it is *necessary*."'[52] The memory of the meals becomes part of a motif of taste which draws out the shifting provenance of Petronella's depression brought about by the events of the holiday.

Adulterous male English desire, associated with extreme whiteness, exoticizes its objects, wanting them to be 'gay' (bohemian), not 'drab affairs'; however, Rhys invites the knowing reader to identify the homosocial bond between Marston and Julian as being secured by repressed gayness.[53] (The *Oxford English Dictionary Online* gives 1922 as the date of the first published instance of gay meaning homosexual.) While not taking up the thematic of repressed homosexuality, Judith Kegan Gardiner observes the relative indifference of Marston and Julian towards Petronella and Frankie, pertinently describing their relationship as 'a sexual and professional competition, that resembles a courtship'.[54] Marston does try to deflect Julian's attack on Petronella, saying it is 'not being fair to the girl'. Through allusion to T. S. Eliot's 'The Love Song of J. Alfred Prufrock' ('That is not it at all') Rhys suggests that Marston finds it 'impossible to say just what' he 'mean[s]'.[55] Petronella calls Marston and Julian's relationship '"a mutual admiration society"'.[56] Casually assuming secure heteronormativity in a reading of 'Till September Petronella' as a short story *à clef*, Angier argues that Heseltine 'desired' Rhys, 'What else could the explosion between Marston and Julian mean? "You're letting your jealousy run away with you," says Marston: "Jealousy?" Julian shrieks. "Jealous of what?"'[57] There is a gay subtext to the scene that includes this exchange. Julian, who has been reading a book about the 'biological inferiority of women', insults Petronella, calling her 'fifth rate', a 'ghastly cross between a barmaid and a chorus-girl', a 'female spider' who instead of acting as Marston's sexual muse has stopped 'him from working', and tells her: '"And then I try to get him away from you, of course you follow him down here."'[58] When Marston mentions Julian's jealousy, the reference may be to Petronella as object of his

(Marston's) sexual interest. Julian points out to Marston that Petronella does not desire him sexually, which implies that he (Julian) has no sexual rival. The worldly Frankie tells Julian, 'you hate girls really'. The place of the sexualized bodies of women in the subtext of the homosocial bond between the two men is a reassuring display of heteronormativity on the parts of Marston and Julian, for themselves, each other and the locals. The momentary exposure of the subtext transforms Julian's 'beautiful eyes' to 'mean, little pits' of rage and denial.[59] The scene is part of a thematic around the idea of blind eyes: Petronella resisting the implication of being seen as a 'drab' affair; Julian insisting that Marston cannot recognize Petronella's use of him; hypocrisy.

The image of the transformation of Julian's eyes reworks the moment in the Hebertson chapter of 'Triple Sec', set a year later than 'Till September Petronella', when Forrester becomes incandescent with anger after Suzy asks why he and Hebertson have not enlisted to fight in the war. Suzy's relationship with Hebertson is placed in the contexts of wartime romance, Suzy's sentimentalization of soldier heroes and her falling out with a soldier fiancé at the front. She agrees to join a house party in a bungalow near Cheltenham, only to find that both Forrester and Hebertson attack and pressure her because she refuses to have sex with Hebertson.[60] Suzy observes aspects of Forrester's and Hebertson's performances of manliness, neither of which accords with the civic norms of masculinity embodied in the soldier hero which Graham Dawson argues sustain the British 'national epic' of progress in liberal interpretations of history.[61] In *The Gender of Modernity*, Rita Felski usefully elaborates the way in which femininity became available as a set of mimicable signs for male aesthetes. '[J]ust as nineteenth-century ideals of progress, heroism, and national identity became identified with a somatic norm of healthy masculinity, so the motif of the feminized male offered a provocative refusal of such ideals,' she argues.[62] The performance of femininized masculinity may not necessarily, however, indicate the emergence of an authentic homosexual identity.[63] Heseltine's feminized masculinity would lead many people who met him in this period to suspect homosexuality;[64] his biographer Barry Smith concludes that Heseltine may have had 'a touch of unacknowledged homosexuality in his make-up' and 'some slight sexual ambivalence'.[65]

Aesthetes Forrester and Hebertson other Suzy by marking her out as vulgar. Felski argues that 'the notion of vulgarity reveals its symbolic centrality, as the epitome of everything that aestheticism is not'.[66] The vulgar becomes 'the site of dreaded identification against which – and by virtue of which – the domain of the subject', here the aesthete as conscientious objector, 'will circumscribe its own claim to autonomy and life'.[67] For Suzy that site is that of the prostitute, although she is sexually experienced. In aestheticism, the vulgar comprises a dreaded materiality – 'nature, matter, brute fact – but also the realm of popular (that is, nonelite) culture, the coarse, unrefined, tawdry life of ordinary individuals'. The excoriation of the vulgar is marked by specific class and gender investments, with 'women and the masses merg[ing] as twin symbols of the democratizing mediocrity of modern life, embodying a murky threat to the precarious status and identity of the artist'.[68] Forrester berates Suzy for hurting Hebertson by not becoming his muse and lover, while Hebertson's pressuring of her is more passively aggressive. Forrester, who whistles opera, and speaks of his involvement in establishing a new avant-garde musical magazine, excoriates Suzy as a loathsome chorus girl. Assuming positions of highbrow male reason, Forrester finds Suzy's deflective comments on the war mindless and Hebertson argues with her about the logical and moral defensibility of war. Their conscientious objection is grounded in a heroic distancing of themselves from a feminized pro-war mass culture in wartime. The irony is that neither Hebertson nor Forrester respects Suzy's refusal to be coerced into sex by the popular war mood or by their assumption of her sexual availability as model and former chorus-girl. The language used to describe the conduct of Forrester, Hebertson and Billie – the Indian friends are yet to arrive – is full of military metaphors. The metaphors highlight, in particular, that Forrester's pacifism does not extend to his patterns of response to tensions in personal relations.

In 'Till September Petronella', Rhys does not suggest that the 'desire for annihilation' in Wagnerian opera corrupts Julian's 'civic and manly virtues' (in Cecil Gray's interpretation of Heseltine). Rather, she indicates that Julian's upper-class values, which link 'natural and cultural breeding, pedigree and good taste',[69] and his self-comforting conceptualization of women as a biologically inferior class of human beings to men underpin his attack on Petronella as 'fifth rate'.[70] Wagnerian opera and his work as a music critic are markers for him of his superior cultural breeding. Philip Cohen argues that the aristocratic code of breeding (articulated, too, as an aristocracy of reason as a *practice of refined sensibility*), implicated in the development of Anglo-Saxon racism, was

> modelled on feudalism's three estates. At the top were the English ruling class 'the naturally cultured,' who bore the indelible marks of superior breeding in both senses of the word [pedigree and good taste]; below them were a class of uncultivated humans, who shared the status of domesticated pets or well-bred farm animals, occupying a space midway between the salon and the jungle; this was the group who might be civilised. And at the bottom were those subhumans of entirely savage disposition, wild beyond any possible redemption.[71]

For Julian, Petronella belongs to the third group and Frankie to the second. Julian processes his sense of Frankie's inferiority through an othering discourse of racial ancestry, calling her a 'Phoenician from Cornwall, England'. He insists, according to Frankie, who mocks the class pretensions of his family, that she 'go and be patronized and educated by his detestable mother in her dreary house in the dreary country', knowing that his mother will play the dismissive guardian of the bloodline.[72] When she argues with him he derides her intelligence.

Rhys uses allusion to draw out Marston's badgering of Petronella. When Petronella, who has been dazzled by Julian's classical good looks and whistling of the love duet in Wagner's *Tristan and Isolde*, is cold towards Marston, he plays out his disappointment theatrically by reciting the final verse of Paul Verlaine's 'Il pleure dans mon coeur' ('It rains in my heart') and, more aggressively, lines from Robert Browning's satirical 'A Pretty Woman':

'But for loving, why you would not, Sweet, …
    Though we prayed you,
      Paid you, brayed you. [sic]
In [sic] a mortar – for you could not, Sweet'.[73]

Marston's recitation of Verlaine invokes the 'fatigued heart', a 'conventionally postured sentiment of decadent weariness'.[74] Cecil Gray holds up Verlaine as having, like Warlock, a supreme 'talent … exclusively miniaturist and lyrical'.[75] 'A Pretty Woman' takes up the question of unreciprocated love for a woman whose 'grace' is her 'sweet face' and finally recommends that 'the rose' not be 'gather[ed]' but rather 'throw[n] away'.[76] The voice of Browning's poem asks at one point of 'Sweet',

Shall we burn up, tread that face at once
    Into tinder
    And so hinder
Sparks from kindling all the place at once?[77]

Petronella feels 'shut in' by the 'hot', 'white' 'glare' of the summer's day, Julian and Marston. After Julian's damnation of her, Petronella walks out 'dazed', 'feeling, as if somebody had hit' her 'on the head' and decides to return to London. While Marston worries that the downhearted Petronella might have 'made away with herself', Julian is nonchalant: 'She's not the sort to kill herself. I told you that.'[78]

It is implied through a story Frankie tells about Petersen, a new playwright, that the bohemian circle to which Marston and Julian belong takes up people as new talent, exploiting their entertainment value, encouraging them to make spectacles of themselves and dropping them when they become in its eyes 'really sordid'. This consumption of people is represented metaphorically as the action of a 'gigantic maw'.[79] This ironically counterpoints Julian's sense of Petronella's sordidness compressed in his spider image, a conflated figure of predation, 'engulfing femininity'[80] and a 'devouring' mass culture.[81] In *Spider*, Katarzyna Michalska and Sergiusz Michalska note the association of the female spider from the beginning of the seventeenth century in Europe with the femme fatale and her web with the 'art of seduction', 'erotic entrapment', death and 'sexuality as such, including the inner erotic demons of males'. These symbolic resonances have largely fallen out of use since the Second World War. The Michalskas draw attention to the emergence in 1850s France of an 'image of the – mostly clandestine – prostitute as a spider-like seductress seated in a café'.[82] This image resonates with Julian's claim to Marston that Petronella is only after his 'money'.[83]

To set up the 1940s version of 'Till September Petronella' as a narrative about a depressive rite of passage, Rhys takes from 'Triple Sec' an image of a pervasive cultural menace by which Suzy Gray feels threatened. Both Heseltine and Suzy experience the menace integral to their depressions as a predatory creature poised to pounce on them.[84] The image in 'Triple Sec' compresses the beastliness of the men among whom Suzy circulates and reworks the usual imperial association of the centre of empire with light. The sexuality of the white men who consume Suzy sexually is represented as largely vampiric and predatory. The men operate outside the codes of 'moral' or 'domestic manliness' which developed under evangelical influence through the nineteenth century.[85] The darkness of the sexuality has principally Christian, but also racial referents, and accords with established melodramatic conventions in which London is represented as a place of sexual danger.[86] The effect on Suzy of the sense of menace and of her assimilation as innocent colonial into a disciplining set of class and gender relations in England is depression, which develops after an abortion into a major depressive episode. Suzy becomes severely depressed again during the winter of 1914/15.

Petronella's depression is linked echoingly through the word '*nothing*' with the angry transformation of Julian's 'beautiful eyes' to 'little, mean pits' – 'you looked down them into nothingness'.[87] Rhys reworks from 'Triple Sec' the butchery motif which references colloquial language about prostitution. Back in London in her now 'crumpled white dress', and desperate not to return to the greyness of her room, Petronella is picked up by Melville.[88] Petronella's sex with Melville is not pleasurable, not the modern, sexualized 'good time' slyly hinted at by her landlord or promised by the farmer. She plays the part scripted by masculine expectations of the amateur, her performance characterized by a depressive and demoralized '*exhaustion of erotic drives*'.[89] Positioning him and herself as butchered meat, Petronella acknowledges that their consumption of sex in a private club bedroom of the kind 'that always looks as if its ostentatious whiteness hides dinginess' '*tastes of nothing*', not even the physicality of sweat. Sharing a taxi with Melville that will take her home, Petronella again starts to sing 'Ragtime Violin', this time to stay 'awake'. With authorial irony, Rhys has Melville formulaically tell Petronella as he departs, '"And you've been so sweet to me"', and she responds in kind, '"The pleasure was all mine."'[90] The memory of the sexual encounter with Melville begins with her memory of a snippet of conversation between Frankie and the largely vegetarian Marston, who 'says he can't touch any meat except cold ham' – a conversation which over a short time has acquired sexual innuendo, with tasting beef becoming a euphemism for having sex. When Frankie urges Marston, '"You must have your first bite [of steak] tonight"', he responds, '"It won't be my first bite … I've been persuaded to taste beef before. … I thought it would taste like sweat … and it did."'[91] Petronella remembers: '"*I've been persuaded to taste it before*," Marston said. "*It tasted exactly as I thought it would.*" … *But Marston should have said, "It tastes of nothing, my dear, it tastes of nothing …* "'[92] The allusion to the apples of the Hesperides in the story draws out the contrast between their promise of immortality and nothing and nothingness as death and contempt. In *Black Sun: Depression and Melancholia*, Julia Kristeva points to the significance of such iteration of the word 'nothing': 'As if overtaxed or destroyed by too powerful a breaker, our symbolic means find themselves hollowed out, nearly wiped out, paralyzed. On the edge of silence the word "nothing" emerges, a discreet defense in the face of so much disorder, both internal and external, incommensurable.'[93]

In 'Tigers Are Better-Looking', Mr Severn, the weekly London correspondent for an Australian newspaper, struggles to write a column about a grand imperial occasion, the celebration of George V and Queen Mary's Silver Jubilee, which commenced on 6 May 1935: 'He couldn't get the swing of it. The swing's the thing, as everybody knows – otherwise the cadence of the sentence. … Words whirled round in his head, but he could not make them take shape.'[94] Like Petronella vis-a-vis Julian, Severn has been dazed by personal rejection. Severn's flatmate or partner Hans has moved out abruptly the morning after a party, leaving a letter in which he dubs Severn both 'a tame grey mare' and one of 'a pack of timid tigers waiting to spring the moment anybody is in trouble or hasn't any money. *But tigers are better-looking, aren't they?*'[95] 'Grey mare' is a term for 'a wife who is the dominant or more competent partner in a marriage'.[96]

Tropicality is invoked in the contrast between the tiger and the mare, with the tiger serving as a foil to the temperate ('tame') mare.[97] The phrase '*tigers are better-looking*' particularly haunts Severn. In a story which plays heavily on euphemism, toeing lines of propriety, conditions of sayability and knowing readers, Hans's multilingual salutation 'Mein Lieb, Mon Cher, My Dear, Amigo' and innuendo ('much that it is *better* not to go into', 'you'll have to have your tea straight, my dear', effeminizing a man by calling him a 'mare') leave open the distinct probability that they have been lovers. At the least, Hans has found himself an object of Severn's sexual desire. Severn thinks, 'He had always known Hans would hop it sooner or later, so why this taste in his mouth, as if he had eaten dust', an allusion to Gen. 3.14, God's condemnation of the serpent which tempted Eve to eat forbidden fruit: 'dust shalt thou eat all the days of thy life'.[98] Severn is concerned about divine and social judgement for not 'toe[ing] the line. You will be slain and not spared. Threats and mockery, mockery and threats.'[99] 'Threats' may be a euphemism for blackmail or homophobic violence.

As well as the protagonist's repressed homosexuality and his visit to a jazz club, what is particularly new in the story published in the *London Magazine* compared with fragmentary draft material for the story in the Black Exercise Book of the late 1930s and the subsequent Orange Notebook is Rhys's sharp emphasis on the cultural pervasiveness of 'desolat[ing]' ideas of sin and damnation,[100] and the biblical, vernacular and gestural languages of salvation and damnation, including sneers. In exploring the boundaries between the licit and the illicit and the orderly and the disorderly, Rhys crosses freshly a range of sites of law and policing: sexuality, alcohol licensing, conduct in public places, police cell, Bow Street Magistrate's Court and generalizations about people. Rhys even draws attention in her telling of the narrative to the euphemisms for swear words she as author has to employ to preserve propriety in the 1960s – 'basket' for bastard, 'sugars' for shits, 'blank' for an oath or profanity and 'something somethings'.[101] The curses 'bloody', 'damned', 'Go to hell' and 'To hell with' are useable.[102] This reflexivity resonates with Severn's need as a journalist to censor his political views in deference to publisher and audience expectations. By story's end, '[w]ords and meaningless phrases' no longer 'whirl tormentingly round' in Severn's 'head' and he begins afresh writing a suitably patriotic article about the royal jubilee.[103]

Rhys presents Severn as 'educated, settled, white',[104] living with Hans after offering him hospitality during his convalescence after having broken a leg. The scenario is another variation of the good Samaritan motif in *Quartet* (the Heidlers helping Marya when she is in difficulty). As with Marya, Hans attracts the sexual interest of his host. 'Mr Severn is *severed* and *severe*, a case of destructive isolation and detachment whose interiority corrodes social relations,' observes Rishona Zimring.[105] For Nadia Ellis, Severn would be the 'kind of gay man' who 'helped pave the way for legal inclusion. The image of men living companionably together in arrangements not unlike heterosexual marriages varied from images of male queerness that often gathered around the theatrical, the outlandish, and the outlawed.'[106] Severn's flat is decorated with 'woodcuts from Amsterdam, … chintz covered armchairs, the fading bowl of flowers in the long mirror', oilskin curtains (suggested by Hans) and Severn shows a will to aestheticize the view from it.[107] While Severn might be a figure of private sexual dissidence from heteronormativity and more open Leftish political dissidence – 'talk about Communism' and anti-royal leanings – Rhys exposes the limits of his acceptance of difference by highlighting his racism and class snobberies. In his letter, Hans confronts Severn over the ferocity of the 'sneers' at him, 'enough to last … for the next thirty years'; his circle would 'would pine to death if' it 'hadn't someone to look down on and insult'.[108] Disconcerted by Hans's rebuff, Severn, later that evening, in the company of Heather and Maidie Richards (the alias of Gladys Reilly), women he has met at his local Bloomsbury pub, visits the Jim-Jam Club, a cosmopolitan jazz club in Soho, thinking sardonically, 'The things one does on the rebound.'[109] Severn is ejected from the club by a bouncer and he and Maidie are arrested during a melee outside, kept in police cells overnight and fined in court the next day. Having read on his cell wall, '"Lord save me; I perish" and underneath, "SOS, SOS, SOS" (signed G. R.)', he adds the graffiti 'SOS, SOS, SOS (Signed N. S.)'.[110] SOS is often said to be an abbreviation of Save Our Souls.

That Rhys had frequented the Shim Sham Club is suggested by the accuracy of architectural detail in 'Tigers Are Better-Looking'. On 14 June 1935 she and husband Leslie Tilden Smith were arrested at 4 am in Wardour Street, Soho on the charge of being 'Drunk and Disorderly'.[111] Opening at 37 Wardour Street in March 1935, the Shim Sham Club operated as a bottle party, an arrangement that circumvented liquor licensing laws, allowing alcohol to be consumed after hotel closing hours. The name Shim Sham plays on the bottle party's relation to the law, one of the meanings of shim-sham being '[s]omething that is intended to be mistaken for something else, or that is not really what it purports to be; a spurious imitation, a counterfeit'.[112] Judith Walkowitz explains the operation of bottle parties:

> In commercial venues, the bottle party worked as follows: individuals were invited to a 'party' and would arrange with wine agents to order drinks for themselves in advance. As participants in a private party, revelers were outside

the law and could drink as late into the night as they wished. In practice strangers gained admission to these resorts by paying money at the door; once inside, they could obtain drinks from a hostess who had reserved bottles in advance. Once the legality of bottle parties was upheld in a 1932 court case, they proliferated across the West End by 1934. In 1935, police estimated fifty known bottle parties in and around Soho, but press estimates far exceeded that number.[113]

By October 1935 Jack Isow and Ike Hatch, the proprietors of the Shim Sham, were convicted of 'operating an unlicensed club'.[114] Marc Matera notes that Isow was 'a Polish Jew born in Russia', and Ike Hatch was an 'African American singer'. 'Isow brought significant capital and experience to the venture; well known from the variety stage, records, and radio, Hatch served as the public face of the club.'[115] Writing in 1936 for *Melody Maker,* Rudolph Dunbar hails Hatch's success with the Shim Sham Club, relating it to the 'enhanced status of the Negro' brought about by Paul Robeson's role in *Sanders of the River*; the establishment of Aggrey House, 'named after the distinguished African philosopher, Dr James Emman Kwegyir Aggrey', 'to develop a better understanding between whites and blacks'; the profile of boxer Joe Louis; and the Italo-Abyssinia War.[116] George 'Happy' Blake's band performed at the Shim Sham in its earliest days. Happy Blake and his brother, musician Cyril Blake, were from Trinidad. Matera notes of Soho that by the 1930s a

> 'queer migration' to its black after-hours clubs was well under way. The presence of black bodies and music in the district's nightclubs also linked these urban spaces to colonial settings across the empire, underscoring the intimate relationship between them as if instantiating a sort of return of the repressed colonial Other. The specters of unconventional sexuality and of blacks mixing with whites threatened to invert the racial order of empire.[117]

The moral panic produced by the spectres underpinned anonymous complaints to the police about the Shim Sham Club. Judith Walkowitz outlines the reported grievances:

> 'The patter of the cabaret' was 'an absolute scandal' while 'the encouragement of Black and White intercourse is the talk of the town,' declared one anonymous writer in April 1935. A second anonymous letter, from a 'neighbour in the rear of Wardour Street,' declared the Shim Sham to be a 'den of vice and iniquity': 'there is a negro band, white woman [sic] carrying on perversion, women with women, men with men, a second Caravan Club.' (This refers to a 'queer' club closed in 1934 … ) Some 'obnoxious things' happened in the lavatories, the letter writer added. 'One who has been there' alleged that 'Snow' and 'hashish' were sold in the form of cigarettes.[118]

Walkowitz also notes the mixing in the club of 'Jewish anti-fascists and Communists, as well as black pan-Africanists'.[119] Matera draws out the importance of the black clubs in the development of a pan-African international political consciousness among the black clientele and in the transnational circulation of black musical forms.

In 'Tigers Are Better-Looking', Rhys's character Heather calls the club she, Severn and Maidie struggle to find the Jim-Jam Club, although she declares that the club to which she takes them has changed its name. Heather's acquaintance with the host of the Jim-Jam Club and payment of entrance fees gain the trio access. Like shim-sham, jim-jam is a 'reduplicated term, of which the elements are unexplained; ... compare *flim-flam, trim-tram, whim-wham*, etc.'.[120] Rhys's naming of the bottle party the Jim-Jam Club highlights jazz (jam) and its expressive styles (including swing) as the club's musical idiom.[121] The Shim Sham (or Shim Sham Shimmy) is a tap dance routine developed in the late 1920s (as the Goofus) and performed on Harlem stages in the early 1930s, including at Dickie Wells's Shim Sham Club and the 101 Ranch. There are several accounts of its origins. In *Tap Dancing America*, Constance Valis Hill states: 'While Leonard Reed claimed to have created this routine combination with his partner Willie Bryant, it is more likely that it evolved in collaboration with the female sisters of the Whitman Sisters troupe.'[122] Under racial segregation Reed, Bryant and the Whitman Sisters performed on the black vaudeville circuit. Howard 'Stretch' Johnson claims:

> [T]he Shim-Sham or Shimmy was a dance invented by homosexuals from the chorus line at the 101 Ranch. 'Shim' was a contraction of the term *'she-him,'* and the 'sham' was a word serving the dual purpose of denoting the female role played by males, as well as the shambling nature of the steps, particularly the first eight bars. The Shimmy combined a hip and shoulder wiggle that was part of the opening movements.[123]

Rhys uses Severn's social interactions at the Jim-Jam Club to expose his boorish racism and the brittleness of the veneer of interwar cosmopolitanism at English jazz clubs. Talking to himself, Severn identifies Heather as '[d]isdainful, debonair and with a touch of the tar brush too, or I'm much mistaken. Just my type. One of my types. Why is it that she isn't quite – Now, why?' He then starts drawing pictures of *'face, faces, faces'* in 'yellow pencil' on a tablecloth, faces '[l]ike hyaenas, like swine, like goats, like apes, like parrots. But not tigers, because tigers are better-looking'.[124] The hybrid animalized faces are reminiscent of Julian's classed excoriation of Petronella as a 'ghastly cross between a barmaid and chorus-girl', a 'female spider'.[125] Severn's doodles suggest an underlying racism, especially about the 'bit mixed'.[126] In 'Pornography and Obscenity', with which I have shown Rhys was familiar, Lawrence suggests that obscenity is in the eye of the beholder and that people should make individual judgements on what is obscene or not rather than unquestioningly follow 'mob-indignation, mob-condemnation'.[127] Severn insists that his doodles are not 'obscene'; Rhys shows them to be part of a pattern of churlish and racist behaviour at the club. Bouncers remove Severn from the club for his insistence on his right to doodle after being asked to desist and drunken shouting and swearing at the orchestra. On being forced to leave, he gives Heather a 'hideous grimace', causing her to avert 'her eyes', and exclaim 'My Lawd!'[128] Gregg notes that Severn's 'confusion over the pronunciation of her name' – he hears it at one point as Hedda – suggests Heather's West Indian heritage: 'In West Indian Creoles, the Received Standard English sound *th* is often changed to *d*.'[129] He has met Heather at a Bloomsbury pub, which suggests that she is part of 'the significant African, Caribbean and Asian presence in interwar Bloomsbury, which included students, anti-colonial activists, writers, poets, musicians, artists and actors.... Bloomsbury was a cosmopolitan space, and far more diverse than has been remembered, partly due to the prevailing historical memory which often defines Bloomsbury in relation to the "Bloomsbury Group."'[130] The third-person narrator of 'Tigers Are Better-Looking' describes the host of the club as 'yellow' and the saxophonist as 'mulatto'. Severn demands of the orchestra, '"Play *Dinah, is there anyone finer? That's a good old tune*", shouting, '"I hate that bloody tune you keep playing."'[131] 'Dinah', a jazz standard, with lyrics by Sam M. Lewis and Joseph Young and music by Harry Akst, was popularized by Ethel Waters in 1926. It was also recorded by Josephine Baker in 1926, Louis Armstrong in 1930 and Cab Calloway, Duke Ellington and His Orchestra and Bing Crosby and the Mills Brothers in 1932.[132] Severn is initially more at ease with a 'lovely dark brown couple' he spoke to 'at the bar' while Maidie had spent a great deal of time in the toilet ostensibly talking with a female 'friend' of hers. He tells Maidie that they had rebuffed his invitation to visit him at home, with the woman denigrating a Bloomsbury address. But he had racializingly pilloried her query, 'Is that in Mayfair?' with a play on the idea of darkest Africa: 'Good Lord, no; it's in the darkest, dingiest Bloomsbury.' The woman turned on 'the most perfect British accent, high, sharp, clear and shattering', saying, 'I didn't come to London to go to the slums.' He does not deign to tell Maidie what he thought he 'palled up with the man' over.[133]

Maidie functions in the story as a symbol of a colonial white diaspora, a monitory image of a dishevelled female drunk and a mouthpiece for hasty generalizations about people. Her real family name, Reilly, and drunken cry, 'God save Ireland', indicate Irish heritage. Severn and she drink at the same local pub; he finds her 'good-natured' and 'pleasant to talk to' there, imagining 'her epitaph: "I have never made anybody feel nervous – on purpose." Doomed, of course, for that very reason.' Her presence is benign. He dismisses her when she plays into his anxiety about damnation and offends his vanity by referring to them both as aging. The cultural milieu is saturated with phrases and sayings about damnation, for example, an ad in 'the personal column, in small print, "I will slay in the day of My wrath and spare not, saith the Lord God"' and police cell graffiti: '"Be sure your sins will find you out. B. Lewis."'[134] Maidie compares and judges the capacities of Heather, 'a very dark girl' reminiscent of beautiful Mexican actress Dolores del Rio, and a woman with 'great hairy legs and no stockings' to 'get on' in life. The hairy-legged woman, who 'didn't care a damn' about appearances and was 'laughing and joking' in the vicinity of Bow Street Magistrates Court would, Maidie thinks, always 'come out all right'. Heather is 'too ambitious' and the 'lovely' woman is too anxious. 'And it isn't any good *wanting* to be adapted, you've got to be born adapted,' Maidie opines.[135] Maidie is suggesting that breeding is paramount.

The process of Severn finally recovering his 'swing', 'phrases, suave and slick' rather than 'tormenting', is catalysed by the spectacle of an elderly male busker performing an acrobatic trick with a 'walking-stick' outside his block of flats and no passer-by thinking him 'worth a penny'. Severn's trick of turning out 'swell' columns is a paying proposition, will keep him from begging on streets. He recomposes his I/'eye' 'in the mirror' and rejoicingly types 'JUBILEE ... '[136]

In 'Till September Petronella' Rhys resites and revises materials from several versions of a narrative begun forty-five years earlier to tell another fictional side to Gray's and John's narratives of Peter Warlock, and contrapuntally to plumb the depths of female depression and demythologize the legend of the season of 1914 being 'a positive frenzy of gaiety'. Colloquial usages of words like 'gay' and 'good time' are key markers of historical temporality and meaning. With alertness to irony, Rhys works to make sense, in particular, of the class and gender issues at stake in her material and the ways in which these are articulated through discourses of taste and breeding. In the Hebertson chapter of 'Triple Sec', English misogyny and homosociality are articulated through a class discourse of modernist aestheticism, which also structures the subjectivities of conscientious objectors. Rhys introduces a thematic of repressed, and by virtue of this, repressive homosexuality in 'Till September Petronella'. The misogyny and homosociality of Julian and Marston are articulated here through an aristocratic code of breeding. Suzy and Petronella become for them, especially for Forrester and Julian, figures of the 'democratized mediocrity of modern life' which threatens to engulf the highbrow artist. The trauma of the holiday for Suzy is not highlighted in 'Triple Sec'. In 'Till September Petronella' Rhys draws out the 'aching affects' of Petronella's depression, particularly through the language of nothingness. In *Wide Sargasso Sea*, Rhys would later use the language of nothingness, by contrast, to draw out her Rochester figure's psychological disorientation in the tropics. Rhys worked on 'Tigers Are Better-Looking' between the late 1930s and 1960, when it was accepted for publication by the *London Magazine*. It was for a time misplaced '*in an obscure file in the London Magazine office*'.[137] Through revision, Rhys develops fine narrative layers around inhospitality to the 'stranger' (non-white, non-English, non-heteronormative and the busker) at personal and civic levels. She brings out the vitiating milieu generated by conservative and fixed ideas of salvation and damnation. In post-Windrush Britain, she highlights the continuity of black migration and travel to London across the twentieth century and of anti-cosmopolitan racism.

# Notes

1  Walkowitz, *Nights Out*, 243.
2  Michael Pickering, *Blackface Minstrelsy in Britain* (Aldershot: Ashgate, 2008), 196.
3  Cecil Gray, *Peter Warlock: A Memoir of Philip Heseltine* (London: Jonathan Cape, 1934), 103; Kristeva, *Black Sun*, 246; Rhys, 'Till September Petronella', 10.
4  Rhys, letter to Diana Athill, 11 June 1959, *Letters 1931–1966*, 167.
5  Betty May, *Tiger Woman: My Story* (1929; repr., London: Duckworth Overlook, 2014), 35.
6  Douglas Goldring, *South Lodge: Reminiscences of Violet Hunt, Ford Madox Ford and the* English Review *Circle* (London: Constable, 1943), 148.
7  Nina Hamnett, *Laughing Torso* (New York: Ray Long and Richard R. Smith, 1932), 47, 44.
8  Jean Rhys, 'Till September Petronella', in *Tigers Are Better Looking: With a Selection from* The Left Bank, by Jean Rhys (1968; repr., Harmondsworth: Penguin, 1972), 16, her emphasis.
9  Ibid., 10–11.
10 Ibid., 26.
11 Marilyn Lake gives many instances of this in 'Female Desires: The Meaning of World War II', *Australian Historical Studies* no. 95 (October 1990), 267–84.

12 Nathan Waddell, 'Bohemian Retrospects: Ford Madox Ford, Post-War Memory and the Cabaret Theatre Club', in *Modernist Party*, ed. Kate McLoughlin (Edinburgh: Edinburgh University Press, 2013), 198.
13 Augustus John, 'Foreword', in *Peter Warlock: A Memoir of Philip Heseltine*, by Cecil Gray (London: Jonathan Cape, 1934), 11–15.
14 Barry Smith, *Peter Warlock: The Life of Philip Heseltine* (Oxford: Oxford University Press, 1994), 71.
15 Cecil Gray, *Peter Warlock: A Memoir of Philip Heseltine* (London: Jonathan Cape, 1934), 290.
16 Quoted in ibid., 100.
17 Quoted in ibid., 101.
18 Quoted in ibid., 103–4.
19 Ibid., 59–60.
20 John Daverio, '*Tristan und Isolde*: Essence and Appearance', in *The Cambridge Companion to Wagner*, ed. Thomas S. Grey (Cambridge: Cambridge University Press, 2011), 116.
21 Gray, *Peter Warlock*, 103.
22 Quoted in Smith, *Peter Warlock*, 110.
23 Gray (*Peter Warlock*) includes an 'excellent little poem in Latin' by Heseltine on 151, not noting its virulent misogyny; Smith (*Peter Warlock*) translates it on 123–4. Heseltine's humour is particularly misogynistic. In 1917 the amateur was excoriated in the *Times* as a vampire. See Thomas, *Worlding of Jean Rhys*, 68. Heseltine's comments about Channing, then his wife, and about H. D. around this time use this trope viciously (Smith, *Peter Warlock*, 107).
24 John, Foreword, in *Peter Warlock*, by Gray, 15.
25 Eugene Goossens also mentions Heseltine's holiday in the Cotswolds in *Overture and Beginners: A Musical Autobiography* (London: Methuen, 1951), 111–12. He mentions Cecil Gray, Allinson, himself and Heseltine's 'East Indian mistress (whose dusky charms caused considerable comment among the neighbours)' as being in the party (111).
26 Rhys, 'Till September Petronella', 9.
27 In a letter to Francis Wyndham on 8 July 1959, Rhys asks: 'Would it be possible to alter the name *Harmer* – make it say *Marston*? It was written long before my own name was Hamer!' *Letters 1931–1966*, 169–70. Rhys married Max Hamer in 1947.
28 The Notebook also contains draft material for 'Overture and Beginners Please' in a much later handwriting of Rhys's. This story was published in *Sleep It Off, Lady*.
29 Gray, *Peter Warlock*, 23.
30 Rhys, 'Till September Petronella', 32.
31 Quoted in James Morwood, 'Gilbert Murray's Translations of Greek Tragedy', in *Gilbert Murray Reassessed: Hellenism, Theatre, and International Politics*, ed. Christopher Stray (Oxford: Oxford University Press, 2007), 135.

32  Apart from Brooker's *Bohemia in London*, see, for instance, Richard Cork, *Art beyond the Gallery in Early 20th Century England* (New Haven, CT: Yale University Press, 1985); Lisa Tickner, *Modern Life & Modern Subjects: British Art in the Early Twentieth Century* (New Haven: Yale University Press, 2000); Urmila Seshagiri, *Race and the Modernist Imagination* (Ithaca, NY: Cornell University Press, 2010); and Waddell, 'Bohemian Retrospects'.
33  May, *Tiger Woman*, 45, her emphasis.
34  Gray, *Peter Warlock*, 103.
35  Brooker, *Bohemia in London*, 125–6.
36  Hamnett, *Laughing Torso*, 48.
37  May, *Tiger Woman*, 34–5, 36, 37, 40.
38  Kenneth Hare, *London's Latin Quarter* (London: John Lane, 1926), 38–42, his emphasis.
39  May, *Tiger Woman*, 77.
40  Michael Holroyd, *Augustus John: The New Biography* (1996; London: Vintage, 1997), 418.
41  Rhys, *Smile Please*, 115–16.
42  Brooker, *Bohemia in London*, 107.
43  Rhys, 'Till September Petronella', 15.
44  Ibid., 16.
45  Ibid., 23, 18, 20. In *Jean Rhys* (Basingstoke: Macmillan, 1998), Sylvie Maurel, by contrast, describes the attitude of the locals as 'unmotivated hostility'. She links this to the way that 'the norm' in Rhys's fiction 'is a kind of diffuse menace and is usually endowed with incredible violence' (64).
46  Rhys, 'Till September Petronella', 26, 25.
47  Irving Berlin, 'Ragtime Violin', https://www.oldielyrics.com/lyrics/irving_berlin/ragtime_violin.html, accessed 27 March 2017.
48  Savory, *Jean Rhys*, 86.
49  Jean Rhys, 'I Spy a Stranger', in *The Collected Short Stories*, by Jean Rhys (New York: Norton, 1989), 249. The story was originally published in *Art and Literature*, no. 8 (Spring 1966): 4–53.
50  D. H. Lawrence, 'Pornography and Obscenity', in *Phoenix: The Posthumous Papers of D. H. Lawrence*, ed. Edward D. McDonald (London: William Heinemann, 1936), 176.
51  Rhys, 'Till September Petronella', 10.
52  Ibid., 34, her emphasis.
53  Ibid., 33, 16.
54  Judith Kegan Gardiner, *Rhys, Stead, Lessing, and the Politics of Empathy* (Bloomington: Indiana University Press, 1989), 38.
55  T. S. Eliot, 'The Love Song of J. Alfred Prufrock', in his *Selected Poems* (London: Faber, 1961), 15.

56  Rhys, 'Till September Petronella', 22.
57  Angier, *Jean Rhys*, 91–2.
58  Rhys, 'Till September Petronella', 13, 21.
59  Ibid., 22. Thomas F. Staley reads the eyes as signs of 'malignancy and spiritual emptiness'. Staley, *Jean Rhys: A Critical Study* (Austin: University of Texas Press, 1979), 124.
60  Rhys uses a butchery motif to suggest that the pair expected Suzy to prostitute herself to Hebertson. Newly recruited prostitutes in the period were known colloquially as 'fresh meat'. John Masefield, Preface, *Daughters of Ishmail*, by Reginald Wright Kauffman (London: Stephen Smith, 1911), xi.
61  Graham Dawson, *Soldier Heroes: British Adventure, Empire, and the Imagining of Masculinities* (London: Routledge, 1994), 13.
62  Rita Felski, *The Gender of Modernity* (Cambridge, MA: Harvard University Press, 1995), 95.
63  Ibid., 105.
64  Smith, *Peter Warlock*, 55–6, 77, 81.
65  Ibid., 55.
66  Felski, *The Gender of Modernity*, 105.
67  Judith Butler, *Bodies That Matter: On the Discursive Limits of 'Sex'* (New York: Routledge, 1993), 3.
68  Felski, *The Gender of Modernity*, 106.
69  Philip Cohen, 'The Perversions of Inheritance: Studies in the Making of Multi-Racist Britain', in *Multi-Racist Britain*, ed. Philip Cohen and Harwant S. Bains (Basingstoke: Macmillan Education, 1988), 65.
70  For Staley, Julian is 'an example of the bullying male who, having exploited women, through guilt or perversity has a sadistic desire to show them up as insincere or even villainous' (*Jean Rhys*, 124). He describes the holiday as a 'neurotic gathering' (122), implicitly othering the behaviours of the characters against an unarticulated healthy, respectable norm.
71  Philip Cohen, 'The Perversions of Inheritance', 65–6, his emphasis.
72  Rhys, 'Till September Petronella', 21–2.
73  Quoted in ibid., 20.
74  Sherry, *Modernism and the Reinvention of Decadence*, 77.
75  Gray, *Peter Warlock*, 23.
76  Robert Browning, 'A Pretty Woman', in *Selected Poetry of Browning*, ed. Kenneth L. Knickerbocker (New York: Random House, 1951), 284, 282, 284.
77  Ibid., 283.
78  Rhys, 'Till September Petronella', 20–3, 23, 27.
79  Ibid., 19.
80  Andreas Huyssen, *After the Great Divide: Modernism, Mass Culture, Postmodernism* (Bloomington: Indiana University Press, 1986), 53.

81  Rhys, 'Till September Petronella', 33.
82  Katarzyna Michalska and Serguiz Michalska, *Spider* (London: Reaktion, 2010), 95, 96, 100, 105, 106.
83  Rhys, 'Till September Petronella', 22.
84  Heseltine, letter to Delius, quoted in Gray, *Peter Warlock*, 102; 'Triple Sec', 24.
85  Dawson, *Soldier Heroes*, 65.
86  See Judith R. Walkowitz, *City of Dreadful Delight: Narratives of Sexual Danger in Late-Victorian London* (London: Virago, 1992).
87  Rhys, 'Till September Petronella', 33, 22.
88  Ibid., 25.
89  Kristeva, *Black Sun*, 244, her emphasis.
90  Rhys, 'Till September Petronella', 33, her emphasis, 34, 35.
91  Ibid., 18.
92  Ibid., 33, Rhys's emphasis.
93  Kristeva, *Black Sun*, 223.
94  Jean Rhys, 'Tigers Are Better-Looking', in *Tigers Are Better Looking: With a Selection from* The Left Bank, by Jean Rhys (1968; repr., Harmondsworth: Penguin, 1972), 66.
95  Ibid., 64, Rhys's emphasis.
96  *Oxford English Dictionary Online*.
97  Driver and Martins, 'Introduction', 3.
98  Rhys, 'Tigers Are Better-Looking', 64–5; Gen. 3.14, *King James Bible*.
99  Rhys, 'Tigers Are Better-Looking', 66.
100 Ibid., 66.
101 Ibid., 71.
102 Ibid., 66. Rishona Zimring, by contrast, positions the story as 'Mr Severn's urban *katabasis*, or journey through the underworld', which 'brings him into the London equivalent of Paris cafés and cabarets, an exotic and decadent territory that promises to fertilise the imagination'. She gives the temporal setting as 1934, though the Silver Jubilee took place in 1935. The reading is not attuned to Severn's homosexuality. 'Making a Scene: Rhys and the Aesthete at Mid-century', in *Jean Rhys*, ed. Erica L. Johnson and Moran, 52.
103 Rhys, 'Tigers Are Better-Looking', 73, 77.
104 Nadia Ellis, 'Between Windrush and Wolfenden: Class Crossings and Queer Desire in Salkey's Postwar London', in *Beyond Windrush: Rethinking Postwar Anglophone Caribbean Literature*, ed. J. Dillon Brown and Leah Reade Rosenberg (Jackson: University Press of Mississippi, 2015), 65. Ellis is following, in part, Matt Houlbrook's argument in *Queer London: Perils and Pleasures in the Sexual Metropolis, 1918–1957* (Chicago, IL: University of Chicago Press, 2005).
105 Zimring, 'Making a Scene', 51, her emphasis.
106 Ellis, 'Between Windrush and Wolfenden', 65.

107 Rhys, 'Tigers Are Better-Looking', 76.
108 Ibid., 64.
109 Ibid., 66.
110 Ibid., 73.
111 Angier, *Jean Rhys*, 347–8.
112 *Oxford English Dictionary Online.*
113 Walkowitz, *Nights Out*, 230.
114 Ibid., 244.
115 Matera, *Black London*, Chapter 4.
116 Dunbar, 'Harlem in London', 2.
117 Matera, *Black London*, Chapter 4.
118 Walkowitz, *Nights Out*, 243.
119 Ibid., 240.
120 *Oxford English Dictionary Online*, italics in source.
121 Zimring suggests that the name of the club is 'out of P. G. Wodehouse'. 'Making a Scene', 52.
122 Constance Valis Hill, *Tap Dancing America: A Cultural History* (Oxford: Oxford University Press, 2010), 80.
123 Howard 'Stretch' Johnson, 'From His Unpublished Memoirs', in *Autobiography of a People: Three Centuries of African American History Told by Those Who Lived It*, ed. Herb Boyd (New York: Doubleday, 2000), 260.
124 Rhys, 'Tigers Are Better-Looking', 69, her emphasis.
125 Rhys, 'Till September Petronella', 21.
126 Rhys, 'Tigers Are Better-Looking', 70.
127 Lawrence, 'Pornography and Obscenity', 172.
128 Rhys, 'Tigers Are Better-Looking', 70, 71.
129 Gregg, *Jean Rhys's Historical Imagination*, 171.
130 Gemma Romain, *Race, Sexuality and Identity in Britain and Jamaica: The Biography of Patrick Nelson, 1916–1963* (London: Bloomsbury Academic, 2017).
131 Rhys, 'Tigers Are Better-Looking', 67, 70.
132 'Dinah (1925)', *JazzStandards.com*, http://www.jazzstandards.com/compositions-1/dinah.htm, accessed 12 October 2016.
133 Rhys, 'Tigers Are Better-Looking', 70.
134 Ibid., 66, 73.
135 Ibid., 75–6.
136 Ibid., 76, 77.
137 Rhys, *Letters 1931–1966*, 191n. 2, italics in source.

6

# The *doudou* and doudouism in Rhys's fiction

Jacqueline Couti draws out the different meanings of *doudou* in French-based Caribbean Creole and in standard French. In French Creole it 'means "darling." This term originated from the French word *doux* (soft or sweet) repeated twice … Anyone can be called doudou.… The gallicized *doudou* has come to signify a beautiful, loved French Caribbean woman, most likely light skinned or mixed race.'[1] *Doudou* is also translated as sweetheart or sweetie. The word *doudou* first appeared in 'standard French dictionaries such as *Le petit Robert* in 1929'.[2] The eighteenth-century song '*Adieu madras, adieu foulard*' has been identified as an originary text of the French colonial mythology of the *doudou*,[3] an Antillean mistress who receives gifts from her white lover and is subsequently abandoned by him. This is, pointedly on Rhys's part, one of the songs that the Martinican Christophine Dubois sings to Antoinette Cosway in *Wide Sargasso Sea* and Antoinette sings to her husband. The gallicized *doudou*, Couti explains, is a figure of tropical exoticism – doudouism – which identifies the Antillean mistress with the 'bounty', 'beauty and sensuality' of her home island and projects colonial fealty through the conventions of romance, grounding a representational 'paradigm that intertwines colonial patriarchy, exotic sexuality, entangled female agency, and Edenic feminized Caribbean geography'.[4] Observing the way in which travel writers represent the 'Creole woman's sweet stuff' through 'correlat[ing] language, sexuality, and the sugar trade', Edwin C. Hill, Jr places the '*doudou* in the middle of imperial economies of French-Antillean exchange'.[5] In political terms, the figure has been read as a colonial 'longing for total possession by' the imperial power.[6] For Rhys the provenance of the *doudou* encompasses Dominica's dual French and British colonial heritage, its vernacular and inter-island reaches in Lesser Antillean popular culture and the representational operation of tropicality. A genealogy of the *doudou* and doudouism in Rhys's fiction – from 'Trio' through *Voyage in the Dark*, *Good Morning, Midnight* and 'Let Them Call It Jazz' to *Wide Sargasso*

*Sea* – demonstrates its shaping of strands of her literary imagination and the recyclability of the *doudou* over time and diasporic histories.[7]

Rhys was familiar with the French poetry of the Dominican writer Daniel Thaly (1879–1950), which has been characterized as doudouist.[8] A doctor, as was Rhys's father William Rees Williams, he published two collections in Paris – *Lucioles et Cantharides* (1900) and *La Clarté du sud* (1905) – while Rhys was still living in Dominica and would publish another six before 1938. Noting that he is a man of colour, Rhys very briefly comments in 1936 that he 'has written some poems that aren't bad. Some lines aren't bad.'[9] French Antillean writers began to take a critical interest in the figure of the *doudou* and doudouism in the mid- to late 1920s. That interest is usually traced to African Martinicans Jane and Paulette Nardal. In this period the Nardal sisters were living in Paris, ran a literary salon with their sister Andrée and contributed to the journal *La dépêche africaine* (1928–32). Jane and Paulette Nardal affirm that they worked 'to create a cultural, not political, movement similar to that of the New Negro in America',[10] with Paulette commenting that they 'blazed the trail' for Négritude writers Aimé Césaire, Léon-Gontran Damas and Léopold Sédar Senghor in the 1930s, who 'took up the[ir] ideas … and expressed them with flash and brio'.[11] The term *doudouiste* was used in the single-issue journal *Légitime défense* (1932) 'to denounce the sentimentalist ideology' that reproduced colonial stereotypes of the French Antilles.[12] The manifesto was the joint production of Etienne Léro, Thélus Léro, René Menil, Jules-Marcel Monnerot, Michel Pilotin, Maurice-Sabas Quitman, Auguste Thésée and Pierre Yoyotte, all Martinican students living in Paris. Male writers of the Négritude movement aligned the biguine, a Martinican musical genre, with doudouism.[13] While the sojourns of the Nardals and Rhys in Paris did overlap there is no extant evidence that Rhys knew the sisters personally or their cultural project. Apart from 'Triple Sec', the Rhys archive before 1934 is though, it must be said, sparse. Nor is there evidence that Rhys was familiar with *Légitime défense*, Aimé Césaire, Damas, Senghor and later anti-doudouist writing by Suzanne Césaire and Frantz Fanon.[14] Strikingly, though, in *Good Morning, Midnight* a narrative sequence around singing and dancing to a biguine record takes up questions around primitivism, authenticity and representation of the *doudou*. Over Rhys's career her engagements with the *doudou* and doudouism also address different kinds of issues around the operation of racialized and class thresholds and tropicality. I analyse these engagements in chronological order and separately.

'Trio', set in Montparnasse, concerns sexuality and sexualized consumption, alluding to the *doudou* and French music hall to draw out the affective fabric of the everyday life of a young woman of colour in Paris and to hint at a possible back story of colonial poverty. The unnamed narrator describes three other unnamed patrons of a restaurant dining together – an apparently wealthy 'coal black' man, a 'coffee-coloured' woman and a lighter-skinned girl of 'about fifteen, but probably much younger' – and identifies all four of them in the final paragraph as Antillean 'compatriots'.[15] Judith Raiskin and Leah Rosenberg read the relation of the man, woman and girl as, respectively, one of 'sexual exploitation' and 'sexual abuse' of the girl, rendering her as a tragic mulatta figure.[16] The man and the girl make a highly conspicuous display of sexual consumption: 'long, lingering kisses' in public, with the girl seemingly wanting to 'gather up a tribute of glances and admiration and envy'; and the girl dancing erotically to the song 'J'en ai marre', a performance 'to the huge delight of the coal black man who applauded vigorously'. Her raising of the 'skirt' of her 'short red frock' in the high-kicking dance performance exposes that she is not wearing knickers. The woman looks on 'peacefully' and 'proudly', addressing the girl as '[d]oudou' and commenting to the restaurant manager that she is at least 'cocasse' (amusing).[17] Raiskin identifies 'J'en ai marre' as a 'patois' song and Rosenberg reads just the title ('I'm fed up' in English translation) as an indication of the girl's 'resistance' to the 'mother or female guardian' seemingly 'prostituting the young woman to a man who could easily be her father'.[18] 'J'en ai marre' was, rather, a song written for Mistinguett (1873–1956), the 'queen of post-World War I music hall', an 'incarnation of both Parisian glamour and the plucky, street-wise *parigote*' (Parisian). Indeed, Kelley Conway argues that in the interwar period Mistinguett 'came to stand in for the entire institution of the music hall'.[19] By the early 1920s she was 'the highest paid female entertainer in the world', her trademark legs reportedly insured for 500,000 francs.[20] 'J'en ai marre' (sung in Parisian argot) was her most enduring hit, remaining part of her repertoire for around thirty years.[21]

In accord with Rhys's wider interest in movement across languages in *The Left Bank and Other Stories* and keen ear for vernacular, the identification of the girl as '[d]oudou' draws on Creole and gallicized meanings, Rhys's authorial voice implicitly naming both the affection of the woman for the girl and the exploitative sexual relationship between the girl and the affluent man. The naming is consistent with Rhys's critical interest in the sexual economies in which dancing women circulate. The lover is a black man rather than a white Frenchman, and he has met the girl in Paris or brought her there rather than abandoned her in the Antilles. She is integral to his public performance of upwardly mobile masculinity. The blackness of the man places this twentieth-century exemplar of the *doudou* in a shifting set of class relations in which colonial wealth is no longer synonymous with whiteness and class mobility is not dependent on affiliation with whiteness. On the surface, though, 'Trio' does not particularly unsettle what was by the early 1910s a paradigm of doudouism: 'the literary *doudou* presented as "an erotic object obligingly proposed for the consumption – the textual consumption – of metropolitan readers".[22] Rhys does draw attention to the ways the girl's audience consumes her performance, perhaps inviting some self-reflexivity on the part of readers. She does not, though, undercut tropicalist stereotypes and types: the sexual precociousness of non-white girls and the identification of the skin shades of non-white characters through descriptors of resources extracted from the Caribbean (coal, coffee and, with sweetie, sugar).

'J'en ai marre' was written for Mistinguett to perform in the revue 'Paris en l'air' ('Paris in the Air') staged at the Casino de Paris, a prominent Parisian music hall, from 29 October 1921 until 15 April 1922. Composed by Maurice Yvain with lyrics by Albert Willemetz and Georges Arnould, 'J'en ai marre' was recorded in 1921 by Mistinguett, backed by Mitchell's Jazz Kings, a black band, which played at the Casino de Paris and influenced the development of jazz in France.[23] The combination attests to the cosmopolitanism of French music hall. The first-person voice of the song complains bitterly about a lowly existence governed by a seemingly never-ending and monotonous round of work, not her 'idea of fun', in Lucienne Hill's translation. While abjuring being seen as a 'Red' (Communist), she excoriates the 'fate' that consigns 'some folks' to poverty and 'others' to 'idle' wealth.[24] David Bret characterizes the song as 'so full of Paris slang that parts of it are almost impossible to translate'.[25] 'Paris en l'air' fits the pattern of revue Mistinguett favoured: a programme 'that would allow her to change station (and costume) over and over; this way, audiences could ride with her from poverty and anonymity to the heights of wealth and glory. … Naturally, her shifts in fortune would be marked by the mise-en-scène of the production numbers'.[26] Music hall more generally 'celebrated luxury, cosmopolitan sophistication, and eroticism', 'enact[ing] vivid daydreams', writes Charles Rearick.[27] Mistinguett's 'most important sketch' in 'Paris en l'air', Bret notes, 'involved a train which she had prevented from being derailed … her skirt came off, of course, revealing her fabulous legs, and she and [Earl] Leslie executed a high-kicking routine which all but brought the house down every night'.[28]

During the 1920s Mistinguett performed at the Casino de Paris, the Moulin Rouge and the Folies Bergère in a music-hall era she characterizes as a 'profusion of ostrich feathers, satins, nudes, monumental sets and spectacular transformation scenes'. She tells the story of the revue 'Laissez-les Tombre' (1917/18) triumphantly and daringly rescuing the fortunes of the Casino de Paris by presenting nudes 'climb[ing] up and down a ladder thirty feet in height', 'a far cry from the first appearance for one brief moment of a nude at the Folies-Bergère in 1912'.[29] Nude dancing quickly became a staple element of French music hall. As concessions to modesty, nude female dancers were required to wear a '"triangle oligatoire" [sic], the *cache-sexe*, "'some flowers, a jewel or a bit of lace"'; their bodies were made up with '"a layer of grease and ... a layer of powder"'; and they wore or sported '"accessories, sandals, wig, necklaces, an immense veil, an immense fan, who knows what other immense items!"'[30]

Sporting none of these, Rhys's character crosses a contemporary threshold between the risqué and the indecent. Her erotic performance uncovers the slippage between the older woman's Antillean and Gallicized meanings of *doudou*. That the girl breaks into the song 'J'en ai marre' is a sign of conspicuous cross-cultural consumption of the sexualized glamour of Mistinguett's celebrity and of the compelling popular appeal of the rags-to-riches narrative around it. Concessions to modesty are lost in her performative translation. Further, the performance of Mistinguett's song draws out the centrality of the dancer to the intermedial aesthetic play of the story. By the time Rhys had to make a selection from *The Left Bank and Other Stories* for inclusion in the 1968 collection *Tigers Are Better-Looking* the slippage and Mistinguett's celebrity would have been dated, no longer legible for readers. 'Trio' was not chosen.

In *Voyage in the Dark*, Anna Morgan remembers from her childhood in fin-de-siècle Dominica family servant Francine's only English song, 'Adieu, sweetheart, adieu', a modern variant of '*Adieu madras, adieu foulard*', possibly ironic. Chorus dancer Anna remembers Francine's song after she has spent her future lover Walter Jeffries's first gift of money on clothes, been called a tart and given notice by her landlady, sent for Walter and taken medication for possible influenza.[31] With the surfacing of the memory here, Rhys implies Anna's latent awareness of the Antillean meaning of the acceptance of the gift (taking on the mantle of the *doudou*) and the potential for the relationship to fail. Anna's first sexual encounter with Walter is depersonalized by her engrossment with a childhood memory of Mother St Anthony's lesson on the 'Four Last Things' ('Death, Judgement, Hell and Heaven'), adopting the recommended posture for contemplating death ('[l]ying down with your arms by your sides and your eyes shut') and experiencing the sexual act through her memory of the name of an eighteen-year-old enslaved woman Maillotte Boyd, thinking '[b]ut I like it like this. I don't want it any other way but this'.[32] The techniques of depersonalization are an abdication of a 'proprietary, rational female self capable of claiming and acting' on sexual desire.[33] The guise of Maillotte Boyd racializes Anna's amateur prostitution, while also drawing attention to the inequalities of power between Walter and Anna, problematizing the question of degree of consent.

As in 'Trio', in *Voyage in the Dark* the narrative arc in which the *doudou* figures is framed by a popular music hall song, the framing here setting up the imagined everyday material life of the cockney as a site of abjection for Anna as she struggles with impoverishment and the prospect of assimilation into the English working class. After her first date with Walter, Anna returns to her room in a boarding house in Judd Street and hears a passerby singing lines from 'Standard Bread' (1911), a music-hall song sung by Harry Champion (1865–1942).[34] Alan Ruston writes that Champion 'appeared grotesque, but was the embodiment of the spirit of the poorer parts of London; there was no refinement or sophistication in his performance, which was above all a vibrant evocation of working-class life'. Food was a prominent theme in Champion's repertoire, Peter Bailey reading it as his distinctive 'variant of the good time', pointing out that for 'working-class audiences ... food deprivation was, if not always an actuality, a folk memory and its fears kept very much alive'.[35] The comic premise of 'Standard Bread' is that eating even small amounts of standard bread transforms and empowers the 'weak', inverting usual patterns of dominance. The singer's wife ('weak as any rat') gains strength enough to throw 'the lodger down the stairs' and the singer 'up the flu [sic]' and to get through scrubbing laundry '[l]ike a lion'; the family fowl grows feathers and marries the rooster who had earlier rejected her for being 'much too bald'; and a mouse who eats the bread from a mousetrap kills and eats the family cat.[36] After thinking the song 'Standard Bread' '[m]ad as a hatter', rejecting its comic fantasy of empowerment, but then 'breath[ing] in time' to the lyrics, Anna turns to her distress at the way people 'sneer, sneer all the time' at poorly dressed women and settles momentarily on the fact that her 'clothes are cheap', that she is one of the 'ones without any money, the ones with beastly lives.' The clothes Anna buys with Walter's gift of money empower her to transform her wardrobe and the way people look at her. Her landlady, though, concerned about the propriety of the transformation, gives her notice to move, telling her, '"I don't want no tarts in my house."' Ill, Anna remembers that she 'always wanted to be black' – a sign of her modernist primitivism – and then remembers Francine singing 'Adieu, sweetheart, adieu.'[37]

By the twentieth century '*Adieu madras, adieu foulard*' 'was often sung and played to bid farewell when transatlantic ships left the [Caribbean] port' bound for Europe.[38] Anna's memory of family servant Francine's song –

Adieu, sweetheart, adieu,
Salt beef and sardines too,
And all good times I leave behind,
Adieu, sweetheart, adieu[–]

cuts to a memory of her 'crying' on her departure for England by ship, suggesting that this song, too, was played when ships departed Dominica.[39] In the first version of the ending of *Voyage in the Dark*, the last two lines resurface in the delirium caused by Anna's post-abortion haemorrhage, reframed as a farewell to Dominica and implicitly childhood, her stepmother Hester's policing of racialized thresholds of respectability and a reasonably affluent life.[40] The luxuries enjoyed by the mistress of the Frenchman in the earlier '*Adieu madras, adieu foulard*' – 'madras', 'scarf', 'silk dress', 'necklace' – contrast with the '[s]alt beef', 'sardines' and 'good times' to which the mistress bids farewell in 'Adieu, sweetheart, adieu', suggesting the economic decline of what had once been wealthy plantation slavery economies. Vincent calls serial promiscuity 'good times' for men of his class; 'Adieu, sweetheart, adieu' points to the potential economic basis of sexual relationships for their partners. While in '*Adieu madras, adieu foulard*' and Francine's variant the abandoned mistress addresses the departing lover as *doudou*, 'the *doudou* mythology designates *her* as the *doudou* and leaves *him* unnamed'.[41] In relation to Rhys's translation of the French imperial mythology of the *doudou* across racialized and ethnic thresholds, it is significant that Walter, like the Frenchman abandoning his mistress in '*Adieu madras, adieu foulard*', uses an overseas trip to help effect a break with Anna. Anna's first-person narrative voice positions her as melancholic subject rather than erotic object for the novel's readers.

Engaging with aspects of the *doudou* stereotype in Anna's early conversations with Walter as lover in Chapter 5 of the novel, Rhys juxtaposes Anna's sense of loss as a Dominican woman and her stilted efforts to articulate her West Indian identity to him. Walter positions Anna not as a *doudou* – in spite of calling her 'a baby', 'my sweet' and 'rum' at separate points – but as one of his serial mistresses. 'I don't like hot places much. I prefer cold places. The tropics would be altogether too lush for me,' Walter tells Anna.[42] He takes her to see the Savernake Forest, an experience which highlights for Anna the lack of 'fit' between the tropics and temperate England. For her, while the forest is 'so beautiful', 'something had happened to it. It was as if the wildness had gone out of it.'[43] But not for Walter, who is moved to propose outdoor sex. Even in the early stages of their relationship, Walter imagines a future for Anna in which she will 'get on' by improving her singing skills through lessons for which he will pay; relishing the prospect of dependency, though, Anna tells him, 'I want to be with you. That's all I want.' She thinks to herself here that she is 'hopeless, resigned, utterly happy' in the relationship.[44] Rhys does not generalize her desire for dependency as a colonial condition. What Anna impresses on Walter most in conversation is that she is 'the fifth generation born out there, on my mother's side', a 'real West Indian'.[45] Anna's sense of loss is registered as sensuous memories of tropical gardens, flowers, vibrant colours, smells, sound, feeling the 'earth' 'breathe', and of an estranging corporeal memory of difference: 'The colours are red, purple, blue, gold, all shades of green. The colours here are black, brown, grey, dim-green, pale blue, the white of people's faces – like woodlice.' She is unable to voice these memories to Walter. They are too intimate and, bringing the past into her present, provide a melancholic warmth in relation to perceived sneers at her new status as mistress on the part of servants and of Walter. The image of the white faces being 'like woodlice' loops back to her earlier anxiety about becoming 'one of the ones with beastly lives. They swarm like woodlice when you push a stick into a woodlice-nest at home. And their faces are the colour of woodlice.'[46] Her affective and corporeal memories become caught up with an acknowledgement of having become a 'bad' woman. What gives her role as mistress meaning though is less a moral line she has crossed than 'something about the darkness of the streets': the abjection of poverty and the prospect of working the streets as a prostitute.[47] Rhys implicitly sets the worldliness of Francine's song 'Adieu, sweetheart, adieu' against the naïve bookishness of Anna's initial abject response to Walter's dismissal of her in an unsent letter: 'My dear Walter I've read books about this and I know quite well what you're thinking but you're quite wrong.'[48] In the longer narrative frame, Anna's melancholy is grounded in a loss of home and class dispossession rather than being cast off by a European lover.

In *Voyage in the Dark*, the demand for Standard English is a marker of British colonization in Dominica and of colonial assimilation in England. Anna remembers 'Adieu, sweetheart, adieu' as Francine's 'only English song'. English began borrowing 'adieu' from French in the middle ages.[49] Rhys simply designates Francine's everyday speech patois, including only Francine's untranslated ritual invocations around storytelling in the novel. In the first version of Anna's post-abortion delirium, Rhys has Anna recall singing another Creole, though not *doudou*, song 'Ma belle ka di maman li / Petit ke vini gros' and translating the lines for Hester. In delirium, Anna remembers defying Hester, who is appalled by her Caribbean accent and amicable relations with Francine, by singing twenty folkloric songs, 'negro tunes', 'one after another all the songs I knew and my voice went thin thin but I went on singing until the steamer started to whistle'.[50] This and her identification of landmarks by their French names – Morne Anglais, Morne Piton, Diablotin and the Crète – stake a claim to a cross-racial and inter-imperial Dominican cultural inheritance and belonging. This narrative arc is cut in the revised published version of the ending.

The scene in *Good Morning, Midnight* in which the Russian Jewish émigré artist Serge Rubin plays a gramophone record '*Maladie d'amour, maladie de la jeunesse*' for Sasha Jensen when she visits his studio has emerged as a crux in the interpretation of Sasha's depressive malaise. The music and the spectacle of Serge's dance seemingly transport her in imagination to a location redolent of the tropics: 'I am lying in a hammock looking up at the branches of a tree. The sound of the sea advances and retreats as if a door were being opened and shut. All day there has been a fierce wind blowing, but at sunset it drops.'[51] For Savory, GoGwilt and Erica L. Johnson, among others, the tropical scene is a memory, rather than a daydream. Savory reads it as a sign of Sasha's West Indian origin, GoGwilt as a 'lost Antillean memory as the clue to the narrative's melancholic formation' around the 'impossibility of white middle-class identity' which he projects as Rhys's 'reading of English modernism', and Johnson as an 'unexplained, unshuttered memory' of 'abysmal loss' from 'a very distant, colonial childhood' in which, in Johnson's conflation of Rhys and her character, Sasha has experienced 'the trauma of childhood abuse'.[52] The function of the scenes around the biguine is, rather, a critique of doudouism.

'*Maladie d'amour, maladie de la jeunesse*', recorded in 1931 by Léona Gabriel, an African Martinican living in Paris and working at the Boule Blanche at that time,[53] became, like a newly arranged '*Adieu madras, adieu foulard*', also recorded by Gabriel, a biguine standard. Hill argues that the commercial popularization of the biguine in France has led to it being 'positioned at the temporal, cultural, geographic, and linguistic borders of authenticity and legitimacy for the colonial and anti-colonial alike'.[54] The origins of the biguine have been traced to the St Pierre region of Martinique in the wake of the eruption of Monte Pelée in 1902. Given the largely shared popular culture between Dominica and Martinique (which are only 50.57 nautical miles apart), Rhys, who moved to England in 1907 to continue her secondary schooling, would have been familiar with its early Antillean iterations.[55] Though the biguine had been introduced to Paris by Antillean musicians before the 1931 Exposition Coloniale Internationale (being played, for instance, at the Bal nègre),[56] Ernest Léardée remembers that the exposition led to 'a craze for exoticism' that saw the biguine become an 'institution' caught up in what Hill describes as the 'alienating dynamics of an emergent French pleasure industry'.[57] Hill points out that 'imperially framed representations of the biguine in the metropolis focus on the bodies on the dance floor', a 'hypersexualization'.[58] Serge and Sasha's discussion of 'negro music' and Montparnasse nightclubs in which it can be heard and danced to[59] shows Rhys extending standard cultural geographies of the US category 'negro music' to the African-Caribbean (Martinique and Cuba) and siting the biguine and African Cuban music as transatlantic African diasporic 'commodity-form[s]'.[60] Rhys situates this music in a culturally appropriative European metropolitan context, with the narrative arc around the biguine being pointedly framed by Serge's acknowledgement to Sasha that he makes 'West African masks' 'straight from the Congo'.[61] That Serge processes the biguine as primitive is suggested by his wearing of one of the masks while dancing to it.

The lyrics of '*Maladie d'amour, maladie de la jeunesse*' place the voice of the singer as a *doudou*, singing of her sorrow.[62] While Serge dances to the record, Sasha improvises on the song in English in her mind:

Pain of love,
Pain of youth,
Walk away from me,
Keep away from me,
Don't want to see you
No more, no more.... [63]

Sasha's improvisation on the vernacular lyrics – rather than translation of them – highlights her desire to distance herself from distressing memories. The *doudou* of the biguine sequence is rather an unnamed drunken weeping Martinican woman, whom Serge met in his London rooming house, an encounter he relates to Sasha after she starts crying in his studio. Serge distinguishes the Martiniquois from Sasha, who has also requested alcohol, by noting that she was a woman of colour rather than white. Like Paulette Nardal in her Parisian story 'In Exile' (1929), Rhys highlights that the 'rhythm of imperial modernity' for the Antillean woman in the metropole 'can be counted by the daily insults and misrecognitions she suffers'.[64]

The social ostracism and persecution Serge's acquaintance has experienced as the black mistress of a white Englishman she met in Paris are so acute that 'she had got so that she would do anything not to see people ... she hadn't been out, except after dark, for two years'. The woman gets drunk after apparently being told by a young girl of 'seven or eight' 'that she was a dirty woman, that she smelt bad, that she hadn't any right in the house. "I hate you and wish you were dead."' Serge is appalled by the everyday racism of their neighbours in the house, but recoils from the woman he identifies as 'half-negro – a mulatto', the 'expression' in her 'eyes' giving him 'an extraordinary sensation, as if [he] were looking down into a pit'.[65] In the context of Rhys's allusion to *Lady Windermere's Fan*, discussed in Chapter 4, the word pit resonates with the woman's status as an outcast. In the French mythology of the *doudou*, the Frenchman acts on an imperial miscegenation taboo in abandoning his concubine in the Caribbean rather than returning to France with her (and possibly their mixed-race children). The Martinican woman's English partner in *Good Morning, Midnight* inauthenticates her experience of the operation of the 'huge machine of law, order, respectability' around the miscegenation taboo and common-law relationships in London, telling her she is 'imagin[ing] everything'. His discrediting of her experience – it is she who is scapegoated over their relationship – is an excruciating form of emotional abandonment of her. '[S]he stayed with him because she didn't know where else to go, and he stayed with her because he liked the way she cooked,' Serge recalls her telling him.[66] Diasporic labour migration has cut the woman off from kinship and friendship networks; she does not stay with her partner out of loyalty. *Doudou* songs, Rhys suggests, romanticize the conditions of women abandoned by their white partners.

Hypersexualizing the woman through racial stereotype, having recourse to gender stereotype in warning her about becoming 'hysterical', unable 'to tell whether she was pretty or ugly, young or old' because '[s]he had been crying so much', Serge is certain that she wants him to 'make love to her'. 'But alas, I couldn't', he tells Sasha.[67] His experience of the woman makes him feel as though he 'were being suffocated, as if a large derriére was sitting' on him;[68] the 'large derriére' became over the course of the nineteenth century, as Sander Gilman has shown, a stereotypical 'sign of the promiscuity of the black woman and the prostitute'.[69] Linda Camarasana and Jess Issacharoff raise the possibility that Serge's sexual rebuff of the woman is a sign of homosexuality rather than the operation of a miscegenation taboo, a reading, though, that takes his hypersexualization of her to be a truth about her.[70] While Serge identifies the young girl's ascription of dirtiness to the woman as racist, in discussing the Highball with Sasha he calls it 'a dirty place', not 'nice any more'.[71] His hypersexualization of the dancing in a mixed-race venue indicates his disgust at the prospect of miscegenation.

Rhys suggests though her representation of Serge that the 1930s vogue for the biguine in France might coexist with a visceral racism, ironic given that he too has experienced racial persecution; in Sasha it inspires a tropicalist daydream. In a 1928 essay 'Pantins exotiques', Jane Nardal identifies 'the decor of the past, the rococo of hammocks, palm trees, virgin forests, etc' as doudouist tropes of 'exotic literature'.[72] A hammock, trees and the sounds of the sea on a beach feature in Sasha's daydream that takes her to a place of sunshine, a 'sweet place' in the language of the Emily Dickinson poem Rhys chose as the epigraph of the novel.[73] The easing of the 'fierce wind' at nightfall positions the wind as a metaphor of Sasha's characteristic despair. In a subjective context, her tropicality is not as egregious as Serge's or René's. In René's account of himself, he has been a Foreign Legionnaire in Morocco (helping to suppress the Comité d'Action Marocaine, a nationalist party campaigning for indirect rule from France). He boasts of his own hypersexuality there: gang raping locals and sampling homosexual sex with young boys.

In 'Let Them Call It Jazz' (1962), written in the 1950s, Rhys uses a *doudou* song in treating thresholds of sexual respectability, of language and of social, cultural and political belonging for people of colour. The story addresses the racism experienced by the first-person narrator Selina Davis, a light-skinned post-Windrush Caribbean immigrant to England, who speaks what Rhys calls an English 'stylized patois'. This English vernacular troubled her, for, as she acknowledges in a 1960 letter to Francis Wyndham, a French Creole is spoken in Dominica. 'Does it sound right? I've not read any of the "West Indian" people. It's by ear and memory,' she comments to him.[74] Thomas S. Davis has argued that the 'invented vernaculars' of post-Windrush authors of the late 1940s and 1950s 'figure the lived experiences of colonial and migrant populations as sites where the constraints and possibilities of political belonging come into being'. The vernaculars are used 'to familiarize the reader with their story worlds without altogether eliminating the strangeness and difference' the language 'carries with it', not to 'ethnographically record or aesthetically alienate'.[75] Rhys uses Selina's memory of her grandmother's song about a *doudou* to indicate how the woman who raised her inculcated a sense of sexual propriety. The context for the memory is post-Windrush British racism and moral panics around accommodation of West Indian migrants and the prospect of miscegenation. Rhys's authorial voice in the story cuts across the racist neighbours' stereotypical association of Selina's blackness with promiscuity and their invocation of a miscegenation taboo.

Of her grandmother's song, a late-nineteenth- or early-twentieth-century Antillean reworking of the Gallicized *doudou* that foregrounds shifting racialized class formations, Selina explains, 'It's about a man whose doudou give him the go-by when she find somebody rich and he sail away to Panama.' When the man returns home having made money working on construction of the Panama Canal, 'the girl meet him on the jetty, all dressed up and smiling'. The action of the *doudou* of the song, initially a companionate sweetheart, exposes her as mercenary. There are puns on go-by (go bye, go buy). The blackness of the male character of the song is indicated by his labour, not by a racial descriptor. The choric voice of the song dramatizes the man's repudiation of the *doudou* at the dock, singing

> Don't trouble me now
> You without honour
> Don't walk in my footstep
> You without shame.[76]

Selina knows the song in English, but has heard it, too, in Martinican Creole, a sign of Caribbean cultural traffic across neighbouring imperial and linguistic borders. While she dances and sings barefoot in the garden, white neighbours, offended by her breach of their ideas of respectability, accuse her of being the tart of Mr Sims, a shadowy seeming good Samaritan figure who has offered her lodging: 'At least the other tarts that crook installed here were *white* girls.' After retaliating by throwing a stone which breaks a window of the neighbours' house, Selina sings the lines of her grandmother's song to dress down their 'shameless' conduct. The song and the intonations of the grandmother's voice have been lifted from their informal pedagogic context in Selina's relationship with her grandmother, so Selina's 'voice don't sound right'. The song also functions in the story as a reminder – alongside Selina's migration to England and her mother's to Venezuela – of the depressed economic conditions that are a driver of labour migration from Caribbean islands. For a neighbour who testifies against Selina in court, the lyrics represent 'insulting' and 'filthy language', a misrecognition that is a sign of the stakes of her patois (and cultural heritage).[77] Here the gap between Selina's vernacular and Standard English figures her experiences of community racism. Selina's dancing bodily and cultural presence in the street incites a panic in her xenophobic neighbours around racialized hygiene.

'Don't trouble me now' is not the only song reframed for Selina in the story.[78] Imprisoned for breaking the window, Selina hears a Holloway Prison song sung 'from the punishment cells' to other inmates – 'cheerio and never say die' – an idiomatic message which sharpens her determination to make more of her life as an immigrant in England.[79] Historically, Holloway is remembered for the imprisonment of suffragettes (and their Holloway song). The Holloway of 'Let Them Call It Jazz' is haunted by the figure of the suffragette (being jailed for breaking a window and disorderly conduct, a prison song, attempted suicide by throwing oneself over a prison railing, hunger-striking), the spectrality being an axis of racialized and contemporary translation in the story. Enfranchisement of British women, Rhys implies, has not addressed racism and ethnocentrism.[80] After Selina's release, a guest at a party hears Selina whistling the Holloway song she prizes, 'jazz[es] it up' and sells it, giving Selina part of the proceeds. The musician seems stereotypically to associate a black patois voice with jazz and translates the song into this marketable musical form. While initially upset at the appropriation of a song that has had a deeply personal impact on her, Selina is reconciled to cherishing the memory of hearing the lyrics, a gift of solidarity: '"So let them call it jazz," I think, and let them play it wrong. That won't make no difference to the song I heard.'[81]

Writing to Francis Wyndham in May 1964, Rhys avers of Part Two of *Wide Sargasso Sea* that it 'was so impossibly difficult. I had no facts at all.... The characters though had to be imagined – not one real fact. Not one. No dialogue. Nothing.' In April she had told him of a breakthrough occasioned by Athill's suggestion that Antoinette and her husband experience 'a few weeks of happiness ... before he gets disturbing letters': 'As soon as I wrote that bit I realised that he must have fallen for her – and violently too. The black people have a good word for it – "she *magic* with him" or "he *magic* with her". Because you see, that is what it is – magic, intoxication. Not "Love" at all.'[82] Antoinette singing to the Rochester figure in the voice of the *doudou* is her magic; her mother Annette's seduction of Mr Mason, by contrast, is figured through dance, though the locals also pointedly comment that 'he came to make money as they all do. Some of the big estates are going cheap.'[83] The remark implies that Annette is 'going cheap' in her pursuit of a new husband and the capital he would bring to a marriage. The fineness of Rhys's design and stitching of musical allusion in *Wide Sargasso Sea* is illustrated by Antoinette's song, '*Adieu foulard, adieu madras*', which the Rochester figure remembers as being among the songs she tried to 'teach' him, 'for they haunted' him.[84] While authorship of the song has usually been credited to the eighteenth-century French governor of Guadeloupe François Amour, Marquis de Bouillé, he may have merely written down an Antillean Creole song or had it transcribed.[85] Among Rhys's papers there is a page on which she has written out a version of the song and noted his authorship.[86]

Christophine, who, like Antoinette's mother Annette, is from Martinique, sings French Antillean Creole songs to Antoinette when she is a child. Hill points out that the 'movement of thirds in the melody' of '*Adieu madras, adieu foulard*' 'suggests hearing the song as a lullaby ... Consideration of *Adieu madras* as a lullaby ... suggests the role musical culture assumes in the pedagogy of colonial sentiment'.[87] In addition to what Antoinette remembers as '*Adieu foulard, adieu madras*', Christophine's repertoire includes 'The little ones grow old, the children leave us, will they come back?' ('*Ma belle ka di maman li*' – 'My beautiful girl is singing to her mother')[88]

> and the one about the cedar tree flowers which only last for a day.
> The music was gay but the words were sad and her voice often quavered and broke on the high note. 'Adieu.' Not adieu as we said it, but *à dieu*, which made more sense after all. The loving man was lonely, the girl was deserted, the children never came back. Adieu.[89]

The song about the cedar tree flowers alludes to 2 Peter 3.8 – 'one day *is* with the Lord as a thousand years, and a thousand years as one day' – suggesting divine consolation in the face of the fragility of natural beauty.[90] Etymologically 'adieu' derives from *à dieu,* meaning 'I commend you to God'.[91] Christophine's critical inflection of the word(s) differs from Antoinette's as remembered by the Rochester figure. To commend to God (Acts 20.32) is to refer to a divine grace that will 'keep from sins and corruptions of the times'.[92] Christophine's quaver *à dieu* positions the *doudou* as in need of that grace and in doing so critiques an aspect of French regional imperialism.

Christophine addresses Antoinette familiarly as '*doudou*', '*doudou ché*' and '*Doudou, ché cocotte*'.[93] The first instances of Christophine calling Antoinette '*doudou*' and '*doudou ché*' follow Antoinette's request that she supply an obeah remedy for the loss of love between her and the Rochester figure and Christophine advising her not to cry. Through this form of address Rhys is both representing French-based Creole endearments as a legacy of the nurse–child relationship and, within the wider scene, implicitly drawing a contrast between Antoinette's initial Gallicized *doudou*-like response to a perceived loss of love and Christophine's injunction to her, 'Have spunks and do battle for yourself.'[94] Antoinette, though, will come to mourn not the Rochester figure but a loss of home.

For Rhys's Rochester figure the *doudou*, though, is also part of the menace, the exoticism, that so troubles him in Dominica. He first articulates this to himself in thinking of his new wife: 'Long, sad, dark alien eyes. Creole of pure English descent she may be, but they are not English or European either.'[95] Antoinette's songs entrance him 'as a sign for the desire of the other' and because he is seemingly the colonizing 'creative force' behind the performances.[96] In the scenes of emotional parting (drawing her future as a prisoner in Thornfield Hall) and departure from Granbois, he veers between longing to be addressed again in the voice of the *doudou* and emotional and epistemic battery of Antoinette, now renamed Bertha. I discuss his estrangement from and violence towards Antoinette in Chapter 7.

Scholarship on the *doudou* and doudouism has to date been conducted in the field of Francophone Caribbean Studies. Dominica, Rhys's birthplace, is one of several Caribbean countries with a French and English imperial history. One of the legacies of Dominica's inter-imperial history has been the proximity of Dominican and Martinican Creole language and popular culture. Rhys's writerly interest in the figure of the *doudou* and *doudou* songs – formed by this proximity – spans a period of around forty years. Thacker and Lopoukhine, Regard and Wallart highlight Paris of the 1920s and 1930s and metropolitan French writing as nodes of French/English 'transcultural' passage in Rhys's oeuvre, rather than her Dominican upbringing.[97] The scope of Rhys's interest in the *doudou* and doudouism (a manifestation of tropicality) demonstrates the proximity of her concerns and those of diasporic anti-colonial French Caribbean writers of the 1920s and 1930s. It reveals a complex site of regional and transatlantic translation and transculturation that crosses imperial and linguistic boundaries, speaking across French Antillean Creole, French, English, stylized West Indian patois and, in its relation to music hall, Parisian argot and London cockney. Further, it evinces traces of regional Lesser Antillean (rather than Gallic) reinvention of the figure over time, including taking it into a pedagogic context and beyond Gallic melancholic formations.

## Notes

1   Jacqueline Couti, 'The Mythology of the Doudou: Sexualizing Black Female Bodies, Constructing Culture in the French Caribbean', in *Provocations: A Transnational Reader in the History of Feminist Thought*, ed. María Cristina Alcalde, Susan Bordo and Ellen Bayuk Rosenman (Oakland: University of California Press, 2015), 132.
2   Couti, 'The Mythology of the Doudou', 132.
3   Régis Antoine, *Les Ecrivains français et les Antilles, des premiers pères blancs aux surrealists noirs* (Paris: G. P. Maisonneuve et Larose, 1978), summarized by Edwards, *The Practice of Diaspora*, 159.
4   Couti, 'The Mythology of the Doudou', 133; Anny Dominique Curtius, 'Cannibalizing *Doudouisme*, Conceptualizing the *Morne*: Suzanne Césaire's Caribbean Ecopoetics', *South Atlantic Quarterly* 115, no. 3 (2016): 513.

5   Hill, *Black Soundscapes White Stages*, 37.
6   Richard D. E. Burton, '"Maman-France Doudou"', 81.
7   In 'Lost Island', revellers at Masquerade sing of a *doudou*, but, in the absence of lyrics, whether it is used in a Creole or Gallicized sense is unclear. Jean Rhys Papers.
8   Hill, *Black Soundscapes White Stages*, 23. Here he is identified as white.
9   Rhys, letter to Evelyn Scott, 1936, *Letters 1931–1966*, 29.
10  T. Denean Sharpley-Whiting, *Negritude Women* (Minneapolis: University of Minnesota Press, 2002), 44.
11  Sharpley-Whiting, *Negritude Women*, 17. Sharpley-Whiting is quoting Paulette Nardal from Jacques Louis Hymans, *Léopold Sédar Senghor: An Intellectual Biography* (Edinburgh: Edinburgh University Press, 1971), 36.
12  Hill, *Black Soundscapes White Stages*, 22.
13  Ibid., 49.
14  On Suzanne Césaire, see Curtius, 'Cannibalizing *Doudouisme*, Conceptualizing the *Morne*'. On Frantz Fanon and the *doudou*, see Hill, *Black Soundscapes White Stages*, 24–32.
15  Jean Rhys, 'Trio', in her *The Left Bank and Other Stories*, 83–6, 83, 85.
16  Judith Raiskin, 'Jean Rhys: Creole Writing and Strategies of Reading', *Ariel: A Review of International English Literature* 22, no. 4 (October 1991): 62; Rosenberg, *Nationalism and the Formation of Caribbean Literature*, 192.
17  Rhys, 'Trio', 84, 85.
18  Raiskin, 'Jean Rhys', 61; Rosenberg, *Nationalism and the Formation of Caribbean Literature*, 193.
19  Kelley Conway, *Chanteuse in the City: The Realist Singer in French Film* (Berkeley, University of California Press, 2004), 63, 65, 63.
20  David Bret, *The Mistinguett Legend* (London: Robson, 1990), 91; Mary McAuliffe, *Paris on the Brink: The 1930s Paris of Jean Renoir, Salvador Dali, Simone de Beauvoir, André Gide, Sylvia Beach, Léon Blum, and Their Friends* (Lanham, MD: Rowman & Littlefield, 2018), 64.
21  Bret, *The Mistinguett Legend*, 94.
22  Edwards, *The Practice of Diaspora*, 159.
23  William H. Kenney III, '*le hot*: The Assimilation of American Jazz in France, 1917–1940', *American Studies* 25 (1984): 6.
24  Mistinguett, *Mistinguett: Queen of the Paris Night*, trans. Lucienne Hill (London: Elek Books, 1954), 109.
25  Bret, *The Mistinguett Legend*, 94.
26  Dudley Andrew and Steven Ungar, *Popular Front Paris and the Poetics of Culture* (Cambridge, MA: Harvard University Press, 2005), 215.
27  Charles Rearick, *The French in Love and War: Popular Culture in the Era of the World Wars* (New York: Yale University Press, 1997), 69–70.

28  Bret, *The Mistinguett Legend*, 94.
29  Mistinguett, *Mistinguett*, 104.
30  Julie Townsend, *The Choreography of Modernism in France*, 114. She is quoting Collette Andris, *Une Danseuse nue, roman* (Paris: Flammarion, 1933).The translation is Townsend's.
31  Rhys, *Voyage in the Dark*, 27.
32  Ibid., 48, Rhys's emphasis.
33  Haag, 'In Search of "The Real Thing"', 550.
34  Mary Lou Emery identifies the song as a street cry in 'Caribbean Modernism: Plantation to Planetary', 65.
35  Alan Ruston, 'Champion, Harry [*real name* William Henry Crump], *Oxford Dictionary of National Biography* (Oxford University Press, 2019); Bailey, 'Fats Waller Meets Harry Champion', 501–2.
36  'Standard Bread', https://monologues.co.uk/musichall/Songs-S/Standard-Bread.htm, accessed 17 March 2019.
37  Rhys, *Voyage in the Dark*, 22–3, 26, 27.
38  Hill, '*Adieu Madras, Adieu Foulard*', 22.
39  Rhys, *Voyage in the Dark*, 28.
40  Jean Rhys, '*Voyage in the Dark*. Part IV (Original Version)', ed. Nancy Hemond Brown, in *The Gender of Modernism: A Critical Anthology*, ed. Bonnie Kime Scott, 381–9 (Bloomington: Indiana University Press, 1990), 382.
41  Hill, *Black Soundscapes White Stages*, 32.
42  Rhys, *Voyage in the Dark*, 44, 47, 48, 46.
43  Ibid., 67.
44  Ibid., 44, 49.
45  Ibid., 45.
46  Ibid., 47, 23.
47  Ibid., 49.
48  Ibid., 90.
49  Ibid., 28; *Oxford English Dictionary Online*.
50  Rhys, *Voyage in the Dark*, 382.
51  Rhys, *Good Morning, Midnight*, 75.
52  Savory, *Jean Rhys*, 117; GoGwilt, *The Passage of Literature*, 106, 108; Erica L. Johnson, 'Haunted', 30, 20, 29, 33. 'Abysmal loss' is a misquotation from Maslen, *Ferocious Things*, 125. On Rhys's account in her Black Exercise Book of having been sexually abused by an elderly male family friend see Thomas, *The Worlding of Jean Rhys*, 27–47; Moran, *Virginia Woolf, Jean Rhys, and the Aesthetics of Trauma*, 89–114; and Leah Rosenberg, '"The Rope, of Course Being Covered with Flowers": Metropolitan Discourses and the Construction of Creole Identity in Jean Rhys's "Black Exercise Book"', *Jean Rhys Review* 11, no. 1 (1999): 5–34.

53　On Léona Gabriel, see Hill, *Black Soundscapes White Stages*, 51–4. Hill lists her among performers at the Boule Blanche in 1931 on p. 67.
54　Hill, *Black Soundscapes White Stages*, 73. These days béguine is usually spelt biguine.
55　For Simon Cooke, who is unaware of Dominica's inter-imperial history and its legacies, the biguine 'resists assimilation into Rhys's own biography, shifting from Dominica to the French Caribbean'. '"Parler de soi": Jean Rhys and the Uses of Life Writing', in *Transnational Jean Rhys*, ed. Lopoukhine, Regard and Wallart, 70.
56　Berliner, *Ambivalent Desire*, 208.
57　Hill, *Black Soundscapes White Stages*, 66–7.
58　Ibid., 68–9.
59　Rhys, *Good Morning, Midnight*, 75.
60　Ronald Radano, 'Black Music Labor and the Animated Properties of Slave Sound', 206–7. Biguine, Edwards observes, 'emerged in the first decades of the twentieth century at the same time as jazz in the United States, *paseo* in Trinidad, tango in Argentina, and *son* and *danzon* in Cuba' and 'underwent a transformation through the influence of the black transnational music scene … in the cauldron of metropolitan music culture' in Paris. Edwards, *The Practice of Diaspora*, 171–2.
61　Rhys, *Good Morning, Midnight*, 74.
62　Gabriel's 1931 recording of 'Maladie d'amour' may be heard at *SecondHandSongs*, https://secondhandsongs.com/performance/516591/versions, accessed 17 July 2019.
63　Rhys, *Good Morning, Midnight*, 75.
64　Hill, *Black Soundscapes White Stages*, 64. Sharpley-Whiting, *Negritude Women*.
65　Rhys, *Good Morning, Midnight*, 78, 80,79, 78.
66　Rhys, 'Vienne', 241; Rhys, *Good Morning, Midnight*, 78.
67　Gilman, *Difference and Pathology*, 90, 99. For a fuller reading of Serge being sexually repulsed by the black woman, see Thomas, *The Worlding of Jean Rhys*, 127.
68　Rhys, *Good Morning, Midnight*, 80.
69　Thomas, *The Worlding of Jean Rhys*, 127.
70　Linda Camarasana, 'Exhibitions and Repetitions: Jean Rhys's *Good Morning, Midnight* and the World of Paris, 1937', 63; Jess Issacharoff, '"No Pride, No Name, No Face, No Country": Jewishness and National Identity in *Good Morning, Midnight*', in *Rhys Matters*, ed. Wilson and Johnson, 123.
71　Rhys, *Good Morning, Midnight*, 75.
72　Edwards, *The Practice of Diaspora*, 168–9. Quotation from p. 168. Nardal's essay was first published in *La Dépêche africaine* 8 (October 1928). The translator is Edwards.
73　Rhys, *Good Morning, Midnight*, [v].
74　Rhys, letter to Wyndham, 6 December 1960, *Letters 1931–1966*, 197. The question of the authenticity of a stylized English patois (an axis of translation) was also

raised for her by the character Christophine Dubois in *Wide Sargasso Sea*. In a published letter of 20 February 1966 to Athill, Rhys expresses the doubt as a question of Christophine being 'too articulate' (*Letters 1931–1966*, 297); in an unpublished letter of 1 April 1966 to Athill, she clarifies that her reservation concerns articulacy in English, given that a French Creole was the everyday language of Dominica. Jean Rhys Papers. The published letters conclude on 9 March 1966, as Rhys delivered the text of *Wide Sargasso Sea* to Andre Deutsch, her publisher.

75 Thomas S. Davis, *The Extinct Scene: Late Modernism and Everyday Life* (New York: Columbia University Press, 2016), 188, 191.
76 Rhys, 'Let Them Call It Jazz', 55.
77 Ibid., 54, 55, 56, Rhys's emphasis.
78 In a reading of Selina Davis's 'private acoustic space', Zimring does not discuss 'Don't trouble me now'. She focuses entirely on the Holloway song. Zimring, 'Making a Scene', 49–51.
79 Rhys, 'Let Them Call It Jazz', 60.
80 Sue Thomas, 'Modernity, Voice and Window-Breaking: Jean Rhys's "Let Them Call It Jazz"', in *De-scribing Empire: Colonialism and Textuality*, ed. Alan Lawson and Chris Tiffin (London: Routledge, 1994), 191–4.
81 Rhys, 'Let Them Call It Jazz', 63.
82 Rhys, *Letters 1931–1966*, 277, 262, her emphasis.
83 Rhys, *Wide Sargasso Sea*, 17.
84 Ibid., 54.
85 Edwin Hill, '"*Adieu Madras, Adieu Foulard*"', 20.
86 Jean Rhys Papers. The shaky handwriting would suggest that it was transcribed after 1964.
87 Hill, '"*Adieu Madras, Adieu Foulard*"', 25.
88 Rhys gives the translated title in the first version of the ending of *Voyage in the Dark* (Part IV, 382).
89 Rhys, *Wide Sargasso Sea*, 11.
90 Rochester overhears the song 'about one day and a thousand years' when Christophine is trying to comfort Antoinette and alludes to the lyrics when he thinks about Baptiste's indifference to the age of the rum at Granbois: 'A hundred years, a thousand all the same to *le bon Dieu* and Baptiste too'. Rhys, *Wide Sargasso Sea*, 90, 98.
91 *Oxford English Dictionary Online*.
92 Acts 20.32, John Gill's Exposition of the Bible, https://www.biblestudytools.com/commentaries/gills-exposition-of-the-bible/acts-20-32.html, accessed 23 September 2019.
93 'doudou': Rhys, *Wide Sargasso Sea*, 68, 90, 91. 'doudou ché': 68, 90. 'Doudou, ché cocotte': 43.

94  Ibid., 69.
95  Ibid., 39.
96  Hill, "'*Adieu Madras, Adieu Foulard*'", 29, 34.
97  Andrew Thacker, '"Also I Do Like the Moderns": Reading Rhys's Reading', in *Transnational Jean Rhys: Lines of Transmission, Lines of Flight*, ed. Lopoukhine, Regard and Wallart, 59–63. Lopoukhine, Regard and Wallart, 'Introduction', 8.

# 7

# Hurricane poetics in *Wide Sargasso Sea*

Charlotte Brontë's Rochester tells Jane Eyre that he resolved to return from Jamaica to England with his 'maniac' wife Bertha on a 'fiery West-Indian night; one of the description that frequently precedes the hurricanes of those climates', the oppressiveness of which was alleviated by '[a] wind fresh from Europe': 'the storm broke, streamed, thundered, blazed, and the air grew pure'. '[T]rue Wisdom … showed' him 'the right path to follow'. He 'saw Hope revive – and felt Regeneration possible'. Hope advises him: 'Place her in safety and comfort; shelter her degradation with secrecy, and leave her.'[1] In stitching *Wide Sargasso Sea* into *Jane Eyre*, Rhys reads Rochester's representation of the Caribbean weather as symptomatic of a self-justifying psychogeographical memory. She takes it as a point of departure to engage with Brontë's invocation of a stereotypical discourse of tropicality which others the Caribbean, in this instance climatically, as distinct from temperate Europe. Brontë interprets the Caribbean region through 'an imperial ecological myth', 'a geographical symbolics of air and atmosphere' framed, Alan Bewell notes, by 'ideological values, of liberty, purity, and health'.[2] 'Climate', David N. Livingstone observes, 'became an exploitable hermeneutic resource to make sense of cultural difference and to project moral categories into global space.'[3] Departing Granbois in Dominica, Rhys's Rochester figure filters Antoinette's stories of hurricanes which buffet the 'royal palms' and 'bamboos' and contemplates 'hurricanes' and his 'revenge' against Antoinette: 'Words rush through my head (deeds too). Words. Pity is one of them. It gives me no rest.' The word 'Pity' leads him to recall through association William Shakespeare's Macbeth contemplating the murder of Duncan, 'Pity like a naked new-born babe striding the blast.'[4] In an instance of 'tropical turbulence'[5] – where the representation of the hurricane produces 'formal' innovation in 'linear narratives'[6] – pity and self-pity draw Rochester into an internal dialogue with memories of his confrontation with Christophine and of Antoinette he declares to himself: 'I tell you she loves no one, anyone.

I could not touch her. Excepting as the hurricane will touch that tree – and break it. You say I did? No. That was love's fierce play. Now I'll do it.' Of a 'cool wind blowing' later in the scene, 'a cold wind', he thinks, 'Does it carry the babe born to stride the blast of hurricanes?'[7] Hurricane, the combination of 'misfortunes', 'compensation' and 'Nelson's Rest' on the opening page, 'a hut and a bit of land for herself', emancipation, means and property point to a crypt in Lockhart family memory around debt and extravagance in her great grandparents' generation and her slave-owning great-grandfather James Potter Lockhart's will.[8] They are instances of 'haunted language' that 'uses a gap inside speech to point to silenced history'.[9] 'Haunted language', Schwab explains, 'refers to what is unspeakable through ellipsis, indirection and detour, or fragmentation and deformation. A whole range of rhetorical figures may be mobilized to perform the work of crypts in language … figures that all combine concealment and revelation.'[10] Rhys's subconscious working through of Lockhart family secrets, I argue, shapes Antoinette's psychological geography. Rhys conceptualizes Antoinette's anger towards Rochester as a hurricane.[11]

The landscape-function (including climate) in the Rochester figure's narrative is a critique of a Eurocentric discourse of tropicality charted largely through his shifting affective investments in the figure of the *doudou*. Rhys's representation of the escalating turbulence of her Rochester's feeling towards Antoinette draws on a European literary tradition – *Jane Eyre*, William Shakespeare's *Othello* and *Macbeth*, Joseph Conrad's *Almayer's Folly* and *Heart of Darkness* and Charles Baudelaire's 'Le revenant' – and repurposes Charlotte Brontë's allusions to Aesop's fable of the oak and the reeds battered by storm winds. Rhys reframes these intertextual resonances through silent allusion to Derek Walcott's 'The Royal Palms … an absence of ruins' and 'Ruins of a Great House'. To make this allusion or those to Baudelaire and Conrad explicit would be to introduce anachronism into Rochester's point of view. While not making this point, Juliette Taylor-Batty analyses the relation with Baudelaire carefully.[12]

Rochester's disorientation in the Caribbean is part of the process of the making and reinforcement of his sense of tropicality and the familiar desirability of the temperate, in Brontë's Rochester's words, 'the antipodes of the Creole'.[13] His exposure to 'libidinal' and 'material exorbitance' in the tropics unsettles his English identity.[14] His disorientation is expressed through his sense of the excess and threat of its tropical biosphere: 'Everything is too much … Too much blue, too much purple, too much green.' He finds the route to Granbois '[n]ot only wild but menacing. Those hills would close in on you.' He is disconcerted on his walk past 'a sparse plantation of coffee trees, then straggly guava bushes' into a forest of 'enemy trees' to discover ruins of earlier French occupation of the island rather than virgin forest of doudouist provenance: 'part of a paved road', 'the ruins of a stone house and round the ruins rose trees that had grown to an incredible height'. The prospect of engulfment – 'the undergrowth and creepers caught at my legs and the trees closed over my head' – becomes entangled with a sense of the precariousness of European imperial enterprise.[15] After Antoinette confronts and bites him and then withdraws to the bedroom with a comforting Christophine, the Rochester figure remembers '[t]hat green menace. I had felt it ever since I saw this place. There was nothing I knew, nothing to comfort me.' Listening at the door of the bedroom, struggling to distinguish their voices, he hears them singing French Creole songs: '[W]hatever they were singing or saying was dangerous. I must protect myself.'[16]

Filtering his memory of Antoinette's talk of hurricanes through topoi drawn from Aesop's fable of the oak and the reeds, Rhys's Rochester imagines the effect of their violent winds on royal palms and 'abject' bamboos. The hurricane winds, which he promptly Anglicizes as 'blast', become a metaphor of Rochester's battery of Antoinette-renamed-Bertha, identified in Christophine's insistence to him that 'all you want is to break her up'.[17] A blast is a 'blowing or strong gust of wind'.[18] Rhys's Rochester figure thinks:

> Some of the royal palms stand (she told me). Stripped of their branches, like tall brown pillars, still they stand, defiant. Not for nothing are they called royal. The bamboos take an easier way, they bend to the earth and lie there, creaking, groaning, crying for mercy. The contemptuous wind passes, not caring for these abject things. (*Let them live.*)[19]

Stuart B. Schwartz explains that 'salt water driven by the storm winds' of hurricanes 'often stripped trees or blackened those that remained'.[20] The salt water in the passage from *Macbeth* to which Rhys's Rochester alludes are the 'tears' that 'shall drown the wind' when 'Pity' 'blow[s]' Macbeth's 'horrid deed in every eye'.[21] Blackened at this point through racialized othering by Rochester in the wake of his meeting with Daniel Cosway, Antoinette stands defiant, like the royal palms, with 'hatred in her eyes' for him.[22]

In having her Rochester figure allude to the fable of the oak and the reeds, Rhys is carefully stitching him into the design of *Jane Eyre*, in which Brontë also draws on topoi from the fable. The trunk of the horse-chestnut tree in *Jane Eyre* is split by lightning in a storm, foreshadowing the parting of Jane and Rochester brought about by the revelation of an impediment to their marriage in the existence of Bertha and an impediment to co-habitation in the form of

Jane's sense that her spiritual freedom encompasses living according to Christian precepts. After Rochester claims God's sanction for proposing to Jane, the narrating Jane remembers asking herself, 'And what ailed the chestnut tree? It writhed and groaned; while wind roared in the laurel walk, and came sweeping over us.'[23] When Jane resists Rochester's demand that she become his mistress, she remembers his 'fury', 'A wild look raised his brows – crossed his features … I shook, I feared – but I resolved.' Rochester sees her as 'at once so frail and so indomitable. A mere reed she feels in my hand! (and he shook me with the force of his hold.) I could bend her with my finger and thumb: and what good would it do if I bent, if I uptore, if I crushed her.' Recognizing that it is her 'spirit – with will and energy, and virtue and purity', and not the 'brittle' bodily 'frame' that he 'want[s]', Rochester lets her go and tries – unsuccessfully – to elicit her pity. In Jane's dream after she extricates herself from this encounter, a dream that reworks elements of Rochester's narrative of the 'fiery West Indian night' and 'sweet wind from Europe', a radiant white moon (rather than blood-red moon as in Rochester's account) takes the form of a protective maternal figure, which tells her, 'My daughter, flee temptation!'[24] Christian civility – in the name of which she has refused Rochester – is articulated through images of racialized purity. As Bewell points out, 'the "sweet wind from Europe" passage' also 'anticipates and is structurally revised by the mythic communication between Rochester and Jane that will ultimately bring them together'.[25]

The theme of Aesop's fable is how to survive the threat of personal, social and political upheaval, a threat represented by a strong wind. The gist of the fable is summed up in the proverbial saying, 'A reed before the wind lives on, while mighty oaks do fall.'[26] In Samuel Croxall's translation the 'prudent' reed responds to the uprooted oak, 'I secure myself by putting on a Behaviour quite contrary to what you do; instead of being stubborn and stiff, and confiding in my Strength, I yield and bend to the Blast, and let it go over me: knowing how vain and fruitless it would be to resist it.'[27] As Annabel Patterson observes, fables are 'weak against injustice … the fable's power resides precisely in the powerlessness of those who speak its language'.[28]

Recalling the seductiveness of Antoinette singing '*Adieu foulard, adieu madras*', Rhys's Rochester figure recalls of Antoinette during the departure from what Amélie calls the '"honeymoon house"':

> I'll watch for one tear, one human tear. Not that blank hating moonstruck face. I'll listen.... If she says good-bye perhaps adieu. *Adieu* – like those old-time songs she sang. Always *adieu* (and all songs say it). If she too says it, or weeps, I'll

take her in my arms, my lunatic. She's mad but *mine, mine*. What will I care for gods or devils or for Fate itself. If she smiles or weeps or both. *For me*.[29]

She refuses to yield to him as he imagines the bamboos do to the hurricane.[30] Rhys implicitly draws an analogy between the *doudou* and the bamboos. Royal palms are native to parts of the Caribbean and circum-Caribbean; bamboos are exotics. '[O]nce there was an avenue of royal palms' at Coulibri, Antoinette tells Rochester in her story of Annette, 'but a lot of them had fallen and others had been cut down and the ones that were left looked lost. Lost trees.'[31] At Coulibri bamboos are grown beside the great house and the *glacis*, a terrace used for drying coffee beans,[32] repurposed as plantation work cycles came to a halt. Rhys subtly suggests that, like bamboo, the *doudou* is an exotic import of plantation culture. The Rochester figure sees Antoinette, rather than yielding, instead 'staring out to the distant sea. She was silence itself.' He remembers thinking, 'Sing, Antoinetta. I can hear you now.' He silently wills her, 'Do not be sad. Or think Adieu. Never Adieu.' 'And you must laugh and chatter as you used to do.'[33]

The Rochester figure's articulation of Granbois's 'dangerous' situation resonates with images in Conrad's *Almayer's Folly* and *Heart of Darkness*, novels to which Rhys alludes in her fiction of the early 1930s. Leaving Granbois, the Rochester figure notices Antoinette 'there in the *ajoupa*', his reversion to French perhaps signalling an exoticizing recognition of her, and looks back at the 'shabby white house ... More than ever it strained away from the black snake-like forest. Louder and more desperately it called: Save me from destruction, ruin and desolation. Save me from the long slow death by ants. But what are you doing here you folly? So near the forest. Don't you know that this is a dangerous place? And that the dark forest always wins?'[34] The word 'folly', too, draws out the fragility of colonial enterprise; for the Rochester figure, though, the 'shabby white house' comes to stand for Antoinette. Folly refers to a disproportionately 'costly structure'; yet folly in other senses – 'madness' and 'lewdness'[35] – becomes the tenor of Rochester's representation of Antoinette. Almayer's 'half finished' home in Borneo – with 'neatly-fitting floors' and 'sashless windows' – is surrounded by 'forest', and jocularly named 'Almayer's Folly' by visitors, suggesting both overpricing and madness. The folly, too, is his faith in regeneration of his prospects through English investment.[36] David Arnold has read Joseph Conrad's *Heart of Darkness* as exemplary of a 'dark side of tropicality', 'an abiding sense of danger, alienation and repugnance'.[37] Marlow focalizes that darkness through representation of the tropical 'forest'[38] as a site of mystery, the unknown and the unknowable. He remembers, for instance, the 'ruinous aspect' of Kurtz's house: 'The woods were unmoved like a mask – heavy like the closed door of a prison – they looked with their air of hidden knowledge, of patient expectation, of unapproachable silence.'[39] And of his character: 'a flabby, pretending, weak-eyed devil of a rapacious and pitiless folly'. A lurid sign of his depravity are the heads on poles around his house, which Marlow describes as 'food for thought and also for vultures if there had been any looking down from the sky; but at all events for such ants as were industrious enough to ascend the pole'.[40]

In a study of the sublime in postcolonial fiction, Philip Dickinson draws out a 'tension between the imperative to represent' and the 'possible encounter with unrepresentability', arguing that the sublime in *Heart of Darkness* is centrally processed through 'a larger aesthetic of unrepresentability'.[41] Rhys, too, riffs on unrepresentability. In her Rochester's narrative Rhys uses the words 'blanks', 'blank', and 'nothing' in a variety of contexts to convey his affective encounters with unrepresentability. Shortly after arriving at Granbois, he attributes his inability to write coherently of Jamaica and Dominica to the '*illness*' which has been his rite of passage on arrival in the West Indies: 'As for my confused impressions they will never be written up. There are blanks in my mind that cannot be filled up.' For him, 'It was all very brightly coloured, very strange, but it meant nothing.'[42] The West Indies – and the tropics more generally – were often represented as places of disease for Europeans. Writing of the early modernist period, Homi Bhabha states: 'There is a conspiracy of silence around the colonial truth, whatever that might be.' He notes that a 'silence' of 'colonial "otherness", that speaks in riddles, obliterating proper names and proper places … turns imperial triumphalism into the testimony of colonial confusion and those who hear its echo lose their historic memories'.[43] Notably the proper name obliterated in *Wide Sargasso Sea* is Edward Fairfax Rochester. Antoinette does not address him by his first or family name in her narrative; for readers, he implicitly names himself Edward Rochester at the moment he renames Antoinette Bertha.

The hurricane winds of revenge are represented in the traducing of Antoinette's humanity in the 'child's scribble' of a future he anticipates for her:

> I drew a house surrounded by trees. A large house. I divided the third floor into rooms and in one room I drew a standing woman … a dot for a head, a larger one for the body, a triangle for a skirt, slanting lines for arms and feet. But it was an English house.
> English trees.

The pun on 'dot' (a spot and a dowry) is surely deliberate on Rhys's part. 'Howling, shrieking, laughing the wild blast passes', he thinks. The adjective 'wild' tropicalizes 'blast', a term that Brontë uses three times in *Jane Eyre*. Rhys's Rochester acknowledges that his desire for revenge against Antoinette originates in his sense that the Mason family 'bought' him with their 'paltry money', that Antoinette 'deceived' and 'betrayed' him and that she refuses to yield to him like the bamboo by 'smil[ing]' or 'weep[ing] or both. *For me*', Rochester demands.[44] He is tapping into an 'imperialist imaginary' of hurricanes as metaphors for slave 'rebellion'.[45] More subtextually, processing the tropics stereotypically as 'a pathological space of degeneration',[46] he fears adulteration and the violence '"bound up with his own experience of sexual pleasure"' with Antoinette, '"while he must destroy"' her '"both for her excessive experience of pleasure and for awakening such sensations in himself"'.[47] A catalyst for his reassertion of his English manhood, the 'child's scribble' acts as Rhys's ironic intertextual authorial comment on Brontë's Rochester's explanation of his incarceration of Bertha: 'Place her in safety and comfort: shelter her degradation with secrecy, and leave her.'[48] The language of moral legitimation here constructs the imprisonment as an act of what Upamanyu Pablo Mukherjee characterizes as 'palliative imperialism' in the wake of construction of the 'tropics as a disaster zone': 'the idea of imperialism as an act of care, in fact, a relief effort ... undertaken to fulfil Europe's historical mission of rescuing the native inhabitants from their own habitat'.[49] Rhys travesties Rochester's rationalization of his plans for Bertha, the 'child's scribble' implying that his reassertion of English manhood is psychologically regressive and crude.

In formal turbulence, Rhys dramatizes Rochester's 'giddy change, remembering, the sickening swing back to hate' in the final section of Part Two. Here the language of blankness and nothing intensifies. The effect of Rochester's hurricane of revenge on Antoinette is to make her interiority unreadable by him from her face: 'that blank hating moonstruck face'; 'her face blank, no expression at all'; 'blank indifference'; '[b]lank lovely eyes.' The word 'nothing' reverberates through the remembered scene of departure: 'Keep nothing back'; 'You will have nothing'; 'Nothing left but hopelessness'; 'I know nothing about you'; 'For nothing. Nothing.'[50] Given the stock representation of the moon 'as a powerful icon of female sensibility',[51] Rochester's adjective 'moonstruck' shows his clear association of Antoinette's insanity with her gender. When, in 1964, Rhys first started to develop her sense of Rochester's 'giddy change', she thought of Antoinette as 'angry too. Like a hurricane. Like a Creole.'[52]

In the short story 'Temps Perdi' (1967) Rhys identifies the spirit of place in colonial Dominica with the patois phrase that is the story's title, translating it as 'wasted time, lost labour', aligning that spirit with 'natural' catastrophe ('hurricane', 'a disease of the crops').[53] In Rhys's unpublished poem 'Tourists', the steadfast mountains of Dominica deliver the phrase as a judgement on human dreaming of a better life there.[54] Schwartz points out that, in contrast to colonial plantation agriculture, indigenous peoples of the Caribbean hurricane belt chose crops for 'their resistance to wind-storm damage' and adopted 'field management' and 'forest usage and maintenance' strategies to 'adjust their lives to the storms'.[55] In Rhys's story, 'temps perdi' is, then, a 'social construction of "natural disaster" … largely hidden from view' as such by colonial land and plantation crop management practice 'that simultaneously imposes false expectations on the environment and then explains the inevitable disappointments as proof of a malign and hostile nature'.[56] Fire, as in Brontë's Rochester's narrative of his departure from Jamaica, is part of the figurative field of hurricanes; so, too, are '[m]odalities' of slave '[r]evolt'.[57] The words 'blast' and 'blasted' were used in the eighteenth- and nineteenth-century West Indies to describe the destruction caused by hurricanes after they made landfall. Landscapes suffering devastation were seen to have the appearance of being 'burnt over',[58] 'as if a fire had gone through and blasted' them.[59] In *Wide Sargasso Sea*, Rhys's Rochester simply assumes that the appearance of ruined estate houses 'all over the place' are signs of enslaved or formerly enslaved people having 'burned' them in insurrection;[60] the possibility of hurricane damage does not cross his mind. The phrase 'temps perdi' maps the political and cultural ecology of plantation capitalism in economic decline. Rhys's memories of her great-aunt Jane Woodcock's oral stories and songs are, she suggests in a 1959 letter, helping her develop and hone a more precise sense of place, situation and history, located in the subjective points of view of characters.[61]

Within Lockhart family history, the crypt around which Rhys begins negotiating in *Voyage in the Dark*, her Black Exercise Book and the manuscripts she calls 'Creole' conceals and compresses aspects of her great-grandfather James Potter Lockhart's slide into massive debt: plantations owned by him were severely affected by hurricanes in 1825, 1833 and 1834;[62] his business interests were also damaged by the effects on coffee planters of the blight which affected the 1829 crop. He did not report the extent of the 1825 hurricane damage to William King, his chief creditor even then. On 16 June 1825, James asked King to 'befriend' him 'by *managing* for' him with creditors William Coles and Barclays, stating that he expected £15,000 from a settlement with former business partner Charles Court, and citing difficulties in collecting payments from coffee planters because of a poor crop. He wanted time for the settlement to be reached, monies from it to be paid, and to collect debts and proposed to sell his half-share of the estate Bonny and Moore Park. Between 1826 and 1829 E. M. Casey did acquire full title to Bonny and Moore Park.[63] In his next letter of 9 October 1825, James writes to King that Mr Bevan holds the 'deeds of Geneva' as surety on a loan and asks King, out of '[k]indness' to him, to use his '[i]nfluence' with Bevan and Co. to secure 'another years [sic] credit' for him.[64] In 1827 King lent James Lockhart a further £10,964 5s. 3d. at interest of 5 per cent.[65] By 1829 James's silver – including enough cutlery for thirty-two diners – was apparently 'placed with Messrs Cavan & Co. as part Security … for a Loan of £3616.7.6'.[66] In 1836 James demanded of his wife Jane Maxwell Lockhart, who was then based in Plymouth, that she 'live quietly and economically' on less than £500 a year in England (in 2011 economic status terms £559,700 a year); he 'would sooner learn the Death of all' his five '[d]aughters' than have to bring them and Jane back to Dominica because of her inability to do so.[67] A balance sheet produced by James's eldest son by his first marriage William Brade Lockhart in 1838, which may date to 1832, shows other large loans dating from 1823 and 1827 with interest still owing: loans from J. Blackburn of £4,617 13 3 and Page and Son of £603 2 1 in 1823, and from Thomas Coles of £2,259 2 8, Henry St Hill of £2,024 6 8, and J. Gordon of £310 in 1827.[68] Antoinette attributes the decline of family fortune to the emancipation of an enslaved workforce: 'All Coulibri Estate had gone wild like the garden, gone to bush. No more slavery – why should *anybody* work? This never saddened me. I did not remember the place when it was prosperous.'[69] Rhys writes of ruins to Morchard Bishop in 1953, 'There are so many in the West Indies. I grew up with them.'[70]

The representation of the royal palms in *Wide Sargasso Sea* is part of a pattern of engagement with Derek Walcott's 'The Royal Palms … an absence of ruins', a poem published in the February 1962 issue of the *London Magazine* which also featured Rhys's 'Let Them Call It Jazz', and 'Ruins of a Great House', published in Walcott's *In a Green Night: Poems 1948–1960* (1962). In his Nobel Lecture, Walcott elaborates the pertinence of the topos of ruin in Caribbean literature: 'The sigh of History rises over ruins, not over landscapes, and in the Antilles there are few ruins to sigh over, apart from the ruins of sugar estates and abandoned forts.'[71] Walcott's meditations on ruins are so pervasive in his oeuvre that Bruce King opens the first chapter of his biography of him: 'Derek Walcott has often written in a very New World way against the burden of History. For Walcott it is entangled with claims that the West Indies has no history or that it has no major events and achievements on which to build, or that its events and achievements have mostly to do with, or build upon, slavery, racism, and violent conquest.'[72] Inspired by English historian James Anthony Froude's claim in *The English in the West Indies: or, The Bow of Ulysses* (1888) that in the West Indies '[t]here are no people ... in the true sense of the word, with a character and purpose of their own', Walcott writes in 'Air', a poem first collected in *The Gulf* (1969):

> The unheard, omnivorous
> jaws of this rain forest
> not merely devour all,
> but allow nothing vain[.]

The poem, which wryly addresses Indigenous genocide and Eurocentric erasures of Caribbean history, concludes with the line, 'There is too much nothing here.'[73] The poem is also a riposte to V. S. Naipaul's now-infamous comment in *The Middle Passage* (1962): 'The history of the islands can never be satisfactorily told. Brutality is not the only difficulty. History is built around achievement and creation; and nothing was created in the West Indies.'[74] The epigraph of *The Middle Passage* and 'Air' draw on the same passage in Froude's travel narrative. Dania Dwyer points out that '[f]or Walcott, ruins represent the muse through which the poet guesses about and ultimately rewrites history with a difference. This new history challenges the Eurocentric representations of the Caribbean by speaking to the Caribbean writers' postcolonial reality and not necessarily seeking to recreate historical events as they occurred.'[75]

The poetic voice of Walcott's 'The Royal Palms ... an absence of ruins' avers that in the Caribbean 'there are no heroic palaces' or pyramids as monumental 'architecture' in 'praise' of Caribbean civilizations. The region's history has been marked by violent conquest, sexual abuse, 'lust' and enslavement. Using poetic conceit, Walcott represents the royal palms – 'With their Corinthian plumes and earthen plinth' and 'columns' – as metonyms of the Caribbean 'racial labyrinth'. Rhys's image of the trunks of the royal palms as 'pillars' catches up Walcott's 'columns'; hurricane damage strips her royal palms of their branches/plumes. 'If art is where the greatest ruins are, / Our art is in the ruins we became', Walcott writes. The 'ravage[d]' 'Flesh' of conquest, both socio-political and sexual, 'built its ruin in the conqueror's blood'.[76] Walcott is elaborating poetically a stereotype of the white Creole here. Brontë's and Rhys's Rochesters and Rhys's Daniel Cosway attribute Antoinette's degeneracy to her family's Creole blood. Referring to Annette, Antoinette's mother, Daniel writes to Rochester of '*the madness that is in her, and in all these white Creoles*'.[77] The young Antoinette is most at home on ruinate lands – plantation lands reverting to tropical vegetation and local market economies around provision grounds worked by ex-slaves. It is on ruinate lands that 'Tia and Antoinette's relationship develops' and that she experiences moments of 'transcend[ing] the materiality of place and her isolation by "[w]atching the red and yellow flowers in the sun thinking of nothing"'[78] and 'razor grass cut[ting]' her 'legs and arms', the spectacle of 'swarming' ants, and 'rain that soaked' her 'to the skin'.[79]

The elegiac voice of Walcott's 'Ruins of a Great House' contemplates 'Stones only, the *disjecta membra* of this Great House',[80] moving beyond anger at the slave trade and plantation slavery to consolation at the idea of the transience of empires and life. At the time the poem was written neither St Lucia, Walcott's birthplace, nor Trinidad, where he worked during the 1950s, had achieved independence. St Lucia would do so in 1979; Trinidad in 1962. Walcott's measured meditation on transatlantic history contrasts sharply with Rochester's disorientation when he encounters the stones of the paved road and the ruins of the house and garden of Père Lilièvre.[81] For Rhys, the Sargasso Sea of her novel's eventual title was synonymous with wreckage and detritus.[82]

Walcott's image of Caribbean history as a 'racial labyrinth' has many resonances. The word 'labyrinth' is borrowed from the Latin '*labyrinthus*', meaning 'place from which one cannot escape', 'also complicated idea'.[83] The image suggests that the racial formations of Caribbean history are difficult to negotiate; that people are susceptible to becoming bewildered by or entangled in their intricacies. The labyrinth at Knossos was built to house the Minotaur, a creature half-man and half-bull. In *Wide Sargasso Sea* the incommensurability of English Historical and Caribbean historical consciousness is drawn out on the journey to Granbois when locals, including Antoinette, cannot or will not tell Rochester what event was commemorated in the naming of a village Massacre. The event, which occurred in 1674, was a massacre of a 'party of 60–70 Carib men, women, and children including Thomas "Indian" Warner, the supposed half-Carib son of one of the foremost English colonists in the West Indies, Sir Thomas Warner, Governor of St Kitts'.[84] Philip Warner, Sir Thomas's legitimate white child, reportedly ordered the killing; he was tried for and acquitted of fratricide in Barbados in 1676. The place name Massacre identifies the honeymoon island as Dominica. As I have noted in *The Worlding of Jean Rhys*, 'A set of stories surrounding Massacre', shaped by the racial formation of Caribbean history, 'features, like *Wide Sargasso Sea*, the betrayal of a half-sibling, racial tension exacerbated by the shame of miscegenation and illegitimacy, vengeance, and doubt over the paternity of the mixed-race illegitimate child'.[85] One of the signs of Rochester being lost in the labyrinth of history as he prepares to leave Dominica is his interpretation of the memory of Christophine's 'contempt' when she serves him coffee: '"Taste my bull's blood." Meaning that will make you a man. Perhaps.'[86] His explanation is grounded in his sense of his sovereign manhood being threatened by the tropics. Bull's blood was used in the clarifying of liquid sugar in the milling process.[87] Christophine was referring to the preparation of sugar for consumption as a sweetener of coffee and the racialized labour of sugar cultivation and the sugar boiling house. While Antoinette remembers walking 'past the old sugar works and the water wheel that had not turned for years' at Coulibri,[88] Christophine's mention of bull's blood draws out the continuity of a racialized plantation labour system after slave emancipation.

The Lockhart family memory of its ruin was profoundly shaped by what Gordon K. Lewis calls the 'myth of King Sugar': sugar cultivation under plantation slavery not only as a 'tropical capital-labor regime', but 'also, in the imaginary world that the plantocracy constructed, a sort of divine, mystical cult'.[89] In reality, in 1835 James Lockhart's financial affairs were such that he had to transfer the slave compensation monies for his Geneva workforce to William King to offset monies recoverable through a bond of obligation of £21,928 10s. 6d.[90] In 2021 terms that sum has a historic relative income value of £16,530,000.[91] James's will refers to ownership of two Dominican estates: Geneva and Nelson's Rest. In 1840, King and James Parkinson, James' executors, reported to the Lord Chancellor of England that they could not establish his unencumbered title to either. Under the terms of James' will, all of his assets apart from his plate were to be sold to settle his debts and to provide annuities of £300 sterling for Jane while she remained his widow, £100 for Lavinia Parke (the daughter of Rachel Parke) and £75 for his mother Bridget. His mother, though, had predeceased him.[92] The apprentice Eliza (understood by King to be his mistress) was to be allowed possession of 'her House then occupied by her Mother and the piece of Ground fenced in adjoining the said House for her use during her life'.[93] In *Wide Sargasso Sea*, Rhys's Rochester figure remembers Daniel, old Cosway's illegitimate son, Antoinette's half-brother, a man of colour, mentioning an additional more generous gift of freedom in a conversation about the lies on his father's memorial tablet:

> 'Pious,' they write up. 'Beloved by all'. Not a word about the people he buy and sell like cattle. 'Merciful to the weak,' they write up. Mercy! The man have a heart like stone. Sometimes when he gets sick of a woman which is quickly, he free her like he free my mother, even he give a hut and a piece of land for herself (a garden some call that), but it is no mercy, it's for wicked pride he do it.[94]

As there were no grandchildren of James by any deceased legitimate children at his death, the remainder of the monies and plate were to be divided equally among his legitimate adult or married children, apart from William Brade Lockhart, whom he had disinherited. The two youngest children Richard Hooton Lockhart (b. 1817) and Rhys's grandfather Edward Lockhart (b. 1820) were neither twenty-one nor married at their father's death, so, like William, they inherited no property or wealth.[95] The class trappings of their upbringings and their education would, though, have been valuable cultural capital.

The Lockhart family estate Geneva is transposed from Dominica to Jamaica under the toponym Coulibri in the novel.[96] During civil unrest in Dominica in 1844 (La Guerre Negre), estate workers ransacked the great house at Geneva for Jane Lockhart's personal effects (all she owned) and burned them in the grounds. They pointedly did not burn the great house; estate workers fire the great house at Coulibri in *Wide Sargasso Sea*. La Guerre Negre was provoked by a controversial census which would reify the offensive racial categories of the plantation slavery period. Provocatively, Richard and Edward Lockhart had damaged worker dwellings.

In the legitimate Lockhart children's generation, the dramas of shame and trauma contingent on James and Jane's debts, on a façade of wealth and prestige having been underpinned and undermined by debt, on legitimate children having to adjust to very different expectations in their lives because of parental debt may have been screened somewhat from later generations. Abraham suggests that loyalty to 'the fictitious yet necessary integrity of the parental figure' is at stake in the keeping of family secrets.[97] Notably, in this instance what was sayable about compensation monies and family fortunes also conformed to planter ideology: that the economic viability of its class was shattered by outside interference around the abolition of slavery. It is a view of history, both familial and more general, that keeps the cult of 'King Sugar' and its sustaining myths of wealth and grandeur intact. Rhys represents it critically in *Wide Sargasso Sea*.

As first-person narrator of Part One Antoinette remembers a conversation that she overheard her mother Annette have with Mr Luttrell of Nelson's Rest, 'our neighbour and her only friend. "Of course they have their own misfortunes. Still waiting for this compensation the English promised when the Emancipation Act was passed. Some will wait for a long time."'[98] Who 'they' are is not specified. There is an authorial pun on 'misfortunes'. Having overheard this snippet of conversation, Antoinette assumes that Luttrell's suicide was motivated by his having grown 'tired of waiting' for the compensation monies. '[S]trangers from Spanish Town' visit Nelson's Rest to 'gossip' about 'the tragedy'. She remembers them saying, '"Live at Nelson's Rest? Not for love or money. An unlucky place."' Luttrell's house is temporarily unoccupied, 'left empty'. 'Soon the black people said it was haunted, they wouldn't go near it. And no one came near us.'⁹⁹ Antoinette's '[a]nd no one came near us' sets up an analogy between Nelson's Rest and Coulibri as houses 'haunted' by missed fortune. Mardorossian argues perceptively:

> Rhys distances herself from her protagonist through formal patterns, ellipses, and repetitions that expose Antoinette's colonialist assumptions.... In the first section of the novel, the young Antoinette's perceptual and psychological point of view ... seems to function merely by internalizing others' – especially her mother's – language and contradictory values....[T]he novel offers a narrator-focalizer whose own limited knowledge and problematic values highlight her unreliability as she is shown desperately trying to patch together the fragments of her disintegrating world.¹⁰⁰

The technique fits with Rhys's sense of her artistic practice in the novel involving 'a lot of cutting, joining up'. Annette's understandings of her '*lowering*' social and economic position as a widow of limited financial means¹⁰¹ and its broader contexts are strongly shaped by self-pity, racial stereotyping, and colonial ideology that Maslen has analysed as a 'nostalgic' and 'melancholic' longing for her 'family's former affluence and prestige'.¹⁰² The language haunted by Lockhart family secrets here – 'misfortunes', 'compensation' and 'Nelson's Rest', and perhaps Annette's sense of having been 'abandoned' in its meaning of having been profligate¹⁰³ – is crucially imbricated in this mode of relation to a slave-owning family history, and as author Rhys subjects it to critical scrutiny and irony.

Puns encrypt Lockhart family history. Nelson's Rest was 'left', in the sense of bequeathed, 'empty'.¹⁰⁴ The syllable Nel might also be read as a pun on knell, 'A sound announcing the death of a person or the passing away of something; an omen of death or extinction', 'To strike with a resounding blow'.¹⁰⁵ Read in this way the name Nelson's Rest encrypts the predicaments of James Lockhart's sons after his death. Brought up accustomed to luxury, they then had to worry over and work to pay their father's debts. Rhys's grandfather Edward (b. 1820) died young in *c.* 1860, when her mother Minna was seven.¹⁰⁶

The social world of the Luttrells who inherit Nelson's Rest in *Wide Sargasso Sea* draws Annette into the narrative reach of *Jane Eyre*, for she meets and captivates Mr Mason at its 'dance[s]' and 'moonlight picnic[s]'. Christophine says to Antoinette of the 'very beautiful' and well-dressed Luttrells who laugh at her when she returns home in Tia's clothes: 'Trouble walk into the house this day. Trouble walk in.'¹⁰⁷ Through Annette's second marriage Antoinette will acquire the last name Mason, for readers familiar with Charlotte Brontë's novel an early point of recognition that she might become Bertha Mason Rochester. In relation to Rhys's inscription of *Jane Eyre* in *Wide Sargasso Sea*, Nelson's Rest is a palimpsest of Lockhart family history of the late plantation slavery period.

Brontë's uses of the word blast may have suggested to Rhys her Rochester's allusion to *Macbeth* and her pursuit of a countervailing hurricane poetics. Blasts feature in *Jane Eyre* in two narrative sequences marked by stark shifts in generic register which culminate in Jane becoming 'insensible from terror': the narrative of events which lead to her syncope in the red room; and Jane's prophetic dream of Thornfield Hall as ultimately 'a dreary ruin, the retreat of bats and owls' from which she wakes to see Bertha Mason Rochester tearing her bridal veil.[108] The blast in the opening chapter of *Jane Eyre* accompanies what feminist critics have read as Jane's assumption of voice-agency in defying John Reed, 'the mood of the revolted slave … bracing me with its bitter vigour', a 'heart in insurrection', 'damp[ened]' in the red-room, in Jane's narration, by an abject whiteness of 'humiliation, self-doubt, forlorn depression'.[109] Both Jane and author Brontë are tropicalizing revolt. For Virginia Woolf, Brontë's conflation of natural and psychological landscape in the pathetic fallacy of the blast is a sign of the Yorkshire moors and of Brontë's distinctive regional feminist voice in English fiction. The blast is, in her view, an 'exhilaration' that 'rushes us' common readers 'through the entire volume, without giving us time to think, without letting us lift our eyes from the page'.[110]

Sally Shuttleworth has shown that the 'organising psychological assumptions' in *Jane Eyre* 'are drawn directly from the energy dynamics of nineteenth-century economic and psychological discourse'. She focuses, in particular, on images of fire and 'social turbulence', and refers briefly to the language of 'earthquakes and tremors'.[111] But in the first chapter the child Jane, sitting on the window-seat reading Thomas Bewick's *History of British Birds*, '[a]t intervals … studied the aspect of that winter afternoon. Afar, it offered a pale blank of mist and cloud; near, a scene of wet lawn and storm-beat shrub, with ceaseless rain sweeping away wildly before a long and lamentable blast', climatic turbulence.[112] A girl's or woman's look from a window (or the roof as later in *Jane Eyre*) is a common literary motif, a spatialized figure of desire for transcendence of the materiality of her sequestered domestic condition. Recently Justine Pizzo has coined the term 'atmospheric exceptionalism' to describe Jane Eyre's 'sensual and intellectual receptivity to climate', noting Brontë's interest in 'affinity with meteorological energy'. Jane's 'atmospheric sensitivity' is coupled from the novel's beginning, she argues, with 'a profound interest in pictorial representation' of air and sky, initially in the illustrations of Bewick's book and later in the paintings Rochester admires. The sensitivity is shown in 'unmistakable physical and psychological expansiveness'.[113] Rhys's Rochester seizing on the fury of the hurricane as described by Antoinette is a regressive cover for his own violence.

Jane's dream of Thornfield Hall in ruin is seemingly provoked by anxiety about her material dependence on Rochester, a social disparity highlighted in his present of an extravagant wedding veil. In dream, thinking the 'gallop[ing] … horse' she hears might be Rochester, 'departing for many years, and for a distant country', she struggles to climb the 'shell-like wall' of the ruin with an 'unknown little child' in her arms. 'The blast blew so strong' she is forced to sit down and calm 'the scared infant'. '[T]he wall crumbled; I was shaken; the child rolled from my knee; I lost my balance, fell and woke.' And it is then that she sees the reflection of Bertha in the mirror as Bertha dons, removes, rends and tramples on her bridal veil. Bertha pauses at Jane's 'bedside' when leaving the room: 'the fiery eye glared upon me … I was aware her lurid visage flamed over mine, and I lost consciousness.'[114] For Sandra M. Gilbert and Susan Gubar the 'wailing child' is 'the child Jane herself', 'her orphaned alter ego'.[115] 'When Jane dreams of children', Mary Poovey argues, 'some disaster follows that is a displaced expression of the anger against kin that the character denies … narrative effect is split off from psychological cause … the body of the text symptomatically acts out what cannot make its way into the psychologically realistic narrative'.[116] Shuttleworth's phrase '*lurid hieroglyphics*' points to the enigmatic formal juxtaposition of Jane's dream images and her apprehension of Bertha, which she argues is not 'the intrusion of an out-dated Gothic form into a realist novel; she stands, rather as the crystallization of the negative images of womanhood available in contemporary social and scientific discourse'.[117] 'What crime was this, that lived incarnate in this sequestered mansion, and could neither be expelled nor subdued by the owner?' thinks Jane.[118] For readers of *Wide Sargasso Sea* the answer might be Rochester's 'swing' to hatred of Antoinette and his revenge against her. Rhys's characterization of Rochester's revenge as '[h]owling, shrieking, laughing' suggests that this is what reverberates in the eerie noises Jane hears at Thornfield Hall in *Jane Eyre*.[119] The rereading accords with Rhys's interest in the psychological geography of Brontë's novel.

If the Bertha of Jane's terror and Rochester's story for Jane is framed as his 'horrid deed' by Rhys's allusion to *Macbeth*, the infant of Jane's dream might be reread as 'unknown' pity, not born to stride the blast of her anger, of his vengeance, of her struggle to comprehend the racialized visage.[120] Also Rhys's Grace Poole remembers Mrs Eff (Fairfax) saying of her 'master': 'His stay in the

West Indies has changed him out of all knowledge. He has grey in his hair and misery in his eyes. Don't ask me to pity anyone who had a hand in that.'[121]

In *Wide Sargasso Sea*, the Rochester figure processes the tropical climate and landscape through Eurocentric ideas of tropicality, shifting between two of their registers, the paradisal (the seductiveness of the *doudou*) and the pernicious (the psychological geography of corruption, intemperance, ruin, injury and destruction). These registers underpin and subjectively legitimize for him his cultural and moral othering of Antoinette and Christophine. Rhys's experiment with a hurricane poetics enables her to draw out incommensurabilities between European and local knowledges of the Caribbean and the fragility of imperial ambitions there. Her exploration of the dissonance between English History and Caribbean history, particularly through the experiences of the forest that unnerve Rochester, and the image of the royal palms, is shaped by her reading of Derek Walcott's early poetry, a hitherto unknown influence on her. Rhys's Rochester reads his hurricane of 'revenge' (Rhys's amplification of his memory of a 'fiery West-Indian night' in *Jane Eyre*) as having broken Antoinette: 'She was only a ghost. A ghost in the grey daylight. Nothing left but hopelessness.'[122] '*I'll say one thing for her, she hasn't lost her spirit. She's still fierce*', Grace Poole acknowledges. There are three axes of landscape-function in Rhys's characterization of Antoinette: the encryption of family history, ruinate lands (a sign of the local impact of History) and a nurturant racialized formation of the senses (a sign of history). At Thornfield Hall Antoinette's 'red dress', rather than her 'grey wrapper', becomes the metonym of her sustaining spirit, connected as it is with the tropics through colour ('[t]he colour of flamboyant flowers') and fragrance ('the smell of vetivert and frangipanni, of cinnamon and dust and lime trees when they are flowering ... of the sun and ... the rain').[123] When Antoinette 'look[s] at the dress on the floor ... it was as if the fire had spread across the room' and she has her third prophetic dream – of return to a remembered tropical home.[124] In Antoinette's dream the sky is red – a colour that suffuses Brontë's Rochester's account of the 'fiery West-Indian night; one of the description that frequently precede the hurricanes of those climates' – and she thinks 'all' her 'life was in it'.[125]

# Notes

1   Brontë, *Jane Eyre*, 307–9.
2   Alan Bewell, '*Jane Eyre* and Victorian Medical Geography', *ELH* 63 (1996): 790.
3   Livingstone, 'Tropical Hermeneutics', 93.

4   Rhys, *Wide Sargasso Sea*, 98–9.
5   Upamanyu Pablo Mukherjee, *Natural Disasters and Victorian Empire: Famines, Fevers, and Literary Cultures in South Asia* (Basingstoke: Palgrave Macmillan, 2013), 24.
6   Sharae Deckard, 'The Political Ecology of Storms in Caribbean Literature', in *Caribbean: Aesthetics, World-ecology, Politics*, ed. Chris Campbell and Michael Niblett (Liverpool: Liverpool University Press, 2016), 36.
7   Rhys, *Wide Sargasso Sea*, 99.
8   Ibid., 9, 10, 73.
9   I give a much fuller and detailed sense of this history in Thomas, 'Ghostly Presences'.
10  Schwab, *Haunting Legacies*, 54.
11  Later, and not drawing on Rhys, Kamau Brathwaite uses the hurricane as a metaphor for Caribbean experience and clime which cannot be accommodated in the rhythms of English poetry: 'The hurricane does not roar in pentameter.' 'History of the Voice' (1979/81) in his *Roots* (Michigan: University of Michigan Press, 1993), 265.
12  Juliette Taylor-Batty, '"Le revenant": Baudelaire's Afterlife in *Wide Sargasso Sea*', *Modernism/Modernity* 27, no. 4 (2020): 665–88. I discuss Rhys's allusions to *Othello* in *The Worlding of Jean Rhys*, 172–6.
13  Brontë, *Jane Eyre*, 34.
14  Steven Vine, *Reinventing the Sublime: Post-Romantic Literature and Theory* (Brighton: Sussex Academic Press, 2013), 3.
15  Rhys, *Wide Sargasso Sea*, 41, 62–3, 62.
16  Ibid., 90.
17  Ibid., 98, 98–9, 92.
18  *Oxford English Dictionary Online*.
19  Rhys, *Wide Sargasso Sea*, 98, her emphasis.
20  Stuart B. Schwartz, *Sea of Storms: A History of Hurricanes in the Greater Caribbean from Columbus to Katrina* (Princeton, NJ: Princeton University Press, 2015), 41.
21  William Shakespeare, *Macbeth*, ed. D. R. Elloway (Basingstoke: Macmillan Education, 1971), act 1, scene 7, lines 21–5.
22  Rhys, *Wide Sargasso Sea*, 102.
23  Brontë, *Jane Eyre*, 256.
24  Ibid., 317, 316, 317–18, 319.
25  Bewell, '*Jane Eyre* and Victorian Medical Geography', 791.
26  Jennifer Speake, comp. *The Oxford Dictionary of Proverbs* (Oxford: Oxford University Press, 2015), 264.
27  Samuel Croxall, trans. *Fables of Aesop and Others* (London: W. Strahan, J. and F. Rivington, et al., 1878), 90.

28 Patterson, *Fables of Power*, 30.
29 Rhys, *Wide Sargasso Sea*, 38, 99, her emphasis.
30 Bamboo is in fact far more resilient to hurricane winds than the Rochester figure imagines. Indeed, Martinican intellectual and activist Suzanne Césaire takes bamboo as an emblem of a new anti-doudouist poetics: 'Come on now, real poetry lies elsewhere. Far from rhymes, laments, sea breezes, parrots. Stiff and stout bamboos changing direction, we decree the death of sappy, sentimental, folkloric literature. And to hell with hibiscus, frangipani, and bougainvillea.' Quoted in Anny Dominique Curtius, 'Cannibalizing *Doudouisme*, Conceptualizing the *Morne*', 517.
31 Rhys, *Wide Sargasso Sea*, 78–9.
32 On the structure and use of the *glacis*, see Élie Monnereau, *The Complete Indigo-maker: Containing, an Accurate Account of the Indigo Plant; Its Description, Culture, Preparation, and Manufacture. With Œconomical Rules and Necessary Directions for a Planter How to Manage a Plantation, and Employ His Negroes to the Best Advantage. To Which Is Added, a Treatise on the Culture of Coffee* (P. Elmsly, 1769).
33 Rhys, *Wide Sargasso Sea*, 101.
34 Ibid., 100.
35 'folly, *n.*, 5.a.', 'folly, *n.*, 3.a.', *Oxford English Dictionary Online*.
36 Conrad, *Almayer's Folly*, 29–30.
37 Arnold, *The Problem of Nature*, 150.
38 Conrad, *Heart of Darkness*, 37.
39 Ibid., 57, 56.
40 Ibid., 20, 57.
41 Philip Dickinson, 'Itineraries of the Sublime in the Postcolonial Novel', in *The Cambridge Companion to the Postcolonial Novel*, ed. Ato Quayson (Cambridge: Cambridge University Press, 2015), 153–4.
42 Rhys, *Wide Sargasso Sea*, 45, her emphasis.
43 Homi K. Bhabha, *The Location of Culture* (London: Routledge, 1994), 123.
44 Rhys, *Wide Sargasso Sea*, 98, 102, 99, her emphasis.
45 Deckard, 'The Political Ecology of Storms', 26.
46 Driver and Martins, 'Introduction', 3.
47 Thomas, *The Worlding of Jean Rhys*, 177, drawing on Stephen Greenblatt's analysis of Shakespeare's character Othello in *Renaissance Self-Fashioning from More to Shakespeare* (Chicago, IL: University of Chicago Press, 1980), 250.
48 Brontë, *Jane Eyre*, 309.
49 Mukherjee, *Natural Disasters and Victorian Empire*, 18.
50 Rhys, *Wide Sargasso Sea*, 99, 100, 102, 103, 104.
51 Justine Pizzo, 'Atmospheric Exceptionalism in *Jane Eyre*: Charlotte Brontë's Weather Wisdom', *PMLA* 131, no. 1 (2016): 90.
52 Rhys, letter to Francis Wyndham, 14 April 1964, *Letters 1931–1966*, 263.

53   Jean Rhys, 'Temps Perdi', 155.
54   Jean Rhys, 'Tourists', Jean Rhys Papers.
55   Schwartz, *Sea of Storms*, 5.
56   Mike Davis, *Ecology of Fear: Los Angeles and the Imagination of Disaster* (New York: Vintage, 1999), 9.
57   Deckard, 'The Political Ecology of Storms in Caribbean Literature', 36.
58   Schwartz, *Sea of Storms*, 41.
59   Honychurch, *The Dominica Story*, 120-1. The quotation from an 1825 newspaper report is from p. 120.
60   Rhys, *Wide Sargasso Sea*, 80.
61   Rhys, letter to Maryvonne Moerman, 19 November 1959, *Letters 1931-1966*, 176.
62   On the 1825 and 1834 hurricanes, see Thomas, 'Ghostly Presences'. On the 1833 hurricane, see David Longshore, *Encyclopedia of Hurricanes, Typhoons, and Cyclones*, new ed. (New York: Checkmark, 2008), 137.
63   J. P. Lockhart to King, 9 October 1825, Atkins Collection, Wilberforce House Museum, Hull, UK, KINCM:2006.6949.3. Great Britain, Office of Registry of Colonial Slaves and Slave Compensation Commission, Slave Registration Lists Dominica 1826, T71/360 and Slave Registration Lists Dominica 1829, T71/361, National Archives (United Kingdom), London.
64   J. P. Lockhart to William King, 9 October 1825, Atkins Collection, KINCM:2006.6949.4.
65   Great Britain, Office of Registry of Colonial Slaves and Slave Compensation Commission: Records. Compensation. Registers of Claims. Dominica, T71/881, National Archives (United Kingdom), London.
66   W. B. Lockhart to King, 24 July 1838, Atkins Collection, KINCM:2006.6949.17.
67   J. M. Lockhart to King, 19 April 1836, Atkins Collection, KINCM:2006.6949.14. MeasuringWorth.com, http://www.measuringworth.com/ukcompare/relativevalue.php, accessed 9 January 2013.
68   W. B. Lockhart to King, 24 July 1838, Atkins Collection. The record of these debts in the balance sheet shows the original loan rather than the loan plus interest.
69   Rhys, *Wide Sargasso Sea*, 11.
70   Rhys, letter to Morchard Bishop, 27 January 1953, *Letters 1931-1966*, 99.
71   Walcott, 'The Antilles', 68.
72   Bruce King, *Derek Walcott: A Caribbean Life* (Oxford: Oxford University Press, 2000), 3.
73   Derek Walcott, 'Air', in *The Poetry of Derek Walcott 1948-2013*, ed. Glyn Maxwell (London: Faber & Faber, 2014), 106.
74   V. S. Naipaul, *The Middle Passage* (1962; repr., London: Andre Deutsch, 1963), 29.
75   Dania Dwyer, 'Re-membering History: The Aesthetics of Ruins in West Indian Postcolonial Poetry', in *The Routledge Companion to Anglophone Caribbean Literature*, ed. Michael A. Bucknor and Alison Donnell (London: Routledge, 2014), 435.

76 Derek Walcott, 'The Royal Palms ... an absence of ruins', *London Magazine* 1, no. 11 (1962): 12–13.
77 Rhys, *Wide Sargasso Sea*, 57, her italics.
78 Thomas, *The Worlding of Jean Rhys*, 156. The quotation is from p. 16 of *Wide Sargasso Sea*.
79 Rhys, *Wide Sargasso Sea*, 16.
80 Derek Walcott, 'Ruins of a Great House', in *In a Green Night: Poems 1948–1960*, by Derek Walcott (1962; repr., London: Jonathan Cape, 1969), 19.
81 In 'Ruins of a Great House' the named citrus crop of the estate is limes; in *Wide Sargasso Sea* Père Liliièvre has had an orange tree in his garden.
82 Rhys, letter to Eliot Bliss, 1962.
83 *Oxford English Dictionary Online*.
84 Rhys, *Wide Sargasso Sea*, 38 n.4.
85 Thomas, *The Worlding of Jean Rhys*, 173.
86 Rhys, *Wide Sargasso Sea*, 100.
87 See 'Sugar', *American Magazine of Useful and Entertaining Knowledge* 2, no. 7 (1836): 289–91. The description of the refining process is on p. 291. See also the images 'Des Friches' and 'Sugar Bakers', *Sugar and the Visual Imagination in the Atlantic World*, circa 1600–1860, http://www.brown.edu/Facilities/John_Carter_Brown_Library/exhibitions/sugar/pages,cannibalism.html, accessed 25 January 2018.
88 Rhys, *Wide Sargasso Sea*, 16.
89 Gordon K. Lewis, *Main Currents in Caribbean Thought: The Historical Evolution of Caribbean Society in Its Ideological Aspects, 1492–1900* (Baltimore, MD: Johns Hopkins University Press, 1983), 191.
90 Great Britain, Office of Registry of Colonial Slaves and Slave Compensation Commission: Records. Compensation. Registers of Claims. Dominica, T71/881.
91 MeasuringWorth.com, accessed 1 June 2021.
92 J. M. Lockhart to King, 10 December 1837, Atkins Collection.
93 Indenture between William King and James Parkinson and Frederick Keddell and Alexander Dalrymple, 13 June 1840, M565, Beinecke Lesser Antilles Collection, Hamilton College. The description of the document in *The Beinecke Lesser Antilles Collection at Hamilton College: A Catalogue of Books, Manuscripts, Prints, Maps, and Drawings, 1521–1860*, comp. Samuel L. Hough and Penelope R. O. Hough (Gainesville: University Press of Florida, 1994), 309 is inaccurate.
94 Rhys, *Wide Sargasso Sea*, 73.
95 There is no basis for Victoria Burrows's claim that Edward Lockhart, like his father, 'owned large numbers of slaves'. *Whiteness and Trauma: The Mother-Daughter Knot in the Fiction of Jean Rhys, Jamaica Kincaid and Toni Morrison* (Basingstoke: Palgrave Macmillan, 2004), 33.
96 Hulme, 'The Locked Heart', 79.

97   Abraham, 'Notes on the Phantom', 174.
98   Rhys, *Wide Sargasso Sea*, 9.
99   Ibid., 9–10.
100  Mardorossian, *Reclaiming Difference*, 65, 68.
101  Rhys, *Wide Sargasso Sea*, 17.
102  Ibid.; Maslen, *Ferocious Things*, 189. Burrows, though, collapses Rhys's authorial perspective into Antoinette's. She reads West Indian history of the apprenticeship period back from Annette's and Antoinette's sense of it, locating, for instance, what historians call the flight from the fields, the withdrawal of plantation labour by ex-slaves, in the apprenticeship period – 'why should *anybody* work' voices Antoinette (Rhys, *Wide Sargasso Sea*, 11), echoing Annette – rather than after August 1838 when apprenticeship was abolished. She states that after slavery was abolished in 1834, 'slaves … became worthless' and estates were left 'without a workforce' (Burrows, *Whiteness and Trauma*, 29). As Clinton V. Black points out, legally apprentices had 'to work for their masters for three quarters of every week (40 ½ hours) without wages, the masters on their part being required to continue to provide lodging, clothing, medical attendance and food, or in place of food provision grounds in which apprentices could grow their own food'. *The History of Jamaica* (London: Collins, 1983), 108.
103  Rhys, *Wide Sargasso Sea*, 12.
104  Ibid., 10.
105  knell, *n.*, b.', 'knell, *v.*, 1', *Oxford English Dictionary Online*.
106  Angier, *Jean Rhys*, [xi].
107  Rhys, *Wide Sargasso Sea*, 16, 14–15.
108  Brontë, *Jane Eyre*, 284, 282.
109  Ibid., 14–15.
110  Virginia Woolf, '"Jane Eyre" and "Wuthering Heights"', in *The Common Reader: First Series*, ed. Andrew McNeillie (1925; repr., London: Hogarth Press, 1984), 156.
111  Sally Shuttleworth, *Charlotte Brontë and Victorian Psychology* (Cambridge: Cambridge University Press, 1996), 158, 157, 149.
112  Brontë, *Jane Eyre*, 8.
113  Pizzo, 'Atmospheric Exceptionalism in *Jane Eyre*', 84–5, 87, 95, 88.
114  Brontë, *Jane Eyre*, 282, 283, 284.
115  Sandra M. Gilbert and Susan Gubar, *The Madwoman in the Attic: The Woman Writer and the Nineteenth-Century Literary Imagination* (1979; New Haven, CT: Yale University Press, 1984), 358.
116  Mary Poovey, *Uneven Developments: The Ideological Work of Gender in Mid-Victorian England* (1988; London: Virago, 1989), 141.
117  Shuttleworth, *Charlotte Brontë and Victorian Psychology*, 148, 167, her emphasis.
118  Brontë, *Jane Eyre*, 211.

119 Rhys, *Wide Sargasso Sea*, 102, 98.
120 Brontë, *Jane Eyre*, 282.
121 Rhys, *Wide Sargasso Sea*, 105.
122 Ibid., 99, 102.
123 Ibid., 107, 110, 109, Rhys's italics. The named plants are natives of the global tropics rather than the Caribbean, a sign of ecological imperialism.
124 Rhys, *Wide Sargasso Sea*, 110–11.
125 Brontë, *Jane Eyre*, 307; Rhys, *Wide Sargasso Sea*, 112.

# Coda

*Jean Rhys's Modernist Bearings and Experimental Aesthetics* opens out new ways of locating Rhys in literary histories, ways which may reshape future reading of and scholarship on and around her. Focusing on her novels and a selection of short stories – 'Vienne', 'Tea with an Artist', 'Trio', 'Till September Petronella', 'Tigers Are Better-Looking' and 'Let Them Call It Jazz' – I establish the reach and importance of fresh analytical framings in reading and researching her aesthetics, for example, bearings, depressive time, tropicality, decadence, the experiential dimension of memory and histories in the present, jazz modernity, improvisation, revision as a modernist practice, the *doudou*, countering doudouism, family crypt, hurricane poetics and psychological geographies. The analytical frames warrant further study of her short fiction. They place her in fresh relations of filiation, disaffiliation and contiguity with writers and literary movements, for example, Joseph Conrad, Rudyard Kipling, Michel Leiris, Georges Bataille, Oscar Wilde, Jean Richepin, D. H. Lawrence, Katherine Mansfield, Robert Browning, Derek Walcott, Jane and Paulette Nardal, and the French Antillean literary resistance to doudouism (Etienne Léro, Thélus Léro, René Menil, Jules-Marcel Monnerot, Michel Pilotin, Maurice-Sabas Quitman, Auguste Thésée, Pierre Yoyotte, Aimé Césaire and Suzanne Césaire), and bring new depth to understanding of her allusions to Émile Zola, Heinrich Heine, Charlotte Brontë and William Shakespeare. Her early fiction, I show, is grounded in a sifting through of contemporary aesthetic ideas and practice. Notably, in 'Vienne' she engages intermedially with kineticist interest in the representation of movement, using her translation of practice across art forms to address the aftermath of the collapse of the Austro-Hungarian Empire. Translation, resiting and thinking creatively across art forms remain for Rhys important ways of establishing and developing the bearings of her fiction. The process characterizes, to give just a few examples, the inspiration she draws from Dunning's sonnet 'The Hermit' and puppet theatre in *Quartet*, her treatments of tropicality across the arts in *After Leaving Mr Mackenzie* and of the *doudou* across a range of stories and novels, and her deft engagement with Pablo Picasso's drowning and weeping women of the 1930s and jazz improvisation in *Good Morning, Midnight*. My study of tropicality, diaspora, the *doudou*, inter-imperiality, ruin and hurricane in Rhys's fiction and of contiguity as a form of relation provides further scope for comparative scholarship on her as a Caribbean writer whose work was shaped by the negotiation of racialized cultural inheritances and of decolonial horizons. Rhys does not figure in scholarship on decadence. My reading of *Voyage in the Dark* reveals challengingly the depth and originality of her engagement with decadence and the seriality of moral panics around it. Both *Voyage in the Dark* and *Good Morning, Midnight* are shaped by complex experiment with the proximate temporalities of past and present and temporalities of traumatic memory.

In 'Songs My Mother Never Taught Me', Rhys intimates that her historical memory was shaped by the currency of particular pieces of popular music.[1] Her musical memory is a creative source that draws on the enmeshing of songs in their cultural, political and historical moments. Rhys is interested in the stakes of transatlantic consumption and circulation of popular music of the Americas (ragtime, jazz, swing, hotcha, biguine); the travel of *doudou* songs through cultural and geographical proximity, migration and racialized cross-cultural encounter; and the reach of songs in the affective lives of her characters. She is alert to commercial and primitivist appropriation of musical styles, linking such commodification with the emergence and fashions of jazz modernity, and the fuelling of moral panic around ragtime in pre–First World War England. She remains acutely aware of the complexities of her characters' negotiations of racialized and sexualized thresholds around music marked as African-American and African-Martinican and the limits of the cosmopolitan in relation to these. Rhys limns the more intimate circulation of *doudou* songs in the Caribbean as cross-generational guidance, lullaby and cross-cultural seduction. Her shaping of character, narrative arcs and psychological geographies around *doudou* songs is very finely grained and nuanced.

Tracing allusions in Rhys's fiction – explicit, tacit and silent – reveals the subtlety, depth, breadth, and carefulness of her intertextual and intermedial thinking and reach. Rhys's allusions shape her writing most compellingly as part of complex, often structural allusive patterns. A prime example here is her crafting of the intricate subtextual connections that place details of Wilde's *The Picture of Dorian Gray* and his trial appearances beside the gendered, racialized, diasporic and class experience of Anna Morgan in *Voyage in the*

*Dark*. Her allusions to Wilde and a wider decadent tradition demonstrate that, to reframe Rhys's comment on her experiment with time, the past exists side by side with the present of the novel and the present of its publication. Another is her seamless exploration of her Rochester figure's psychological geography by experimenting with explicit bearings from *Jane Eyre*, *Macbeth* and '*Adieu madras, adieu foulard*', tacit ones from *Othello*, and silent ones from *Almayer's Folly*, *Heart of Darkness*, 'Le Revenant', 'The Royal Palms ... an absence of ruins' and 'Ruins of a Great House'. Caught up with a hurricane poetics, the bearings shift and lift the characterization and the novel's contrapuntal reflection on Caribbean ruin to a 'different plane'.[2] Readerly recognition of allusion is subject to cultural memory, forgetting and specificity. My research restores legibility to historical allusions, from, for instance, the meanings of war material in 'Vienne' and Brazil in *After Leaving Mr Mackenzie* to establishments and sites of sexual dissidence in London – Kettner's, Oddendino's and Berners Street in *Voyage in the Dark*, the Crabtree Club (renamed the Appletree Club) in 'Till September Petronella' and the Shim Sham Club (renamed the Jim-Jam Club) in 'Tigers Are Better-Looking'. Keenly aware of their scope, Rhys intricately works each of her allusions into the design and fabric of narrative and her sharp examinations of gender, class, racial and ethnic politics.

'To give life shape – that is what a writer does. That is what is so difficult,' Rhys explains to Elizabeth Vreeland.[3] Situating her material in relation to literary, historical and intermedial bearings that emerge through the course of writing novels or short stories is, I have argued, crucial to her process of giving it shape. Finding, negotiating and elaborating the bearings – a process that was for her '*mysterious*, not mechanical' – is core to her experimental literary aesthetics.[4] In her Ropemakers' Arms diary, kept in 1951–2, a time when she was trying to recover a sense of literary vocation which collapsed in the late 1940s, she admits to 'forc[ing]' herself 'to write, to write' in search of inspiration: 'the pattern, the clue that can be followed'.[5] Reflecting on her spirit in much older age, she records that aesthetic inspiration grips and absorbs her such that she feels pen-like, posing for her questions around writerly agency.[6] Locating her bearings helps Rhys clarify her project in a work, creatively and critically distance her fiction from the personal, establish a 'smooth firm foundation' for it and layer through telling details contemporary to the settings of her texts.[7] 'I am pretty sure that most people notice details *without knowing it*,' she writes to Wyndham.[8] Synchronic and intermedial allusions do more work in her texts than ground historical accuracy. They may structure thematic and narrative arcs, enrich motifs, nuance and resonance, and inspire experiment with temporalities of memory, melancholy and depression. Berman observes that Rhys's novels are 'often perceived to have been quickly written or without craft'.[9] Rather, Rhys's meticulous crafting and revision of her fiction calls for slow reading, the connective tracing of relation within a novel or short story, across her oeuvre and archives, and to the literary, cultural and historical fields with which she engages.

## Notes

1. Jean Rhys Papers.
2. Rhys, letter to Francis Wyndham, 14 May 1964, *Letters 1931–1966*, 277.
3. Elizabeth Vreeland, 'Jean Rhys: The Art of Fiction LXIV', *Paris Review* 76 (1979): 225.
4. Rhys, letter to Maryvonne Moerman, April 1958, *Letters 1931–1966*, 155, her emphasis.
5. Rhys, *Smile Please*, 147–8. Here the diary is incorrectly dated to the 1940s.
6. Jean Rhys Papers, Series 1, Box 3, Folder 7.
7. Rhys, letter to Selma Vaz Dias, 9 November 1949, *Letters 1931–1966*, 60.
8. Rhys, letter to Francis Wyndham, 8 July 1959, *Letters 1931–1966*, 170, her emphasis.
9. Berman, *Modernist Commitments*, 78.

# Selected Bibliography

## Archival sources

Atkins Collection, Wilberforce House Museum, Hull, UK.
Beinecke Lesser Antilles Collection, Hamilton College, US.
Jean Rhys Papers, Department of Special Collections and University Archives, University of Tulsa, US.
National Archives, United Kingdom, London, UK.

## Databases

*Legacies of British Slave-ownership*. London: University College, London, Department of History, 2013. http://www.ucl.ac.uk/lbs/.
*The Oxford English Dictionary Online*. Oxford: Oxford University Press.
*World's Fairs: A Global History of Expositions*. Marlborough: Adam Matthew Digital, n.d.

## Primary sources

Rhys, Jean. *After Leaving Mr Mackenzie*. 1931. Reprint, Harmondsworth: Penguin, 1971.
Rhys, Jean. *Good Morning, Midnight*. 1939. Reprint, Harmondsworth: Penguin
Rhys, Jean. 'I Spy a Stranger'. In *The Collected Short Stories*, by Jean Rhys, 242–55. New York: Norton, 1989.
Rhys, Jean. 'Let Them Call It Jazz'. In *Tigers Are Better Looking: With a Selection from The Left Bank*, by Jean Rhys, 42–63. 1968. Reprint, Harmondsworth: Penguin, 1972.
Rhys, Jean. *Letters 1931–1966*, edited by Francis Wyndham and Diana Melly. London: Andre Deutsch, 1984.
Rhys, Jean. *Quartet*. 1928 [as *Postures*]. Reprint, Harmondsworth: Penguin, 1973.
Rhys, Jean. *Smile Please: An Unfinished Autobiography*. 1979. Reprint, Harmondsworth: Penguin, 1981.
Rhys, Jean. 'Tea with an Artist'. In *The Left Bank and Other Stories*, by Jean Rhys, 73–82. 1927. Reprint, Freeport, NY: Books for Libraries Press, 1970.
Rhys, Jean 'Temps Perdi'. In *Tales of the Wide Caribbean*, edited by Kenneth Ramchand, 144–61. London: Heinemann, 1986.

Rhys, Jean. 'Tigers Are Better-Looking'. In *Tigers Are Better Looking: With a Selection from* The Left Bank, 64–77. 1968. Reprint, Harmondsworth: Penguin, 1972.

Rhys, Jean. 'Till September Petronella'. *Tigers Are Better Looking: With a Selection from* The Left Bank, by Jean Rhys, 9–36. 1968. Reprint, Harmondsworth: Penguin, 1972.

Rhys, Jean. 'Trio'. *The Left Bank and Other Stories*, by Jean Rhys, 83–6. 1927. Reprint, Freeport, NY: Books for Libraries Press, 1970.

Rhys, Jean. 'Vienne' [1924]. In *The Gender of Modernism: A Critical Anthology*, edited by Bonnie Kime Scott, 377–81. Bloomington: Indiana University Press, 1990.

Rhys, Jean. 'Vienne'. In *The Left Bank and Other Stories*, by Jean Rhys, 193–256. 1927. Reprint, Freeport, NY: Books for Libraries Press, 1970.

Rhys, Jean. *Voyage in the Dark*. 1934. Reprint, Harmondsworth: Penguin, 2000.

Rhys, Jean. '*Voyage in the Dark*. Part IV (Original Version)', edited by Nancy Hemond Brown. In *The Gender of Modernism: A Critical Anthology*, edited by Bonnie Kime Scott, 381–9. Bloomington: Indiana University Press, 1990.

Rhys, Jean. *Wide Sargasso Sea*, edited by Judith L. Raiskin. Norton Critical Edition. New York: Norton, 1999.

## Selected secondary sources

Abraham, Nicolas, and Maria Torok. *The Shell and the Kernel: Renewals of Psychoanalysis*, translated by Nicholas T. Rand. Chicago, IL: University of Chicago Press, 1994.

Allen, Carolyn. 'Creole: The Problem of Definition'. In *Questioning Creole: Creole Discourses in Caribbean Culture*, edited by Verene Shepherd and Glen Richards, 47–63. Oxford: James Currey, 2002.

Amort, Andrea. 'Free Dance in Interwar Vienna'. In *Interwar Vienna: Culture between Tradition and Modernity*, edited by Deborah Holmes and Lisa Silverman, 117–42. Rochester: Camden House, 2009.

Andrew, Dudley, and Steven Ungar. *Popular Front Paris and the Poetics of Culture*. Cambridge, MA: Harvard University Press, 2005.

Angier, Carole. *Jean Rhys: Life and Work*. Rev. edn. London: Penguin, 1992.

Armstrong, Tim. 'Modernist Temporality: The Science and Philosophy and Aesthetics of Temporality from 1880'. In *The Cambridge History of Modernism*, edited by Vincent Sherry, 31–46. Cambridge: Cambridge University Press, 2016.

Armstrong, Tim. 'Technology'. In *A Concise Companion to Modernism*, edited by David Bradshaw, 158–78. Oxford: Blackwell, 2003.

Arnold, David. '"Illusory Riches": Representations of the Tropical World, 1840–1950'. *Singapore Journal of Tropical Geography* 21, no. 1 (2000): 6–18.

Arnold, David. *The Problem of Nature: Environment, Culture and European Expansion*. Oxford: Blackwell, 1996.

Athill, Diana. *Stet*. London: Granta, 2000.
Bailey, Peter. 'Fats Waller Meets Harry Champion'. *Cultural and Social History* 4, no. 4 (2007): 495–509.
Bailey, Peter. '*"Hullo, Ragtime?"* West End Revue and the Americanisation of Popular Culture in Pre-1914 London'. In *Popular Musical Theatre in London and Berlin 1890–1939*, edited by Len Platt, Tobias Becker and David Linton, 135–52. Cambridge: Cambridge University Press, 2014.
Baker, Simon. 'Variety (Civilizing "Race")'. In *Undercover Surrealism: Georges Bataille and Documents*, edited by Dawn Ades and Simon Baker, 65–71. London: Hayward Gallery, 2006.
Baldassari, Anne. *Picasso: Love and War 1935–1945. Life with Dora Maar*. Melbourne: National Gallery of Victoria, 2006.
Barnett, Vincent L., and Alexis Weedon. *Elinor Glyn as Novelist, Moviemaker, Glamour Icon and Businesswoman*. New York: Routledge, 2016.
Barrios, Richard. *A Song in the Dark: The Birth of the Musical Film*. Oxford: Oxford University Press, 1995.
Barty-King, Hugh and Anton Messel. *Rum: Yesterday and Today*. London: Heinemann, 1983.
Bast, Gerald, Agnes Husslein, Herbert Krejci and Patrick Werkner, editors. *Wiener Kinetismus: Eine bewegte modern/Viennese Kineticism. Modernism in Motion*. Wien and New York: Springer, 2011.
Bataille, Georges. 'Black Birds', translated by Iain White. In *Encyclopædia Acephalica*, edited by Alistair Brotchie, 36–7. London: Atlas Press, 1995.
Baucom, Ian. *Spectres of the Atlantic: Finance Capital, Slavery, and the Philosophy of History*. Durham, NC: Duke University Press, 2005.
Bauer, Ralph, and José Antonio Mazzotti. 'Introduction: Creole Subjects in the Colonial Americas'. In *Creole Subjects in the Colonial Americas: Empires, Texts, Identities*, edited by Ralph Bauer and José Antonio Mazzoti, 1–58 (Chapel Hill: University of North Carolina Press for the Omohundro Institute of Early American History and Culture, 2009).
Baxter, Jeanette, Anna Snaith and Tory Young, editors. *Reading Jean Rhys. Women: A Cultural Review*, 23, no. 4 (2012).
Bell, Matthew. *Melancholia: The Western Malady*. Cambridge: Cambridge University Press, 2014.
Bender, Todd. 'Jean Rhys and the Genius of Impressionism'. *Studies in the Literary Imagination* 11, no. 2 (1978): 43–53.
Berlant, Lauren, and Sianne Ngai. 'Comedy Has Issues'. *Critical Inquiry* 43, no. 2 (2017): 233–49.
Berliner, Brett A. *Ambivalent Desire: The Exotic Black Other in Jazz-Age France*. Amherst, MA: University of Massachusetts Press, 2002.
Berman, Jessica. *Modernist Commitments: Ethics, Politics, and Transnational Modernism*. New York: Columbia University Press, 2012.

Bewell, Alan. '*Jane Eyre* and Victorian Medical Geography'. *ELH* 63 (1996): 773–808.

Bhabha, Homi K. *The Location of Culture*. London: Routledge, 1994.

Black, Clinton V. *The History of Jamaica*. London: Collins, 1983.

Blake, Ann, Leela Gandhi and Sue Thomas. *England through Colonial Eyes in Twentieth-Century Fiction*. Basingstoke and New York: Palgrave, 2001.

Bowen, Stella. *Drawn from Life*. 1941. Reprint, London: Virago, 1984.

Bowler, Rebecca. *Literary Impressionism: Vision and Memory in Dorothy Richardson, Ford Madox Ford, H. D. and May Sinclair*. London: Bloomsbury, 2016.

Brathwaite, Kamau. 'History of the Voice'. In *Roots*, by Kamau Brathwaite, 259–304. Michigan: University of Michigan Press, 1993.

Bret, David. *The Mistinguett Legend*. London: Robson, 1990.

Breton, André. 'Crisis of the Object'. In *Surrealism and Painting*, by André Breton, translated by Simon Watson Taylor, 274–80. London: Macdonald, 1972.

Britzolakis, Christina. '"This [W]ay to the [E]xhibition": Genealogies of Urban Spectacle in Jean Rhys's Interwar Fiction'. *Textual Practice* 21, no. 3 (2007): 457–82.

Brome, Vincent. 'A Last Meeting with Dorothy Richardson'. *London Magazine* 6 (June 1959): 26–32.

Brontë, Charlotte. *Jane Eyre*. Edited by Margaret Smith. Introduction and revised notes by Sally Shuttleworth. Oxford: Oxford University Press, 2000.

Brooker, Peter. *Bohemia in London: The Social Scene of Early Modernism*. Basingstoke: Palgrave Macmillan, 2007.

Brown, Nancy Hemond. 'Jean Rhys and *Voyage in the Dark*'. *London Magazine* 25, nos. 1 & 2 (April/May 1985): 40–59.

Browning, Robert. 'A Pretty Woman'. In *Selected Poetry of Browning*, edited by Kenneth L. Knickerbocker, 281–4. New York: Random House, 1951.

Burrows, Victoria. *Whiteness and Trauma: The Mother-Daughter Knot in the Fiction of Jean Rhys, Jamaica Kincaid and Toni Morrison*. Basingstoke: Palgrave Macmillan, 2004.

Burton, Richard D. E. '"Maman-France Doudou": Family Images in French West Indian Colonial Discourse'. *Diacritics* 23, no. 3 (1993): 69–90.

Butler, Judith. *Bodies That Matter: On the Discursive Limits of 'Sex'*. New York: Routledge, 1993.

Camarasana, Linda. 'Exhibitions and Repetitions: Jean Rhys's *Good Morning, Midnight* and the World of Paris, 1937'. In *At Home and Abroad in the Empire: British Women Write the 1930s*, edited by Robin Hackett, Freda S. Hauser, and Gay Wachman, 51–70. Newark: University of Delaware Press, 2009.

Carr, Helen. *Jean Rhys*. 2nd ed. Tavistock: Northcote House, 2012.

Chalk, Bridget T. *Modernism and Mobility: The Passport and Cosmopolitan Experience*. New York: Palgrave Macmillan, 2014.

Clarke, Joseph. 'Caribbean Modernism and the Postcolonial Social Contract in *Voyage in the Dark*'. *Journal of Caribbean Literatures* 3, no. 3 (Summer 2003): 1–16.

Clukey, Amy. '"No Country Really Now": Modernist Cosmopolitanisms and Jean Rhys's *Quartet*'. *Twentieth-Century Literature* 56, no. 4 (2010): 437–61.

Cohen, Philip. 'The Perversions of Inheritance: Studies in the Making of Multi-Racist Britain'. In *Multi-Racist Britain*, edited by Philip Cohen and Harwant S. Bains, 9–108. Basingstoke: Macmillan Education, 1988.

Collett, Anne, Russell McDougall and Sue Thomas. 'Tracking the Literature of Tropical Weather'. In *Tracking the Literature of Tropical Weather: Typhoons, Cyclones and Hurricanes*, edited by Anne Collett, Russell McDougall, and Sue Thomas, 1–24. New York: Palgrave Macmillan, 2017.

Conrad, Joseph. *Almayer's Folly: A Story of an Eastern River*, edited by Floyd Eugene Eddelman and David Leon Higdon. Cambridge: Cambridge University Press, 1994.

Conrad, Joseph. *Heart of Darkness*, edited by Richard Kimbrough. Norton Critical Edition. 3rd ed. New York: W. W. Norton, 2006.

Conway, Kelley. *Chanteuse in the City: The Realist Singer in French Film*. Berkeley: University of California Press, 2004.

Cooke, Simon. '"Parler de soi": Jean Rhys and the Uses of Life Writing'. In *Transnational Jean Rhys: Lines of Transmission, Lines of Flight*, edited by Juliana Lopoukhine, Frédéric Regard and Kerry-Jane Wallart, 65–80. London: Bloomsbury, 2020.

Cork, Richard. *Art beyond the Gallery in Early 20th Century England*. New Haven, CT: Yale University Press, 1985.

Cornell, Drucilla. *The Imaginary Domain: Abortion, Pornography & Sexual Harassment*. New York and London: Routledge, 1995.

Couti, Jacqueline. 'The Mythology of the Doudou: Sexualizing Black Female Bodies, Constructing Culture in the French Caribbean'. In *Provocations: A Transnational Reader in the History of Feminist Thought*, edited by María Cristina Alcalde, Susan Bordo and Ellen Bayuk Rosenman, 131–43. Oakland: University of California Press, 2015.

Croxall, Samuel, translator. *Fables of Aesop and Others*. London: W. Strahan, J. and F. Rivington, et al., 1878.

Curtius, Anny Dominique. 'Cannibalizing *Doudouisme*, Conceptualizing the *Morne*: Suzanne Césaire's Caribbean Ecopoetics'. *South Atlantic Quarterly* 115, no. 3 (2016): 513–34.

Dalberg-Acton, John Emerich Edward, First Baron Acton, *Historical Essays & Studies*, edited by J. N. Figgis and R. V. Laurence. London: Macmillan, 1907.

Darwin, Charles. *The Voyage of the Beagle*. New York: P. Collier, 1937.

Daverio, John. '*Tristan und Isolde*: Essence and Appearance'. In *The Cambridge Companion to Wagner*, edited by Thomas S. Grey, 115–33. Cambridge: Cambridge University Press, 2011.

Davis, Mike. *Ecology of Fear: Los Angeles and the Imagination of Disaster*. New York: Vintage, 1999.

Davis, Thomas S. *The Extinct Scene: Late Modernism and Everyday Life*. New York: Columbia University Press, 2016.

Dawson, Graham. *Soldier Heroes: British Adventure, Empire, and the Imagining of Masculinities*. London: Routledge, 1994.

de Lauretis, Teresa. *Technologies of Gender: Essays on Theory, Film, and Fiction*. Bloomington: Indiana University Press, 1987.

Deal, Laura. 'Zola in England: Controversy and Change in the 1890s'. Honours diss., American University, 2008.

Deckard, Sharae. 'The Political Ecology of Storms in Caribbean Literature'. In *Caribbean: Aesthetics, World-Ecology, Politics*, edited by Chris Campbell and Michael Niblett, 25–45. Liverpool: Liverpool University Press, 2016.

del Pilar Blanco, María, and Esther Peeren. 'Introduction: Conceptualizing Spectralities'. In *The Spectralities Reader: Ghosts and Haunting in Contemporary Cultural Theory*, edited by María del Pilar Blanco and Esther Peeren, 1–36. London: Bloomsbury, 2013.

del Pilar Blanco, María, and Esther Peeren. 'Spectral Subjectivities: Gender, Sexuality, Race/Introduction'. In *The Spectralities Reader: Ghosts and Haunting in Contemporary Cultural Theory*, edited by María del Pilar Blanco and Esther Peeren, 309–16. London: Bloomsbury, 2013.

Dell'Amico, Carol. *Colonialism and the Modernist Moment in the Early Novels of Jean Rhys*. New York: Routledge, 2005.

Dickinson, Philip. 'Itineraries of the Sublime in the Postcolonial Novel'. In *The Cambridge Companion to the Postcolonial Novel*, edited by Ato Quayson, 152–65. Cambridge: Cambridge University Press, 2015.

Dixon, Joe C. *Defeat and Disarmament: Allied Diplomacy and the Politics of Military Affairs in Austria, 1918–1922*. Newark: University of Delaware Press, 1986.

Donald, James. *Some of These Days: Black Stars, Jazz Aesthetics, and Modernist Culture*. Oxford: Oxford University Press, 2015.

Downes, Sara. 'Jean Rhys, William Orpen and the Frames of Modernist Representation'. *Women: A Cultural Review* 27, no. 3 (2016): 280–95.

Driver, Felix and Luciana Martins, 'Introduction: Views and Visions of the Tropical World'. In *Tropical Visions in the Age of Empire*, edited by Felix Driver and Luciana Martins, 3–20. Chicago, IL: University of Chicago Press, 2010.

Dunbar, Rudolph. 'Harlem in London: Year of Advancement for Negroes. Significance of the Shim-Sham'. *Melody Maker*, 7 March 1936: 2.

Dunning, R. C. 'The Hermit'. *transatlantic review* 2, no. 5 (1924): 480.

Dwyer, Dania. 'Re-membering History: The Aesthetics of Ruins in West Indian Postcolonial Poetry'. In *The Routledge Companion to Anglophone Caribbean Literature*, edited by Michael A. Bucknor and Alison Donnell, 432–40. Abingdon, Oxon: Routledge, 2011.

Edwards, Brent Hayes. *The Practice of Diaspora: Literature, Translation, and the Rise of Black Internationalism*. Cambridge, MA: Harvard University Press, 2003.

Eliot, T. S. 'The Love Song of J. Alfred Prufrock'. In *Selected Poems*, by T. S. Eliot, 11–16. London: Faber, 1961.

Ellis, Nadia. 'Between Windrush and Wolfenden: Class Crossings and Queer Desire in Salkey's Postwar London'. In *Beyond Windrush: Rethinking Postwar Anglophone Caribbean Literature*, edited by J. Dillon Brown and Leah Reade Rosenberg, 60–75. Jackson: University Press of Mississippi, 2015.

Emery, Mary Lou. "'Broken Parts': *Wide Sargasso Sea* and the Poetics of Caribbean Modernism". In *Wide Sargasso Sea at 50*, edited by Elaine Savory and Erica L. Johnson, 125–39. Cham: Palgrave Macmillan, 2020.

Emery, Mary Lou. 'Caribbean Modernism: Plantation to Planetary'. In *The Oxford Handbook of Global Modernisms*, edited by Mark Wollaeger and Matt Eatough, 48–77. Oxford: Oxford University Press, 2012.

Emery, Mary Lou. 'Foreword'. In *Rhys Matters: New Critical Perspectives*, edited by Mary Wilson and Kerry L. Johnson, xi–xii. New York: Palgrave Macmillan, 1913.

Emery, Mary Lou. *Jean Rhys at 'World's End': Novels of Colonial and Sexual Exile*. Austin: University of Texas Press, 1990.

Emery, Mary Lou, editor. *Jean Rhys. Journal of Caribbean Literatures* 3, no. 3 (2003).

Emery, Mary Lou. *Modernism, the Visual, and Caribbean Literature*. Cambridge: Cambridge University Press, 2007.

Emery, Mary Lou. 'The Poetics of Labor in Jean Rhys's Caribbean Modernism'. *Women: A Cultural Review* 23, no. 4 (2012): 421–44.

Emery, Mary Lou. 'Taking the Detour, Finding the Rebels: Crossroads of Caribbean and Modernist Studies'. In *Disciplining Modernism*, edited by Pamela L. Caughie, 71–91. New York: Palgrave Macmillan, 2010.

Esty, Jed. *Unseasonable Youth: Modernism, Colonialism, and the Fiction of Development*. Oxford: Oxford University Press, 2012.

Etherington, Ben. *Literary Primitivism*. Stanford, CA: Stanford University Press, 2017.

Evans, David. '*Documents* against Civilization'. In *Empire and Culture: The French Experience, 1830-1940*, edited by Martin Evans, 71–88. Basingstoke: Palgrave Macmillan, 2004.

Felski, Rita. *The Gender of Modernity*. Cambridge, MA: Harvard University Press, 1995.

Ford, Ford Madox. *Henry James: A Critical Study*. New York: Albert and Charles Boni, 1915.

Ford, Ford Madox. 'Paris Letter: Editorial'. *transatlantic review* 2, no. 5 (1924): 547–51.

Ford, Ford Madox. 'Rive Gauche'. In *The Left Bank and Other Stories*, by Jean Rhys, 7–27. 1927; Freeport, NY: Books for Libraries Press, 1970.

Fraser, Graham. 'The Ghost in the Mirror in *Good Morning, Midnight*'. *Modern Language Review* 113, no. 3 (2018): 481–505.

Frattarola, Angela. *Modernist Soundscapes: Auditory Technology and the Novel*. Gainesville: University Press of Florida, 2018.

Frost, Laura. *The Problem with Pleasure: Modernism and Its Discontents*. New York: Columbia University Press, 2013.

Frow, John. *Character and Person*. Oxford: Oxford University Press, 2014.

Fry, Andy. *Paris Blues: African American Music and French Popular Culture, 1920-1960*. Chicago, IL: University of Chicago Press, 2014.

Gardiner, Judith Kegan. *Rhys, Stead, Lessing, and the Politics of Empathy*. Bloomington: Indiana University Press, 1989.

Geiger, Jeffrey. *Facing the Pacific: Polynesia and the U.S. Imperial Imagination*. Honolulu: University of Hawai'i Press, 2007.

George, Alys X. 'Hollywood on the Danube? Vienna and Austrian Silent Film of the 1920s'. In *Interwar Vienna: Culture between Tradition and Modernity*, edited by Deborah Holmes and Lisa Silverman, 143–60. Rochester: Camden House, 2009.

Gilbert, Sandra M., and Susan Gubar. *The Madwoman in the Attic: The Woman Writer and the Nineteenth-Century Literary Imagination*. 1979; New Haven, CT: Yale University Press, 1984.

Giles, Jana. 'The Landscape of the Other: Aesthetics, Representation, and the Post-Colonial Sublime in Jean Rhys's *Wide Sargasso Sea*'. *MaComère* 5 (2002): 156–83.

Gilman, Sander. *Difference and Pathology: Stereotypes of Sexuality, Race, and Madness*. Ithaca, NY: Cornell University Press, 1985.

Glissant, Edouard. *Poetics of Relation*, translated by Betsy Wing. Ann Arbor: University of Michigan Press, 1997.

Glyn, Elinor. '*It*'. New York: Macaulay, 1927.

Glyn, Elinor. *Man and Maid*. New York: A. L. Burt, 1922.

GoGwilt, Christopher. *The Passage of Literature: Genealogies of Modernism in Conrad, Rhys, and Pramoedya*. Oxford: Oxford University Press, 2011.

Goldman, Jonathan. *Modernism Is the Literature of Celebrity*. Austin: University of Texas Press, 2011.

Goldring, Douglas. *South Lodge: Reminiscences of Violet Hunt, Ford Madox Ford and the English Review Circle*. London: Constable, 1943.

Goldsmith, Oliver. *A History of the Earth and Animated Nature*. London, 1774.

González, Octavio R. 'The Narrative Mood of Jean Rhys' *Quartet*'. *Ariel: A Review of International English Literature* 49, no. 1 (2018): 107–41.

Goossens, Eugene. *Overture and Beginners: A Musical Autobiography*. London: Methuen, 1951.

Gordon, Donald E. *Ernst Ludwig Kirchner: A Retrospective Exhibition*. Boston, MA: Museum of Fine Arts, 1968.

Goudie, Sean X. *Creole America: The West Indies and the Formation of Literature and Culture in the New Republic*. Philadelphia: University of Pennsylvania Press, 2006.

Gray, Cecil. *Peter Warlock: A Memoir of Philip Heseltine*. London: Jonathan Cape, 1934.

Gregg, Veronica Marie. 'Jean Rhys on Herself as a Writer'. In *Caribbean Women Writers: Essays from the First International Conference*, edited by Selwyn Cudjoe, 109–15. Wellesley, MA: Calaloux Publications, 1990.

Gregg, Veronica Marie. *Jean Rhys's Historical Imagination: Reading and Writing the Creole*. Chapel Hill: University of North Carolina Press, 1995.

Grieve, Symington. *Notes upon the Island of Dominica (British West Indies): Containing Information for Settlers, Investors, Tourists, Naturalists, and Others*. London: Adam & Charles Black, 1906.

Haag, Pamela S. 'In Search of "The Real Thing": Ideologies of Love, Modern Romance, and Women's Subjectivity in the United States, 1920–40'. *Journal of the History of Sexuality* 2, no. 4 (1992): 547–77.

Haliloglu, Nagihan. *Narrating from the Margins: Self-Representation of Female and Colonial Subjectivities in Jean Rhys's Novels*. Amsterdam: Rodopi, 2011.

Hall, Catherine. 'What Is a West Indian?' In *West Indian Intellectuals in Britain*, edited by Bill Schwarz, 31–50. Manchester: Manchester University Press, 2003.

Halliday, Nigel Vaux. *More Than a Bookshop: Zwemmer's and Art in the Twentieth Century*. London: Philip Wilson Publishers, 1991.

Halliday, Sam. *Sonic Modernity: Representing Sound in Literature, Culture and the Arts*. Edinburgh: Edinburgh University Press, 2013.

Hamnett, Nina. *Laughing Torso*. New York: Ray Long and Richard R. Smith, 1932.

Hare, Kenneth. *London's Latin Quarter*. London: John Lane, 1926.

Hawthorn, Jeremy. 'Travel as Incarceration: Jean Rhys's *After Leaving Mr Mackenzie*'. In *Literary Landscapes: From Modernism to Postmodernism*, edited by Attie de Lange, Gail Fincham, Jeremy Hawthorn and Jakob Lothe, 58–74. Basingstoke: Palgrave Macmillan, 2008.

Herbert, James D. *Paris 1937: Worlds on Exhibition*. Ithaca, NY: Cornell University Press, 2018.

Hext, Kate, and Alex Murray, editors. *Decadence in the Age of Modernism*. Baltimore, MD: Johns Hopkins University Press, 2019.

Hill, Constance Valis. *Tap Dancing America: A Cultural History*. Oxford: Oxford University Press, 2010.

Hill, Edwin C., Jr. '"*Adieu Madras, Adieu Foulard*": Musical Origins and the *Doudou's* Colonial Plaint'. *Ethnomusicology Forum* 16, no. 1 (2007): 19–43.

Hill, Edwin C., Jr. *Black Soundscapes White Stages: The Meaning of Francophone Sound in the Black Atlantic*. Baltimore, MD: Johns Hopkins University Press, 2013.

Holmes, Deborah, and Lisa Silverman, 'Introduction: Beyond the Coffeehouse. Vienna as a Cultural Center between the World Wars'. In *Interwar Vienna: Culture between Tradition and Modernity*, edited by Deborah Holmes and Lisa Silverman, 1–18. Rochester: Camden House, 2009.

Holroyd, Michael. *Augustus John: The New Biography*. Rev. ed. London: Vintage, 1996.

Howells, Coral Ann. *Jean Rhys*. Hemel Hempstead: Harvester Wheatsheaf, 1991.

Huggan, Graham, and Helen Tiffin. *Postcolonial Ecocriticism: Literature, Animals, Environment*. London: Routledge, 2010.

Hulme, Peter. 'The Locked Heart: The Creole Family Romance of *Wide Sargasso Sea*'. In *Colonial Discourse/Postcolonial Theory*, edited by Francis Barker, Peter Hulme and Margaret Iverson, 72–88. Manchester: Manchester University Press, 1996.

Hulme, Peter. *Remnants of Conquest: The Island Caribs and Their Visitors, 1877–1998*. Oxford: Oxford University Press, 2000.

Husslein-Arco, Agnes, Thomas Kühler, Ralf Burmeister, Alexander Klee, and Annelie Lütgens, editors. *Vienna – Berlin: The Art of Two Cities. From Schiele to Grosz*. Munich: Prestel, 2013.

Huyssen, Andreas. *After the Great Divide: Modernism, Mass Culture, Postmodernism*. Bloomington: Indiana University Press, 1986.

Hyman, Jr, Ira E., et al. 'Involuntary to Intrusive: Using Involuntary Musical Imagery to Explore Individual Differences and the Nature of Intrusive Thoughts'. *Psychomusicology: Music, Mind and Brain* 25, no. 1 (2015): 14–27.

Issacharoff, Jess. '"No Pride, No Name, No Face, No Country": Jewishness and National Identity in *Good Morning, Midnight*'. In *Rhys Matters: New Critical Perspectives*, edited by Mary Wilson and Kerry L. Johnson, 111–29. New York: Palgrave Macmillan, 2013.

James, William. 'The Stream of Consciousness'. In *Classics in the History of Psychology*, edited by Christopher D. Green, http://psychclassics.yorku.ca/James/himmy11.htm, accessed 1 October 2017.

John, Augustus. 'Foreword'. In *Peter Warlock: A Memoir of Philip Heseltine*, by Cecil Gray, 11–15. London: Jonathan Cape, 1934.

Johnson, Erica L. 'Auto-ghostwriting *Smile, Please: An Unfinished Autobiography*'. *Biography* 29, no. 4 (2006): 563–83.

Johnson, Erica L. 'Haunted: Affective Memory in Jean Rhys's *Good Morning, Midnight*'. *Affirmations: Of the Modern* 1, no. 2 (2014): 15–38.

Johnson, Erica L. *Home, Maison, Casa: The Politics of Location in Works by Jean Rhys, Marguerite Duras, and Erminia Dell'Oro*. Madison, NJ: Fairleigh Dickinson University Press, 2003.

Johnson, Erica L. '"Upholstered Ghosts": Jean Rhys's Posthuman Imaginary'. In *Jean Rhys: Twenty-First-Century Approaches*, edited by Erica L. Johnson and Patricia Moran, 209–27. Edinburgh: Edinburgh University Press, 2015.

Johnson, Erica L. and Patricia Moran. 'Introduction: The Haunting of Jean Rhys'. *Jean Rhys: Twenty-First-Century Approaches*, edited by Erica L. Johnson and Patricia Moran, 1–17. Edinburgh: Edinburgh University Press, 2015.

Johnson, Erica L. and Elaine Savory, editors. *Wide Sargasso Sea at 50*. Cham: Palgrave Macmillan, 2020.

Johnson, Howard 'Stretch'. 'From His Unpublished Memoirs'. In *Autobiography of a People: Three Centuries of African American History Told by Those Who Lived It*, edited by Herb Boyd, 257–61. New York: Doubleday, 2000.

Johnson, Joanna. *Topographies of Caribbean Writing, Race, and the British Countryside*. Cham: Palgrave Macmillan, 2019.

Johnson, Lonnie. *Central Europe: Enemies, Neighbours, Friends* (Oxford: Oxford University Press, 1996).

Jordan, Matthew F. '*Amphibiologie*: Ethnographic Surrealism in French Discourse on Jazz'. *European Studies* 31 (2001): 157–86.

Jordan, Matthew F. *Le Jazz: Jazz and French Cultural Identity*. Champaign: University of Illinois Press, 2010.

Jordan-Baker, Craig. 'On Cliché: Expression, Cognition and Understanding'. *Journal of Creative Writing Studies* 2, no. 2 (2016): article 1.

'A Journey through the Exhibition: Picasso and Dora Maar – A Mercurial Meeting of Minds'. *Picasso: Love and War 1935–1945: Education Resource*, National Gallery of Victoria, https://www.ngv.vic.gov.au/picasso/education/ed_JTE_MMM.html, accessed 1 July 2018.

Kalliney, Peter J. *Commonwealth of Letters: British Literary Culture and the Emergence of Postcolonial Aesthetics*. Oxford: Oxford University Press, 2013.

Kalliney, Peter J. 'Jean Rhys: Left Bank Modernist as Postcolonial Intellectual'. In *The Oxford Handbook of Global Modernisms*, edited by Mark Wollaeger and Matt Eatough, 413–32. Oxford: Oxford University Press, 2012.

Kargon, Robert H., Karen Fiss, Morris Low, and Arthur P. Molella, *World's Fairs on the Eve of War: Science, Technology, and Modernity, 1937–1942*. Pittsburgh: University of Pittsburgh Press, 2015.

Karl, Alissa G. *Modernism and the Marketplace: Literary Culture and Consumer Capitalism in Rhys, Woolf, Stein, and Nella Larsen*. New York: Routledge, 2009.

Kelly, Veronica. 'Come Over Here! The Local Hybridisation of International "Ragtime Revues" in Australia'. *Popular Entertainment Studies* 4, no. 1 (2013): 24–49.

Kenney III, William H. '*le hot*: The Assimilation of American Jazz in France, 1917–1940'. *American Studies* 25 (1984): 5–24.

Kenney, William Howland. *Recorded Music in American Life: The Phonograph and Popular Memory, 1890–1945*. New York: Oxford University Press, 1999.

King, Bruce. *Derek Walcott: A Caribbean Life*. Oxford: Oxford University Press, 2000.

Kipling, Rudyard. 'The Beginning of the Armadilloes'. In *Just So Stories for Little Children*, by Rudyard Kipling, edited by Lisa Lewis, 75–90. Oxford: Oxford University Press, 1998.

Knoepflmacher, U. C. 'Kipling's "Mixy" Creatures'. *SEL: Studies in English Literature 1500–1900* 48, no. 4 (2008): 923–33.

Kobayashi, Eri. *Women and Mimicry: A Postcolonial Feminist Reading of Jean Rhys's Five Novels*. Okayama, Japan: Fukuro Shuppan Publishing, 2011.

Köhler, Kristina. 'Dance as Metaphor – Metaphor as Dance: Transfigurations of Dance in Culture and Aesthetics around 1900'. *REAL – Yearbook of Research in English and American Literature* 25 (2009): 163–78.

Konzett, Delia Caparosa. *Ethnic Modernisms: Anzia Yesierka, Zora Neale Hurston, Jean Rhys and the Aesthetics of Dislocation*. New York: Palgrave Macmillan, 2002.

Kristeva, Julia. *Black Sun: Depression and Melancholia*, translated by Leon S. Roudiez. New York: Columbia University Press, 1989.

Laird, Ross. *Tantalizing Tingles: A Discography of Early Ragtime, Jazz, and Novelty Syncopated Piano Recordings, 1889–1934*. Westport, CT: Greenwood, 1995.

Lake, Marilyn. 'Female Desires: The Meaning of World War II'. *Australian Historical Studies*, no. 95 (October 1990): 267–84.

Lamberti, Elena. '"Wandering Yankees": The *transatlantic review* or How the Americans Came to Europe'. In *Ford Madox Ford, Modernist Magazines and Editing*, edited by Jason Harding, 215–28. Amsterdam: Rodopi, 2010.

Lane, Christopher. 'Almayer's Defeat: The Trauma of Colonialism in Conrad's Early Work'. *Novel: A Forum on Fiction* 32, no. 3 (1999): 401–28.

Lawrence, D. H. *Lady Chatterley's Lover*. 1928. Reprint, Harmondsworth: Penguin, 1960.

Lawrence, D. H. 'Pornography and Obscenity'. In *Phoenix: The Posthumous Papers of D. H. Lawrence*, edited by Edward D. McDonald, 170–87. London: Heinemann, 1936.

Leiris, Michel. 'Civilisation', translated by Iain White. In *Encyclopædia Acephalica*, edited by Alistair Brotchie, 93–6. London: Atlas Press, 1995.

Leitner, Bernhard. 'Viennese Kineticism'. In *Beyond Art: A Third Culture: A Comparative Study in Cultures, Art and Science in 20th Century Austria and Hungary*, edited by Peter Weibel, 41–2. New York: Springer, 2005.

Lewis, Gordon K. *Main Currents in Caribbean Thought: The Historical Evolution of Caribbean Society in Its Ideological Aspects, 1492–1900*. Baltimore, MD: Johns Hopkins University Press, 1983.

Linder, Douglas O., editor. 'Famous World Trials. The Trials of Oscar Wilde. 1895'. School of Law, University of Missouri-Kansas City, 2015, http://law2.umkc.edu/faculty/projects/ftrials/wilde/wilde.htm, accessed 21 August 2015.

Little, Helen. 'Picasso and Britain: A Selected Chronology of Exhibitions and Acquisitions 1900–1960'. In *Picasso & Modern British Art*, edited by James Beechey and Chris Stephens, 220–27. London: Tate Publishing, 2012.

Livingstone, David N. 'Tropical Hermeneutics: Fragments for a Historical Narrative. An Afterword'. *Singapore Journal of Tropical Geography* 21, no. 1 (2000): 76–91.

Lopoukhine, Juliana, Frédéric Regard and Kerry-Jane Wallart. 'Introduction: On Reading Rhys Transnationally'. In *Transnational Jean Rhys: Lines of Transmission, Lines of Flight*. Edited by Lopoukhine, Regard and Wallart, 1–12. London: Bloomsbury, 2021.

Lopoukhine, Juliana, Frédéric Regard and Kerry-Jane Wallart, editors. *Jean Rhys: Writing Precariously. Women: A Cultural Review* 31, no. 2 (2020).

McAuliffe, Mary. *Paris on the Brink: The 1930s Paris of Jean Renoir, Salvador Dali, Simone de Beauvoir, André Gide, Sylvia Beach, Léon Blum, and Their Friends*. Lanham, MD: Rowman & Littlefield, 2018.

Machacek, Gregory. 'Allusion'. *PMLA* 122, no. 2 (2007): 522–36.

Mahoney, Kristin. *Literature and the Politics of Post-Victorian Decadence*. Cambridge: Cambridge University Press, 2015.

Manning, Susan and Andrew Taylor, 'Introduction: What Is Transatlantic Literary Studies'. In *Transatlantic Literary Studies: A Reader*, edited by Susan Manning and Andrew Taylor, 1–13. Baltimore, MD: Johns Hopkins University Press, 2007.

Mansfield, Katherine. 'The Fly'. In *The Stories of Katherine Mansfield*, edited by Anthony Alpers, 529–33. Auckland: Oxford University Press, 1984.

Mansfield, Katherine. 'A Little Episode'. In *The Collected Fiction of Katherine Mansfield, 1898–1915*, edited by Gerri Kimber and Vincent O'Sullivan, 538–44. Edinburgh: Edinburgh University Press, 2012.

Mao, Douglas, and Rebecca Walkowitz. 'The New Modernist Studies'. *PMLA* 123, no. 3 (2008): 737–48.

Mardorossian, Carine M. 'Caribbean Formations in the Rhysian Corpus'. In *Jean Rhys: Twenty-First-Century Approaches*, edited by Erica L. Johnson and Patricia Moran, 107–22. Edinburgh: Edinburgh University Press, 2015.

Mardorossian, Carine M. *Reclaiming Difference: Caribbean Women Rewrite Postcolonialism*. Charlottesville: University of Virginia Press, 2005.

Marez, Curtis. 'The Other Addict: Reflections on Colonialism and Oscar Wilde's Opium Smoke Screen'. *English Literary History* 64, no. 1 (1997): 257–87.

Marinetti, F. T. 'The Founding and Manifesto of Futurism 1909', translated by R. W. Flint. In *Futurist Manifestoes*, edited by Umbro Apollonio, translated by Robert Brain, R. W. Flint, J. C. Hihggitt, and Caroline Tinsdall,19–24. London: Tate Publishing, 2009.

Marshik, Celia. *British Modernism and Censorship*. Cambridge: Cambridge University Press, 2006.

Masefield, John. Preface. In *Daughters of Ishmail*, edited by Reginald Wright Kauffman, vii–xiv. London: Stephen Smith, 1911.

Maslen, Cathleen. *Ferocious Things: Jean Rhys and the Politics of Women's Melancholia*. Newcastle-upon-Tyne: Cambridge Scholars Publishing, 2009.

Matera, Marc. *Black London: The Imperial Metropolis and Decolonization in the Twentieth Century*. Berkeley: University of California Press, 2015.

Maude, Ulrike. 'Science, Technology and the Body'. In *The Cambridge Companion to Modernist Culture*, edited by Celia Marshik, 33–49. New York: Cambridge University Press, 2015.

Maurel, Sylvie. *Jean Rhys*. Basingstoke: Macmillan, 1998.

May, Betty. *Tiger Woman: My Story*. 1929; London: Duckworth Overlook, 2014.

Mellown, Elgin W. *Jean Rhys: A Descriptive and Annotated Bibliography of Works and Criticism*. New York: Garland, 1984.

Miall, Nina. *Kirchner: Expressionism and The City: Dresden and Berlin 1905–1918*. London: Royal Academy of Arts, 2003.

Michalska, Katarzyna, and Serguiz Michalska. *Spider*. London: Reaktion, 2010.

Miller, Richard Lawrence. *The Encyclopedia of Addictive Drugs*. Westport, CT: Greenwood Press, 2002.

Mistinguett. *Mistinguett: Queen of the Paris Night*. Translated by Lucienne Hill. London: Elek Books, 1954.

Monnereau, Élie. *The Complete Indigo-maker: Containing, an Accurate Account of the Indigo Plant; Its Description, Culture, Preparation, and Manufacture. With Œconomical Rules and Necessary Directions for a Planter How to Manage a Plantation, and Employ His Negroes to the Best Advantage. To Which Is Added, a Treatise on the Culture of Coffee*. P. Elmsly, 1769.

Moran, Patricia. '"The Feelings Are Always Mine": Chronic Shame and Humiliated Rage in Jean Rhys's Fiction'. In *Jean Rhys: Twenty-First-Century Approaches*, edited by Erica L. Johnson and Patricia Moran, 190–208. Edinburgh: Edinburgh University Press, 2015.

Moran, Patricia. *Virginia Woolf, Jean Rhys, and the Aesthetics of Trauma*. New York: Palgrave Macmillan, 2007.
Morris, Mervyn. 'Oh, Give the Girl a Chance: Jean Rhys and *Voyage in the Dark*'. *Journal of West Indian Literature* 3, no. 22 (September 1989): 1–8.
Morrison, Toni. *Playing in the Dark: Whiteness and the Literary Imagination*. Cambridge, MA: Harvard University Press, 1992.
Morwood, James. 'Gilbert Murray's Translations of Greek Tragedy'. In *Gilbert Murray Reassessed: Hellenism, Theatre, and International Politics*, edited by Christopher Stray, 133–44. Oxford: Oxford University Press, 2007.
Mukherjee, Ankhi. 'Creole Modernism'. *Affirmations: Of the Modern* 2, no. 1 (Winter 2014): 25–45.
Mukherjee, Upamanyu Pablo. *Natural Disasters and Victorian Empire: Famines, Fevers, and Literary Cultures in South Asia*. Basingstoke: Palgrave Macmillan, 2013.
Müller-Zettelmann, Eva, and Rudolf Weiss, '"La vie toute faite des morceaux": Intermediality and Impressionism in Jean Rhys's *Quartet*'. In *Rive Gauche: Paris as a Site of Avant-garde Art and Cultural Exchange in the 1920s*, edited by Elke Mettinger, Margarete Rubik and Jörg Türschmann, 79–98. Amsterdam: Rodopi, 2010.
Murdoch, H. Adlai. 'The Discourses of Jean Rhys: Resistance, Ambivalence and Creole Indeterminacy'. In *Jean Rhys: Twenty-First-Century Approaches*, edited by Erica L. Johnson and Patricia Moran, 146–67. Edinburgh: Edinburgh University Press, 2015.
Naipaul, V. S. *The Middle Passage*. 1962; London: Andre Deutsch, 1963.
Nardin, Jane. '"As Soon As I Sober Up I Will Start Again": Alcohol and the Will in Jean Rhys's Pre-War Novels'. *Papers on Language and Literature* 42, no. 1 (2006): 46–72.
Newark, Cormac. '"Ch'hai di nuvo, buffon?" or What's New with *Rigoletto*'. In *The Cambridge Companion to Verdi*, edited by Xiaoxia Wei, 197–208. Cambridge: Cambridge University Press, 2004.
Nicholls, Peter. *Modernisms: A Literary Guide*. Basingstoke: Macmillan, 1995.
Nicoletti, L. J. 'Downward Mobility: Victorian Women, Suicide, and London's "Bridge of Sighs"'. *Literary London: Interdisciplinary Studies in the Representation of London* 2, no. 1 (March 2004), http://www.literarylondon.org/london-journal/march2004/nicoletti.html, accessed 29 July 2015.
O'Connor, Teresa F. *Jean Rhys: The West Indian Novels*. New York: New York University Press, 1986.
Oliver, Vere Langford, comp. *More Monumental Inscriptions: Tombstones of the British West Indies*. Dorchester: F. G. Longman, 1927.
*The Pagan*, directed by W. S. Van Dyke, Metro-Goldwyn-Mayer, 1929. Warner Brothers, 2010.
Paravisini-Gebert, Lizabeth. '"A Forgotten Outpost of Empire": Social Life in Dominica and the Creative Imagination'. *Jean Rhys Review* 10, nos. 1–2 (1998): 13–27.
Paravisini-Gebert, Lizabeth. 'Jean Rhys and Phyllis Shand Allfrey: The Story of a Friendship'. *Jean Rhys Review* 9, nos. 1–2 (1997): 25–36.

Patterson, Annabel. *Fables of Power: Aesopian Writing and Political History*. Durham, NC: Duke University Press, 1991.
Pickering, Michael. *Blackface Minstrelsy in Britain*. Aldershot: Ashgate, 2008.
Pizzo, Justine. 'Atmospheric Exceptionalism in *Jane Eyre*: Charlotte Brontë's Weather Wisdom'. *PMLA* 131, no. 1 (2016): 84–100.
Plock, Vike Martina. *Modernism, Fashion and Interwar Women Writers*. Edinburgh: Edinburgh University Press, 2017.
Poovey, Mary. *Uneven Developments: The Ideological Work of Gender in Mid-Victorian England*. 1988; London: Virago, 1989.
Posmentier, Sonya. *Cultivation and Catastrophe: The Lyric Ecology of Modern Black Literature*. Baltimore, MD: Johns Hopkins University Press, 2017.
Radano, Ronald. 'Black Music Labor and the Animated Properties of Slave Sound'. *Boundary 2* 43, no. 1 (2016): 173–208.
Radden, Jennifer. 'Melancholy and Melancholia'. In *Pathologies of the Modern Self: Postmodern Studies on Narcissism, Schizophrenia, and Depression*, edited by David Michael Levin, 231–50. New York: New York University Press, 1987.
Raiskin, Judith. 'Jean Rhys: Creole Writing and Strategies of Reading'. *Ariel: A Review of International English Literature* 22, no. 4 (October 1991): 51–67.
Raiskin, Judith. *Snow on the Canefields: Women's Writing and Creole Subjectivity*. Minneapolis: University of Minnesota Press, 1996.
Rearick, Charles. *The French in Love and War: Popular Culture in the Era of the World Wars*. New York: Yale University Press, 1997.
Rentzou, Efthymia. 'Animal'. In *A New Vocabulary for Global Modernism*, edited by Eric Hayot and Rebecca L. Walkowitz, 29–42. New York: Columbia University Press, 2016.
Richardson, Dorothy. 'Autobiographical Sketch'. In *Authors Today and Yesterday*, edited by Stanley J. Kunitz, 562–4. New York: H. W. Wilson, 1934.
Richepin, Jean. 'Philistines', translator unknown, http://wulfshead.blogspot.com.au/2013/04/philistines.html, accessed 19 August 2014.
Rochowanski, Leopold Wolfgang. *Der Formwille der Zeit in der Angewandten Kunst*. 1922; repr., München: Klaus Reprint, 1980.
Roditi, Edouard. 'From "Fiction as Allegory"'. In *The Picture of Dorian Gray*, by Oscar Wilde, edited by Donald L. Lawler, 369–70. Norton Critical Edition. New York: W. W. Norton, 1988.
Rogoyska, Jane, and Frances Alexander. *Amedeo Modigliani*. Parkstone International, 2019.
Romain, Gemma. *Race, Sexuality and Identity in Britain and Jamaica: The Biography of Patrick Nelson, 1916–1963*. London: Bloomsbury Academic, 2017.
Rosenberg, Leah Reade. *Nationalism and the Formation of Caribbean Literature*. New York: Palgrave Macmillan, 2007.
Rosenberg, Leah Reade. '"The Rope, of Course Being Covered with Flowers": Metropolitan Discourses and the Construction of Creole Identity in Jean Rhys's "Black Exercise Book"'. *Jean Rhys Review* 11, no. 1 (1999): 5–34.

Rovera, Catherine. *Genèses d'une folie créole: Jean Rhys et 'Jane Eyre'.* Paris: Hermann Éditeurs, 2015.

Rubik, Margarete. 'Jean Rhys's Vision of the Left Bank'. In *Rive Gauche: Paris as a Site of Avant-garde Art and Cultural Exchange in the 1920s*, edited by Elke Mettinger, Margarete Rubik and Jörg Türschmann, 61–78. Amsterdam: Rodopi, 2010.

Ruston, Alan. 'Champion, Harry [*real name* William Henry Crump]'. *Oxford Dictionary of National Biography.* Oxford: Oxford University Press, 2019.

Sacks, Oliver. *Musicophilia: Tales of Music and the Brain.* Kindle Edition.

Said, Edward. *The World, the Text and the Critic.* Cambridge, MA: Harvard University Press, 1983.

Sammells, Neil. *Wilde Style: The Plays and Prose of Oscar Wilde.* 200. Reprint, London: Routledge, 2014.

Saunders, Max. 'Ford and Impressionism'. In *Ford Madox Ford: Literary Networks and Cultural Transformations*, edited by Andrzej Gasiorek and Daniel Moore, 151–66. Amsterdam: Rodopi, 2008.

Saunders, Max. *Ford Madox Ford: A Dual Life. Volume II: The After-War World.* Oxford: Oxford University Press, 1996.

Savory, Elaine. *Jean Rhys.* Cambridge: Cambridge University Press, 1998.

Sax, Boria. *Imaginary Animals: The Monstrous, the Wondrous and the Human.* London: Reaktion, 2013.

Schwab, Gabriele. *Haunting Legacies: Violent Histories and Transgenerational Trauma.* New York: Columbia University Press, 2010.

Schwartz, Stuart B. *Sea of Storms: A History of Hurricanes in the Greater Caribbean from Columbus to Katrina.* Princeton, NJ: Princeton University Press, 2015.

Scott, David. *Conscripts of Modernity: The Tragedy of Colonial Enlightenment.* Durham, NC: Duke University Press, 2004.

Sedgwick, Eve Kosofsky. 'The Beast in the Closet: James and the Writing of Homosexual Panic'. In *Speaking of Gender*, edited by Elaine Showalter, 243–68. New York: Routledge, 1989.

Sedgwick, Eve Kosofsky. *Touching Feeling: Affect, Pedagogy, Performance.* Durham, NC: Duke University Press, 2003.

Seshagiri, Urmila. 'Modernist Ashes, Postcolonial Phoenix: Jean Rhys and the Evolution of the English Novel in the Twentieth Century'. *Modernism/Modernity* 13, no. 3 (2006): 487–505.

Seshagiri, Urmila. *Race and the Modernist Imagination.* Ithaca, NY: Cornell University Press, 2010.

Shakespeare, William. *Macbeth*, edited by D. R. Elloway. Basingstoke: Macmillan Education, 1971.

Shakespeare, William. *The Winter's Tale*, edited by Susan Snyder and Deborah T. Curren-Aquino. Cambridge: Cambridge University Press, 2007.

Sharpe, Christina. *In the Wake: On Blackness and Being.* Durham, NC: Duke University Press, 2016.

Sharpley-Whiting, T. Denean. *Negritude Women*. Minneapolis: University of Minnesota Press, 2002.

Sherry, Vincent. *Modernism and the Reinvention of Decadence*. New York: Cambridge University Press, 2015.

Shires, Linda M. 'Mutual Adaptation in Rudyard Kipling's Letters to His Children and *Just So Stories*'. *Children's Literature* 43 (2015): 182–207.

Shuttleworth, Sally. *Charlotte Brontë and Victorian Psychology*. Cambridge: Cambridge University Press, 1996.

Simpson, Anne B. *Territories of the Psyche: The Fiction of Jean Rhys*. New York: Palgrave Macmillan, 2005.

Slater, Michael. *The Great Charles Dickens Scandal*. New Haven, CT: Yale University Press, 2012.

Smith, Barry. *Peter Warlock: The Life of Philip Heseltine*. Oxford: Oxford University Press, 1994.

Snaith, Anna. *Modernist Voyages: Colonial Women Writers in London, 1890–1945*. Cambridge: Cambridge University Press, 2014.

Snodgrass, Chris. *Aubrey Beardsley: Dandy of the Grotesque*. New York: Oxford University Press, 1995.

Speake, Jennifer, compiler. *The Oxford Dictionary of Proverbs*. Oxford: Oxford University Press, 2015.

Staley, Thomas. *Jean Rhys: A Critical Study*. Austin: University of Texas Press, 1979.

Stam, Robert, and Ella Shohat, 'Transnationalizing Comparison: The Uses and Abuses of Cross-Cultural Analogy'. In *Comparison: Theories, Approaches, Uses*, edited by Rita Felski and Susan Stanford Friedman, 120–46. Baltimore, MD: Johns Hopkins University Press, 2013.

Stead, Lisa. *Off to the Pictures: Cinema-Going, Women's Writing and Movie Culture in Interwar Britain*. Edinburgh: Edinburgh University Press, 2016.

Stepan, Nancy Leys. *Picturing Tropical Nature*. Ithaca, NY: Cornell University Press, 2001.

Straley, Jessica. *Evolution and Imagination in Victorian Children's Literature*. Cambridge: Cambridge University Press, 2016.

Streip, Katharine. '"Just a Cérébrale": Jean Rhys, Women's Humour, and Ressentiment'. *Representations*, 45 (1994): 117–44.

Sullivan, Hannah. *The Work of Revision*. Cambridge, MA: Harvard University Press, 2013.

Taxidou, Olga. *Modernism and Performance: Jarry to Brecht*. Basingstoke: Palgrave Macmillan, 2007.

Taylor-Batty, Juliette. '"Le revenant": Baudelaire's Afterlife in *Wide Sargasso Sea*'. *Modernism/Modernity* 27, no. 4 (2020): 665–88.

Taylor-Batty, Juliette. *Multilingualism in Modernist Fiction*. Basingstoke: Palgrave Macmillan, 2013.

Thacker, Andrew. '"Also I Do Like the Moderns": Reading Rhys's Reading'. In *Transnational Jean Rhys: Lines of Transmission, Lines of Flight*, edited by Juliana

Lopoukhine, Frédéric Regard and Kerry-Jane Wallart, 51–64. London: Bloomsbury, 2020.
Thacker, Andrew. 'The Idea of a Critical Literary Geography'. *New Formations*, no. 57 (Winter 2005/6): 56–73.
Thacker, Andrew. *Moving through Modernity: Space and Geography in Modernism*. Manchester: Manchester University Press, 2003.
Thomas, Sue. 'Genealogies of Story in Jean Rhys's "The Day They Burned the Books"'. *Review of English Studies* 72 (2021): 565–76.
Thomas, Sue. 'Ghostly Presences: James Potter Lockhart and Jane Maxwell Lockhart in Jean Rhys's Writing'. *Texas Studies in Literature and Language* 57, no. 4 (2015): 389–411.
Thomas, Sue. 'Jean Rhys Getting the "Feel" of the West Indies in *Wide Sargasso Sea*'. In *Wide Sargasso Sea at 50*, edited by Elaine Savory and Erica L. Johnson, 111–24. New York: Palgrave, 2020.
Thomas, Sue. 'Jean Rhys's Cardboard Dolls' Houses'. *Kunapipi* 26, no. 1 (2004): 39–53.
Thomas, Sue. 'Jean Rhys Writing White Creole Childhoods'. *a/b: Auto/Biography Studies* 19, nos. 1–2 (2004): 203–21.
Thomas, Sue. 'Modernity, Voice and Window-breaking: Jean Rhys's "Let Them Call It Jazz"'. In *De-scribing Empire: Colonialism and Textuality*, edited by Alan Lawson and Chris Tiffin, 185–200. London: Routledge, 1994.
Thomas, Sue. '"Tearing Me in Two So Slowly So Slowly": Jean Rhys's Representations of Abortion'. *Jean Rhys Review* 12, no. 1 (2002): 7–27.
Thomas, Sue. *The Worlding of Jean Rhys*. Westport, CT: Greenwood Press, 1999.
Tickner, Lisa. *Modern Life & Modern Subjects: British Art in the Early Twentieth Century*. New Haven, CT: Yale University Press, 2000.
Toepfer, Karl. *Empire of Ecstasy: Nudity and Movement in German Body Culture, 1910–1955*. Berkeley: University of California Press, 1997.
Townsend, Julie. *The Choreography of Modernism in France: La Danseuse, 1830–1930*. Leeds: Legenda, 2010.
Toye, Francis. 'Ragtime: The New Tarantism'. *English Review* March 1913: 654–8.
Udovicki-Selb, Danilo. 'Facing Hitler's Pavilion: The Uses of Modernity in the Soviet Pavilion at the 1937 Paris International Exhibition'. *Journal of Contemporary History* 47, no. 1 (2012): 13–47.
Vine, Steven. *Reinventing the Sublime: Post-Romantic Literature and Theory*. Brighton: Sussex Academic Press, 2013.
Voicu, Cristina-Georgiana. *Exploring Cultural Identities in Jean Rhys's Fiction*. Warsaw: De Gruyter Open, 2014.
Vreeland, Elizabeth. 'Jean Rhys: The Art of Fiction LXIV'. *Paris Review* 76 (1979): 218–34.
Waddell, Nathan. 'Bohemian Retrospects: Ford Madox Ford, Post-War Memory and the Cabaret Theatre Club'. In *Modernist Party*, edited by Kate McLoughlin, 193–209. Edinburgh: Edinburgh University Press, 2013.

Wainwright, Laura. '"Doesn't That Make You Laugh?": Modernist Comedy in Jean Rhys's *After Leaving Mr Mackenzie* and *Good Morning, Midnight*'. *Journal of International Women's Studies* 10, no. 3 (2009): 348–57.

Walcott, Derek. 'Air'. In *The Poetry of Derek Walcott 1948-2013*, edited by Glyn Maxwell, 106–7. London: Faber and Faber, 2014.

Walcott, Derek. 'The Royal Palms … an Absence of Ruins'. *London Magazine* 1, no. 11 (February 1962): 12–13.

Walcott, Derek. 'Ruins of a Great House'. In *In a Green Night: Poems 1948-1960*, by Derek Walcott, 19–20. 1962; London: Jonathan Cape, 1969.

Walkowitz, Judith R. *City of Dreadful Delight: Narratives of Sexual Danger in Late-Victorian London*. London: Virago, 1992.

Walkowitz, Judith R. *Nights Out: Life in Cosmopolitan London*. New Haven, CT: Yale University Press, 2012.

Walvin, James. *The Zong: A Massacre, the Law and the End of Slavery*. New Haven, CT: Yale University Press, 2011.

Warner, Marina. *Fantastic Metamorphoses, Other Worlds: Ways of Telling the Self*. Oxford: Oxford University Press, 2002.

Watney, Simon. *Policing Desire: Pornography, AIDS and the Media*, 3rd ed. London: Cassell, 1997.

Weibel, Peter, editor. *Beyond Art: A Third Culture: A Comparative Study in Cultures, Art and Science in 20th Century Austria and Hungary*. New York: Springer, 2005.

Weinstock, Jeffrey Andrew. '*from* Introduction: The Spectral Turn'. In *The Spectralities Reader: Ghosts and Haunting in Contemporary Cultural Theory*, edited by María Del Pilar Blanco and Esther Peeren, 61–8. London: Bloomsbury, 2013.

Weliver, Phyllis. 'Oscar Wilde, Music, and the "Opium-Tainted Cigarette": Disinterested Dandies and Critical Play'. *Journal of Victorian Culture* 15, no. 3 (2010): 315–47.

Whitlock, Gillian. *The Intimate Empire: Reading Women's Autobiography*. London: Cassell, 2000.

Widmaier Picasso, Diana. 'Rescue: The End of the Year'. In *The EY Exhibition. Picasso 1932: Love Fame Tragedy*, edited by Achim Borchardt-Hume and Nancy Ireson, 208–33. London: Tate Publishing, 2018.

Wilde, Oscar. *Lady Windermere's Fan*. In *Five Plays*, by Oscar Wilde, 1–57. New York: Bantam, 1961.

Wilde, Oscar. *The Picture of Dorian Gray*, edited by Peter Ackroyd. Harmondsworth: Penguin, 1985.

Wilde, Oscar. *Poems and Essays*. London: Dent, 1956.

Williams, Tim I. 'The Classification of Involuntary Musical Imagery: The Case for Earworms'. *Psychomusicology: Music, Mind and Brain* 25, no. 1 (2015): 5–13.

Wilson, Mary, and Kerry L. Johnson. 'Introduction: Rhys Matters?' In *Rhys Matters: New Critical Perspectives*, edited by Mary Wilson and Kerry L. Johnson. New York: Palgrave Macmillan, 2013.

Woolf, Virginia. *The Common Reader: First Series*, edited by Andrew McNeillie. London: Hogarth Press, 1984.

Woolf, Virginia. *A Room of One's Own*. 1929. Reprint, London: Grafton, 1978.

Zimring, Rishona. 'Making a Scene: Rhys and the Aesthete at Mid-century'. In *Jean Rhys: Twenty-First-Century Approaches*, edited by Erica L. Johnson and Patricia Moran, 40–58. Edinburgh: Edinburgh University Press, 2015.

Zola, Émile. *Nana*, introduced by Burton Rascoe. New York: Alfred A. Knopf, 1925.

# Index

Abraham, Nicolas 51, 177
Abraham, Nicolas, and Maria Torok 16
Adam, H. Pearl 4–5, 6
'*Adieu madras, adieu foulard*' (song) 15, 143, 147, 157, 168, 191
   ship farewell 149
Aesop 167–9
*After Leaving Mr Mackenzie* 3, 11, 15, 23 n.73, 51–66
Allen, Carolyn 8
Allfrey, Phyllis Shand 9
Allinson, Adrian 7, 13, 118, 122
allusion. *See under* Rhys, Jean, aesthetics and techniques
*Almayer's Folly* (Conrad) 3, 11, 53, 55, 59, 65, 169
Armstrong, Louis 63
Armstrong, Tim 40, 100
Angier, Carole 6, 125
Arnold, David 10
Athill, Diana 15, 118, 156
Austro-Hungarian Empire 27, 28, 118, 189, 191

Bailey, Peter 148
basilisk 62–3
Bataille, Georges 11, 64, 65
Baudelaire, Charles, 'Le revenant' 166
Beardsley, Aubrey 73, 84
bearings 1–2, 9, 10, 11, 28, 66, 67, 73, 76, 189
Beede, Ivan 5
'Beginning of the Armadilloes, The' (Kipling) 11, 52–5, 57, 65
Bell, Matthew 36
Bergson, Henri 110
Berlant, Lauren, and Sianne Ngai 99
Berman, Jessica 192
Bewell, Alan 165, 168
Bhabha, Homi 170
Bible 86, 131, 157
biguine

   coexists with racism 154
   critique of doudouism 144, 151
   internationally commodified 97, 152, 190
   origins 151, 161 n.60
   sexualization 152
'Birthday, The' (Rhys) 8
Black, Clinton V. 186 n.102
*Blackbirds of 1929* 11, 53, 63, 65
Blake, George 'Happy' (musician) 133
Bliss, Eliot 9
Bloomsbury 135
bottle parties 117, 132–3
Boule Blanche 151
Bowen, Stella 38
Brathwaite, Kamau 182 n.11
Brazil 51–2, 54
Bret, David 146
Breton, Andre 66
Brisson, Pierre 64
Brontë, Charlotte, *Jane Eyre* 16, 165–6, 167–8, 171, 174, 178–80, 181
Brooker, Peter 7, 122
Browning, Robert 128
Budapest 28, 29, 31, 32
Burrows, Victoria 186 n.102

Café Royal 7, 119, 122
Camarasana, Linda, and Jess Issacharoff 153
'Camptown Racecourse' (song) 82
*Candide* (newspaper) 64
Cantor, Eddie 38
capitalism 15, 34, 58–9, 78, 106, 172
Carco, Francis, *Perversité* 6
Carr, Helen 3
Casino de Paris 146, 147
Cave of the Golden Calf 118, 119, 122
censorship 37, 79, 88, 95 n.107, 131
Césaire, Aimé 144
Césaire, Suzanne 144, 183 n.30
Chalk, Bridget T. 31

Channing, Puma 118–19
'Christmas Presents of Mynheer van Rooz, The' (Rhys) 66
Cizek, Franz 10, 29, 30
Clarke, Joseph 94 n.100
Clukey, Amy 40
Cohen, Philip 127
Cohen, Stanley 73–4
Collett, Anne, Russell McDougall, and Sue Thomas 10
Conrad, Joseph. *See Almayer's Folly*; *Heart of Darkness*
Conway, Kelley 145
Cornell, Drucilla 84
Couti, Jacqueline 143
Crabtree Club 7, 13, 14, 117, 119, 121, 122, 123
Creole 8–9, 78–9
  white 9, 76, 79, 86–7, 174
crypted language, transgenerational 16–17, 51, 62, 166, 172, 178
Cuba 152, 161 n.60

Damas, Léon-Gontran 144
dance 29, 30
  nude 39, 147
  sexual economies 27, 28, 30, 42, 43, 82, 145, 149
  sexual modernity 58
'Dancer, The' (Rhys) 29
Darwin, Charles 55
Daverio, John 120
Davis, Thomas S. 154
Dawson, Graham 126
'Day They Burned the Books, The' (Rhys) 9
decadence 12, 34, 43, 73–4, 84–90
del Rio, Dolores 136
Delius, Frederick 119, 120
Dell'Amico, Carol 3
*dépêche africaine, La* 144
depression 117–19, 124, 129–30, 151
  articulated as nothingness 117, 129–30, 137
  colours metonymic of, 43, 77, 124
  'rich melancholy' 120
Depression, Great 11, 12, 56, 97, 101
Derrida, Jacques 42
Dias, Selma Vaz 13
diasporas 77, 88, 144, 152, 153

experience in England 135–6
  in Rhys studies 2–3
  writers 10, 14, 53, 158
Dickens, Charles 81
Dickinson, Emily 104, 154
Dickinson, Philip 170
*Die Brücke* 29
'Dinah' (song) 135
Dominica 14, 76
  culturally close to Martinique 14, 67, 151, 158
  La Guerre Negre 177
Donald, James 98
*doudou* 143–58
  colonial resonances 14, 143, 149–50, 153, 157, 169
  etymology and history 143–4
doudouism, countering 14, 154, 183 n.30
Downes, Sarah 34
Driver, Felix, and Luciana Martins 10
Dunbar, Rudolph 133
Dunning, R.C., 'The Hermit' 10, 27, 37–8
Dwyer, Dania 174

economies 143, 155
  artistic 34
  plantation 16, 149, 172–3, 176–7
  sexual 27, 28, 30, 42, 43, 82, 149 *see also* prostitution, amateur
Eliot, T. S. 'The Love Song of J. Alfred Prufrock' 37, 125
Ellington, Duke 63, 135
Ellis, Nadia 132
Emery, Mary Lou 3, 61, 104, 110
England
  grey / white as metonyms of repression 77, 109, 110, 124, 125, 150
  rural idea of 123
Esty, Jed 75, 76
evolution 52, 53, 54, 60, 64, 65, 66
expatriation 6–7, 76
Exposition Coloniale Internationale (1931) 151–2
Exposition Internationale des Arts et Techniques Dans La Vie Moderne (1937) 12, 97, 98, 103

Fanon, Frantz 144
Felski, Rita 126
filiation 85, 105

Flaubert, Gustave 5
Folies Bergère 146, 147
Ford, Ford Madox 5–6, 13, 27, 37, 38
Froude, James Anthony 173–4
Frow, John 31
Fry, Andy 64
futurism 10, 29, 32–3

Gabriel, Léona 151
Gardiner, Judith Kegan 125
Geiger, Jeffrey 59
geographies, psychological 16–17, 166, 180, 181, 190, 191
Gideon, Melville 81, 83, 92 n.55
Gilbert, Sandra M., and Susan Gubar 180
Gilman, Sander 61, 153
Glissant, Edouard 87
'Gloomy Sunday' (Paul Robeson) 106
Glyn, Elinor, *Man and Maid* 31
GoGwilt, Christopher 3, 5, 29, 62, 151
Goldring, Douglas 118
Goldsmith, Oliver 55, 68 n.29
Gomes, Modesto Broco y *The Redemption of Ham* 51
González, Octavio R. 36, 37
*Good Morning, Midnight* 12, 97–110, 117, 144, 151–4
good Samaritan motif 37–8, 102, 131, 155
Goudie, Sean X. 78
Gray, Cecil, *Peter Warlock* 119, 120, 121, 122, 127, 128
Gregg, Veronica 135

Haag, Pamela S. 40
Hall, Catherine 9
Hamilton, Lady Emma 124
Hamnett, Nina 118, 122
Hare, Kenneth 122
Hatch, Ike 14, 133
haunting 2, 16, 42, 82, 87–8, 108, 156, 166, 178
Hawthorn, Jeremy 58
*Heart of Darkness* (Conrad) 57, 76, 169–70
Heine, Henrich, 'Lyrical Intermezzo' 106
Heseltine, Philip (Peter Warlock) 7, 13, 118–20, 121, 122, 125, 126, 129
Hesperides 121, 123, 130
Hill, Constance Valis 134
Hill, Edwin C. Jr 14, 143, 151, 152, 156
Holloway Prison 155–6

Holmes, Deborah, and Lisa Silverman 30
Hood Thomas, 'The Bridge of Sighs' 100–1
hotcha 98, 110, 190
Howells, Coral Ann 3, 38
Hugo, Victor, *Le roi s'amuse* 35
*Hullo, Ragtime!* (Louis Hirsch) 83
Hulme, Peter 16
Hungary 28, 33
hurricane poetics 15–16, 67, 165–6, 170–2, 179–81, 182 n.11
Huxley, Aldous, *Antic Hay* 119
Huysmans, Joris-Karl, *A rebours* 79
hybridity 11, 52, 62, 64, 65–6, 134
Hyman, Ira E. Jr 108

'I Can't Give You Anything But Love, Baby' (Dorothy Fields) 63
identity 35, 62, 121, 151
    artistic 127
    Caribbean 2, 79, 149
    European 10, 57, 87, 166
    sexual 126
'I Do Like a S'Nice, S'Mince, S'pie' (Jay Laurier) 99, 111 n.11
imperialism 59, 157, 158
    fragility 167, 170, 181
    palliative 171
    racism and slavery 12, 129, 152
    in ruins 15, 174–6
impressionism 6, 10, 27, 41
improvisation 106–7, 109, 152
Isow, Jack 14, 133
'I Spy a Stranger' (Rhys) 121, 124
'it' 31

James, Henry 5, 6
James, William 41
Jarry, Alfred, *Ubu Roi* 65
jazz 83, 103, 146, 156
    clubs 132, 134
    evokes loss 64–5
    modernism 12, 98, 106, 108, 190
    provides narrative form 110
'J'en ai marre' (song) 145–7
John, Augustus 13, 119, 120
Johnson, Erica L. 57, 58, 77, 107–8, 151
Johnson, Howard 'Stretch' 134
Johnson, Lonnie 28
Jordan, Matthew F. 65

Kalliney, Peter 6
Kelly, Veronica 83
Kenney, William Howland 108
Kettner's 80–1, 82
kineticism 10, 29–30, 189
King, Bruce 173
King, Tempo 109
Kirchner, Ernst 29, 42
Knoepflmacher, U. C. 53
Konzett, Delia 3
Kristeva, Julia 130

labyrinths 74, 108, 174, 175–6
Lamberti, Elena 6
Lamming, George 9
Lane, Christopher 55
Lawrence, D. H. 101, 119, 124, 135
Léardée, Ernest 152
'Leaving School' (Rhys) 4
*Left Bank and Other Stories, The* 6, 14, 33, 44 n.2, 145
*Légitime défense* 144
Leiris, Michel 11, 64–5, 189
Lenglet, Jean 6, 7, 28, 38
Léro, Etienne 144, 189
Léro, Thélus 144, 189
'Let Them Call It Jazz' 9, 154–6
Lewis, Gordon K. 176
Lewis, Helen Block 63
Lockhart family 166, 172–3, 176–9
London
   darkness and entombment 57–8, 60
   demi-monde 79–84, 118
   menace and sexual danger 129
   middle-class conformist xenophobia 56, 77, 153
   modernist bohemia 121–3
   multi-racial Bloomsbury 135
London clubs. See Café Royal, Cave of the Golden Calf, Crabtree Club, Kettner's, Oddendino's, Shim Sham Club
*London Magazine* 9, 131, 137, 173
Lopoukhine, Juliana, Frederic Regard, and Kerry-Jane Wallart 3, 158
'Lost Island: A Childhood. Fragments of Autobiography' 11, 14, 53, 66–7
Louis, Joe 133

Maar, Dora, *Portrait d'Ubu* 11, 53, 65–6

'*Maladie d'amour*' (song) 151–2
Mansfield, Katherine 75, 107
Mardorossian, Carine M. 15, 178
Marez, Curtis 79–80
Marinetti, Filippo Tommaso 27, 29, 32
marionette theatre 10, 27, 40
   as modernist trope 39, 40–1
Marshik, Celia 37, 87
Martinique
   birthplace of biguine 151
   culturally close to Dominica 14, 67, 151, 158
   musicians considered 'American' 152
Maslen, Cathleen 56, 57, 86, 94 n.100, 105–6, 178
Masquerade 66, 83, 89, 95 n.107
Matera, Marc 133, 134
Maurel, Sylvia 139 n.45
May, Betty 122–3
McCormick, Anne O'Hare 12
McKay, Claude 9
mechanisms of social classification 27–43, 88, 153
memory 15, 108, 147, 151
   depressive 118, 125, 130
   experiential 33, 35, 53–4, 89, 104
   family 15, 16, 166, 176
   musical 81, 97, 107, 149, 154, 156
   traumatic 43, 98, 102, 104
Mendes, Alfred, *Pitch Lake* 9
Menil, René 144, 189
Michalska, Katarzyna, and Sergiusz Michalska 129
migration, labour 14, 153, 155
Miller, Richard Lawrence 80
miscegenation 59, 62, 64, 73, 153, 154, 175
misogyny 120, 121, 124, 136
'Mr. Howard's House. CREOLE' (Rhys) 8
Mistinguett (singer) 145–7
modernism
   aestheticism 136
   car as symbol 29, 32–3
   Creole 2, 3
   drunk narrative 92 n.50
   human-animal dyad 52
   identity-making 121
   jazz 98, 106, 117
   primitivism 58, 62, 66, 76, 148
   revision 13, 189
   temporalities 77

trope of the marionette 27, 39, 40–1
trope of mechanism 27, 29, 39–40
modernist studies 3
modernity
   alcohol as disease of 92 n.50
   fragility 65
   learned responses to 59, 152
   music and dance 12, 58, 83, 98, 190
Modigliani, Amedeo, *Reclining Nude* 11, 53, 60–2
Monnerot, Jules-Marcel 144, 189
moral panics 43, 78, 88, 90, 118, 124, 133, 154, 190
   defined 73–4
Moran, Patricia 58, 63
Morris, Mervyn 88
Morrison, Toni 55–6, 65
Moulin Rouge 63, 146
Mukherjee, Upamanyu Pablo 171
music. *See* biguine; Delius, Frederick; hotcha; jazz; ragtime; swing; Wagner, Richard

Naipaul, V. S. 9, 174
Nardal, Andrée 10, 144
Nardal, Jane 10, 14, 144, 154
Nardal, Paulette 10, 14, 44, 152
Nardin, Jane 92 n.50
Nash, Paul 7, 123
Négritude 144
Nelson, Lord Horatio 124
Nicholls, Peter 32
Nichols, Robert 119, 120
Nicoletti, L.J. 100
nothingness 129, 130, 137, 170–1, 174, 181
Novarro, Ramon 58, 59

Oddendino's 80–1, 83

*Pagan, The* (W.S. Van Dyke film) 11, 53, 58, 64
   compared to *Almayer's Folly* 59–60
   eroticism 59
'Pagan Love Song, The' 56–7, 58–9
pan-Africanism 134
Paris
   Caribbean population 6
   Caribbean writers 10, 144
   clubs and nightspots. (*see* Casino de Paris; dance, nude; Folies Bergère; Moulin Rouge)
   popularizes biguine 151–2
   racial exclusion 152–3
   Rhys in 6–7, 64, 144
   setting for fiction, 12, 55, 97–108
Patterson, Annabel 168
Picasso, Diana Widmaier 103
Picasso, Pablo 102–4
   *Guernica* 103
   rescue from drowning motif 102–3, 190
Pilotin, Michel 144, 189
Pizzo, Justine 179
Poovey, Mary 180
Posmentier, Sonya 67
*Postures* (Rhys). *See Quartet*
Poupeye, Camille 7
Prague 28, 31, 32
prostitution
   amateur 56, 78, 82, 105, 118, 124
   racialized 148, 149
   spider image 129

*Quartet* 27, 36–41, 42–3, 52, 100, 102, 112 n.22, 131
Quitman, Maurice-Sabas 144, 189

Radano, Ronald 83
ragtime 7, 73, 117, 190
   in London 81–4
'Ragtime Violin' (Irving Berlin) 117, 124, 130
Raiskin, Judith 145
Rearick, Charles 146
Rentzou, Efthymia 52
revolt 171, 172, 177, 179
Rhys, Jean, aesthetics and techniques
   allusion 3, 38, 82, 84–5, 100–10, 128, 166–70, 190–1
   revision 2, 13, 117, 118, 192
   temporalities 12, 77, 90, 99, 136
   tropes of mechanism 41, 58, 99–100, 104, 109, 110
   tropes of drowning woman 85–6, 97, 100–3
Rhys, Jean, approaches to
   bohemian modernist 6
   censorship 37, 95n.107, 131
   'difficult canonicity' 2
   expatriate dissident 6–7
   Ford Madox Ford's judgment 6

transnational modernist 3
Rhys, Jean, biography
  ancestors 16, 172–3, 176–7
  Creole 8–9
  observer of London bohemia 7, 13–14
  writerly beginnings 4–10
Rhys Jean, themes and preoccupations
  animal-human dyad 52, 60
  critiques reductive classification 27, 31, 34, 35, 36–7
  depiction of depression 52–8, 60–3, 77–8, 119–20, 124, 128–30, 136–7
  law, order, respectability 27–8, 33–4, 41–3
Rhys, Jean, works
  *After Leaving Mr Mackenzie* 3, 11, 15, 23 n.73, 51–66
  'The Birthday' 8
  'The Christmas Presents of Mynheer van Rooz' 66
  'The Day They Burned the Books' 9
  *Good Morning, Midnight* 12, 97–110, 117, 144, 151–4
  'I Spy a Stranger' 121, 124
  'Leaving School' 4
  *The Left Bank and Other Stories* 6, 14, 33, 44 n.2, 145
  'Let Them Call It Jazz' 9, 154–8
  'Lost Island: A Childhood. Fragments of Autobiography' 11, 14, 53, 66–7
  'Mr. Howard's House. CREOLE' 8
  *Quartet* 27, 36–41, 42–3, 52, 100, 102, 112 n.22, 131
  *Smile Please* 4, 5, 14, 16, 123
  'Songs My Mother Didn't Teach Me' 107, 190
  *The Sound of the River* 8, 13, 121, 124
  'Suzy Tells' 5
  'Tea with an Artist' 27, 33–6, 42, 43
  'Temps Perdi' 171–2
  'Tigers Are Better-Looking' 13, 117, 121, 130–6, 137
  *Tigers Are Better-Looking* 28, 147
  'Till September Petronella' 5, 8, 13, 78, 117–30, 136–7
  'Trio' 14, 43, 144–7
  'Triple Sec' 5, 7–8, 11, 38, 47 n.75, 80, 118–19, 121, 126, 129, 136–7
  'Vienne' 5, 27, 28–33, 36, 42, 44 n.2, 189
  *Voyage in the Dark* 5, 7, 8, 11–12, 15, 43, 66–7, 73–90, 147–51, 190
  *Wide Sargasso Sea* 8, 9, 14–17, 143, 156, 165–81, 186 n.102
Richardson, Dorothy 41
Richardson, John 102
Richepin, Jean 189
Rimbaud, Arthur 114 n.62
Rochowanski, Leopold Wolfgang 30
Roditi, Edouard 80
Rogoyska, Jane, and Frances Alexander 61
Rosenberg, Leah 145
Rubik, Margarete 7
ruins 16, 167, 172–5, 179, 180
Russia 98, 114 n.62
Ruston, Alan 148

Sadlier, Michael 88
Said, Edward 105
Sammells, Neil 99
Saunders, Max 5
Savory, Elaine 3, 6, 99, 151
Sax, Boria 63
Schaeffner, André 11, 64–5
Schwab, Gabriele 16, 166
Schwartz, Stuart B. 167, 172
Scott, David 1
Scott, Evelyn 8
Selvon, Sam 9
Senghor, Léopold Sédar 144
Sexual Offences Act (1967) 117
Shakespeare, William
  *Macbeth* 165, 167, 179, 180
  *Othello* 166, 191
  *Romeo and Juliet* 74
  *The Winter's Tale* 107
Shim Sham Club 13–14, 117, 132–4
Shires, Linda M. 54
Shuttleworth, Sally 179, 180
Slater, Michael 81
slavery
  abolition of 15, 16, 88, 177, 186 n.102
  emancipation 174, 176–7
  plantation 12, 73, 149, 175, 176, 177, 179
  *Zong* massacre 87
*Smile Please* 4, 5, 14, 16, 123
Smith, Barry 120, 126
Smith, Lancelot Hugh 4, 7
Smith, Leslie Tilden 37, 132
Snaith, Anna 3

'Songs My Mother Didn't Teach Me' (Rhys) 107, 190
*Sound of the River, The* 8, 13, 121, 124
Spanish Civil War 98, 103
Stam, Robert, and Ella Shohat 51
'Standard Bread' (Harry Champion) 148
Stepan, Nancy 10, 51
Straus, Ralph 81
Streip, Katherine 99
sublime 66, 170
suffragettes 156
Sullivan, Hannah 13
'Suzy Tells' (Rhys) 5
swing (music and dance) 43, 97–8, 106–7, 109, 117, 134, 190
'Swing High, Swing Low' (song) 12, 98, 99, 106–7, 108–9
*Swing High, Swing Low* (film) 109

Taxidou, Olga 40
'Tea with an Artist' (Rhys) 27, 33–6, 42, 43
temporalities 14, 43, 97–8, 99, 190
    cultural history 74, 90, 136
    past-present fused, 73–5, 77, 90, 98, 100, 107–8, 191
'Temps Perdi' (Rhys) 171–2
Thacker, Andrew 23 n.73, 80, 158
Thaly, Daniel 9, 144
The Hague 98, 104
'There's One More River to Cross' (Paul Tremaine) 99
Thésée, Auguste 144, 189
Thompson, Mary 61
'Tigers Are Better-Looking' 13, 117, 121, 130–6, 137
*Tigers Are Better-Looking* 28, 147
'Till September Petronella' 5, 8, 13, 78, 117–30, 136–7
*Time and Tide* 66
Toepfer, Karl 29
*Tom Jones* (opera) 97
Tomkins, Silvan 58
Toye, Francis 83
*transatlantic review* 5, 27, 29, 37
'Trio' (Rhys) 14, 43, 144–7
'Triple Sec' (Rhys) 5, 7–8, 11, 38, 47 n.75, 80, 118–19, 121, 126, 129, 136–7
tropicality 10–11, 15–16, 51–2, 66, 86–7, 131, 165, 181

compared with Orientalism 10
doudouism 143, 154, 158
imperial politics 165
tropics
    degeneration 51, 73, 79, 171, 174
    excess 87, 149, 166
    sexual exoticism 59–60, 171
    site of miscegenation 51, 62, 64, 153, 175
    threats 166, 170, 176
    unrepresentability 170

vampires 36, 38, 129, 138 n.23
Verdi, Guiseppe, *Rigoletto* 35
Verlaine, Paul 128
Vienna 10, 27, 28, 30, 31
'Vienne' (Rhys) 5, 27, 28–33, 36, 42, 44 n.2, 189
Vizetelly, Henry 79
*Voyage in the Dark* 5, 7, 8, 11–12, 15, 43, 66–7, 73–90, 147–51, 190
Vreeland, Elizabeth 191
vulgarity 123, 126–7

Wagner, Richard, *Tristan und Isolde* 120, 124, 127, 128
Wainwright, Laura 99
'Waiting for the Robert E. Lee' (song) 81
Walcott, Derek 9, 16, 173–5, 181
Walkowitz, Judith 132–3
Waller, Fats 110
Walvin, James 87
war and sexual commodification 28, 43, 73, 118, 123–4, 127
Warlock, Peter. *See* Heseltine, Philip
Waters, Ethel (singer) 135
Watney, Simon 74
Weinstock, Jeffrey Andrew 2
Whitlock, Gillian 3
*Wide Sargasso Sea* 8, 9, 14–17, 143, 156, 165–81, 186 n.102
Wiesenthal, Grete (dancer) 29
Wilde, Oscar
    'The Critic as Artist' 75
    *Lady Windermere's Fan* 12, 99, 102
    *The Picture of Dorian Gray* 74–6, 79–80, 85, 101, 123
    trials of 81, 82, 89
Willemetz, Albert, and Georges Arnould 146

Williams, Clarice Rees 4
Williams, Raymond 75
Williams, Tim I. 106
Williams, William Rees 144
Wolfe, Peter 89
women, tropes of
    fallen, drowned 13, 85–6, 97, 100–2
    outcast 13, 99, 102, 110, 153
    sexually commodified 12, 28, 30, 63, 73

Woodcock, Jane 9, 172
Woolf, Virginia 8, 41, 101, 179
Wyndham, Francis 154, 156, 191

Yoyotte, Pierre 144, 189

Zimring, Rishona 132, 141 n.102
Zola, Émile, *Nana* 73, 76, 79, 80
Zupancic, Alenka 99
Zwemmer Gallery 113 n.38

www.ingramcontent.com/pod-product-compliance
Lightning Source LLC
Chambersburg PA
CBHW062218300426
44115CB00012BA/2115